The Particular and the Public

The Louis I. Kahn Visiting Assistant Professorship
Yale School of Architecture

Yale School of Architecture
180 York Street
New Haven, CT 06520
www.architecture.yale.edu

Distributed by Actar
355 Lexington Avenue, 8th floor
New York, NY 10017
www.actar.com

The Particular and the Public was made possible through an
endowment from the Louis I. Kahn Visiting Assistant Professorship
at the Yale School of Architecture. It is the thirteenth in a series of
publications of the Louis I. Kahn Visiting Assistant Professorship
published through the dean's office.

Editors: Nina Rappaport and Saba Salekfard
Design: Manuel Miranda Practice
Text Editor: Cathryn Drake
Library of Congress Control Number: 2026931089
ISBN: 978-1-63840-227-5

THE PARTICULAR AND THE PUBLIC

Yale School of Architecture

The Louis I. Kahn Visiting Assistant Professorship

RACHAPORN CHOOCHUEY

CARRIE NORMAN
THOMAS KELLEY

CHAT TRAVIESO

Edited by Nina Rappaport and Saba Salekfard

Table of Contents

Preface

Established in 2004, the Louis I. Kahn Visiting Assistant Professorship is Yale's second endowed chair to honor Kahn. It offers young architects who practice and teach the opportunity to lead advanced design studios. The work of the visiting professors and their students is published so that others may benefit from the ideas developed and exchanged in the studios and seminars.

Louis I. Kahn (1901–1974), perhaps the one of the greatest American architects of the post–World War II era, was closely associated with Yale as a teacher and practicing architect. Yale is home to his first important building, the extension to the Art Gallery (1951–53), and his last, the Center for British Art (1969–77). Kahn was new to teaching when he came to Yale in 1947 to begin what would be a ten-year tenure as chief critic in the architecture school. As a teacher he worked closely with students, encouraging them to look beyond their initial ideas about architecture, just as he himself did. Kahn inspired a generation of architects, leading them to new insights that became the basis of their independent work.

The architects included in *The Particular and the Public*—Rachaporn Choochuey, Carrie Norman and Thomas Kelley, and Chat Travieso—each exemplify different directions in architecture, which is a goal of the professorship. They approach process and design from the specific to the vernacular, gaining input from youth perspectives as well as historic contexts, and incorporating local materials relating to the design of the site, formal analysis, and the community.

The Particular and the Public

This publication was made possible through an endowment from the Louis I. Kahn Visiting Assistant Professorship at the Yale School of Architecture. It is the thirteenth in a series published through the dean's office, encompassing thirty-nine studios listed here by year of publication.

Layered Urbanisms, 2007

Gregg Pasquarelli (SHoP Architects)
Galia Solomonoff (Solomonoff Architecture Studio)
Mario Gooden (Huff + Gooden Architects)

Negotiated Terrains, 2009

Jeanne Gang (Studio Gang)
Sunil Bald (Studio SUMO)
Mark Tsurumaki (LTL Architects)

Turbulence, 2011

Christopher Sharples (SHoP Architects)
William Sharples (SHoP Architects)
Ali Rahim (Contemporary Architecture Practice)

Architecture Inserted, 2012

Eric Bunge (nARCHITECTS)
Mimi Hoang (nARCHITECTS)
Chris Perry (Pneuma Studio)
Liza Fior (MUF Architecture and Art)
Katherine Clarke (MUF Architecture and Art)

Renewing Architectural Typologies, 2013

Makram El Kadi (L.E.FT)
Ziad Jamaleddine (L.E.FT)
Tom Coward (AOC)
Daisy Froud (AOC)
Vincent Lacovara (AOC)
Geoff Shearcroft (AOC)
Hernan Diaz Alonso (Xefirotarch)

Cultural Cues, 2015

Joe Day (Deegan Day Design)
Tom Wiscombe (Tom Wiscombe Architecture)
Adib Cúre (Cúre & Penabad)
Carie Penabad (Cúre & Penabad)

Against the Grain, 2016

Marcelo Spina (Patterns)
Georgina Huljich (Patterns)
Dan Wood (WorkAC)
Lisa Gray (Gray Organschi Architects)
Alan Organschi (Gray Organschi Architects)

Future Real, 2018

Kersten Geers (OFFICE Kersten Geers David Van Severn)
Michael Young (Young & Ayata)
David Erdman (davidclovers)

Mexican Social Housing: Promises Revisited, 2019

Tatiana Bilbao (Tatiana Bilbao Estudio)

Within or Without, 2020

Scott Ruff (RuffWorks Studio)
Florencia Pita (Pita Bloom)
Jackilin Hah Bloom (Pita Bloom)
Omar Gandhi (Omar Gandhi Architect)

Reimagining the Civic, 2022

Stella Betts (LEVENBETTS)
Fernanda Canales (Fernanda Canales)
Luis Callejas & Charlotte Hansson (LCLA)

Conscious Community, 2023

Chris Cornelius (studio:indigenous)
Rodney Leon (Rodney Leon Architects)
Abeer Seikaly (Studio Abeer Seikaly)

Introduction

The Particular and the Public brings together the work of three studios taught by the 2022 and 2023 Louis I. Kahn Visiting Assistant Professors at the Yale School of Architecture: Rachaporn Choochuey, Carrie Norman and Thomas Kelley, and Chat Travieso. Although diverse in context and methodology, the studios share an investment in the social and environmental contingencies that inform architectural practice today. Through distinct lenses—youth justice, informal domesticity, and regional specificity—they offer speculative tools for building with purpose, empathy, and precision.

Chat Travieso's Bronx-based studio, "Yes Loitering," centers on youth in public space. Focusing on the South Bronx and working in partnership with WHEDco and DreamYard, students collaborated with teen advisors to design environments responsive to the realities and desires of young people, reframing the city as a place of care, trust, and intergenerational equity.

Rachaporn Choochuey's studio with senior lecturer Michael Surry Schlabs, "Going Home, Again," traveled to Bangkok to examine housing through the lenses of informality, impermanence, and climate resilience. Students explored how mass housing could evolve in the face of urban density, sea-level rise, and the changing concept of family, offering flexible models for dwelling that rethink domestic order as fluid and collective.

Norman Kelley's studio with critic in architecture Violette de la Selle was set in New England and proposed alterations to First Period houses. By converting a private historic house where George Washington slept into a public Athenaeum, students tested ways to build with and against history and its physical context, seeking a "third language" of form that could hold past contradictions while projecting new social futures.

Together these studios question how architecture might move from symbolic gesture toward transformative action. Their work demonstrates, across scales and contexts, that architecture is not a passive reflector of culture but rather an active shaper of equitable and resilient worlds.

We would like to thank the professors and students for making this book possible. From Rachaporn Choochuey's studio we would like to thank Uzayr Agha, Ariel Bintang, Ceyda Gioutzesoi, Carolina Ho, Luyao (Chloe) Hou, Weiqiao (Joe) Lin, Chentian (Serena) Liu, Samantha Ong, Amanda Tian, Huy Truong, and Nohar Zask Agadi. From Chat Travieso's studio we would like to thank Ben Acheampong, Miranda Clark, Odette James, Fuad Khazam, Mariel Lindsey, Barbara Nasila, Precious Ndukuba, Kevin Yan, Chloe Zhang, and Kaiwen Zhao. From Carrie Norman and Thomas Kelley's studio we would like to thank Jerry Chow, Jonathan Chu, Bobby Chun, Benjamin Fann, Tiana Kimball, Calvin Liang, Ingrid Pelletier, Abby Reed, Iris You, and Jessica Zhou.

Special recognition is due to Cathryn Drake for her guiding and precise editorial work. We extend our utmost appreciation to Manuel Miranda Practice for graphic design. This volume represents a movement that is consistently engaged with its context and strives for social relevance and impact within the academic realm of architecture. It stands as a testament to the transformative power of architecture.

—Nina Rappaport and Saba Salekfard

GOING AGAIN

RACHAPORN CHOOCHUEY

MICHAEL SURRY SCHLABS

THE PARTICULAR AND THE PUBLIC

HOME,

Marmalade Sky, Wonderfruit Festival

"Going Home, Again" began by exploring questions related to house and home, family and community, architecture and environment through the lenses of informality and impermanence. This investigation was conducted while considering challenges associated with climate change and its impact on coastal cities like Bangkok, the realities of designing and building for a tropical urban environment, and the ongoing trauma of the COVID-19 pandemic. We used the city of Bangkok as a situational case study to develop alternative models of mass housing and collective living that are capable of adapting to the radical uncertainties inherent in these current crises.

ORGANIZATION

The semester began with a close (and quick) critique of the formal and its inverse, the informal. We discussed a variety of aesthetic and experiential approaches to informality and its relationship to problems of order, clarity, intelligibility, organization, and hierarchy. Students were asked to select, or find, a specific object with formal qualities that are more or less well-defined and then, through a series of discrete actions and operations, transform it. Transformative actions included addition and subtraction, cutting and sanding, casting and sculpting, sewing and weaving, dismembering and re-membering, each executed with an eye (as it were) on the tension between formal and informal, clear and ambiguous, legible and illegible.

Having explored the object's formal character—and, inversely, having worked to obscure its formal clarity through a series of interventions and transformations—the students were asked to draw their object, taking stock not only of its present condition but of its past and future too: that is, of its fundamental adaptability and impermanence over time, of its history, understood generously. Through the process of selecting what to represent in these drawings—and how—students staked out individual positions not only on what their objects were or meant, but on what they could have been and may yet become.

During our studio trip to Thailand we discussed the tectonic and spatial potentials of traditional Thai dwellings and how they adapt to unpredictable climatological conditions; visited squatters' communities and informal settlements in Bangkok's inner city; explored twentieth-century experiments in public housing; and toured new super-high-end residential developments tailored to the desires of the global capitalist elite. We met with local experts, urban historians, neighborhood activists, community organizers, residential architects, and housing developers.

In Bangkok the students collected images, found objects, field recordings, and videos and assembled these, alongside other items and ephemera, into a sort of matrix. After organizing these items in a roughly gridded table, they were asked to identify moments of slippage, "looseness," and ambiguity within the order of the matrix. How and where might these items span or penetrate the boundaries or borders between categories? Where might categories themselves become porous, vague, or nebulous? How might these slippages and ambiguities begin to suggest new forms of material, spatial, and social order?

Finally, with the studio's midterm review just around the corner, students were asked to bring these preliminary explorations of form, category, and order to bear on the question of housing and home, of what it means to live together in the twenty-first century. Conversations about housing—whether "affordable" or "premium"—are fraught with contradiction and uncertainty, and the terminology around which such conversations often develop is sorely inadequate to describing the way people, families, and communities live. The way we talk (and think) matters, and whether one begins at the bottom, with the individual housing "unit," or at the top, with a Students were challenged to develop a position on these issues that falls between individual and collective, public and private, inside and outside, house and community, domestic and urban. What does it mean to live, or dwell, in such an in-between place? What might home, so considered, even look like?

Student projects toyed with the fundamental "looseness" and "fluidity" of domestic experience in the modern city, exploiting the potential of drawing and making—the tools of architectural representation—to illuminate (and celebrate) the various ambiguities inherent in social and spatial relations in contemporary Bangkok.

RACHAPORN CHOOCHUEY

Over seven days in Bangkok we explored a number of different housing typologies, from informal squatters' settlements, to middle-class public housing and high-end real estate developments. We saw the city from the road, the water, and the rooftop. And we ate very, very well.

STUDIO BRIEF

The global COVID-19 pandemic has been utterly devastating, introducing uncertainty into every aspect of modern life. For the urban poor in a dense metropolis like Bangkok, whose lives were already vulnerable, the pandemic compounded and amplified that uncertainty. In many parts of the city, one-room living spaces are shared by many inhabitants. Social distancing, as we have come to understand it, is simply impossible under such conditions, and many people have been forced to live on the street or in their cars, if only to keep their families safe. For too many, "home" is no longer a safe space.

At the peak of the pandemic, it became clear that a major COVID-19 cluster in one of Bangkok's biggest hospitals was being driven not by patients but by the hospital's service employees, many of whom lived in a crowded informal settlement nearby. So the long-ignored problem of affordable housing became critical. The majority of Bangkok's housing is privately developed, and affordable housing isn't profitable. This drives many workers to informal settlements in or near the city center, where most service jobs are located. Of course Bangkok is hardly unique in this respect. The affordable-housing crisis and the emergence of informal housing settlements are challenges faced by cities throughout developing countries. With no realistic end to the pandemic in sight—and with other pandemics/crises on the horizon— the need for innovation in clean, safe, affordable housing has never been more urgent.

The COVID-19 pandemic has prompted a radical reconsideration of certain traditional notions of what it means to make a "home" and create a family. In much of the world, the standard of the nuclear family has become inadequate to the demands of pandemic living; many of the social infrastructures taken for granted as part of pre-pandemic life are absent. This rupture, while traumatic in the extreme, presents an opportunity to reconsider architecture's role in perpetuating a vision of home/family life now proven less than sufficient, if not wholly obsolete, in light of current crises.

By 2050 more than half of Bangkok could be under water. Fifty years later it could disappear entirely, along with many other coastal cities. In this context, mass migration could become a regular part of life for far too many of us. The very concept of "home," to say nothing of "homeownership," will be greatly challenged.

Bangkok's tropical climate invites a range of creative approaches to cooling and ventilation, which will become increasingly necessary in more and more places if the worst effects of climate change are to be averted. Many of these methods are rooted in vernacular building traditions based on light construction and daily adaptability to extreme changes in weather. The fundamental impermanence of architecture is especially evident in this context, where the built environment appears as but a pause in the constant flux and flow of the natural world, subject to the entropic processes of erosion, dissolution, and attrition. This demands of architecture—and of architects—a high degree of flexibility and adaptability. In such a context, informality becomes less a symptom of marginality and precarity and more a matter of necessity. Like all things natural, architecture exists in a constant state of emergence and disappearance, construction and dissolution, solidity and ephemerality. A house, in this view, is not a fixed object or thing unto itself, but a condition—an expression perhaps—of living.

Considering the specter of climate change and the threat it poses to the viability of modern urban life, along with the lingering impact of the global pandemic on human society, the adage that "you can't go home again" may hold more than ever. What is "home," after all, but a manifestation of the familiar, a way of organizing space—be it mental or physical—around notions of the stable, the secure, and the certain?

This studio began by rejecting such assumptions to consider questions of house and home, family and community, and architecture and environment through the lenses of informality and impermanence. This exploration was conducted in light of challenges associated with climate change and its impact on coastal cities like Bangkok, the realities of designing and building for a tropical urban environment, and the ongoing trauma of the COVID-19 pandemic. The students examined several aspects of affordable housing in high-density, tropical urban contexts. We used Bangkok as a case study for developing alternative models of mass housing and collective living capable of adapting to the radical uncertainties inherent in the current crises. To this end, we consulted with and collaborated with representatives of the Bangkok Metropolitan Government and the National Housing Authority of Thailand, among other local institutions and stakeholders.

The world has changed, and continues to change, at a bewildering pace. That in itself is nothing new. What is new is our collective recognition of that change, of change as a fundamental characteristic of the world at large, and of architecture's need to change with it.

In the first part of the studio, the students investigated and developed an individual approach to the question of "home" based on a critical understanding of four key issues: informality, impermanence, uncertainty, and adaptability. The session helped the students to explore the project's conceptual framework. Then the studio spent travel week in Bangkok to experience an actual situation with another set of issues in mind: site, situation, space, and assembly. A "superblock" with mixed developments in the middle of Bangkok was explored as a potential site for the project. In the second half of the studio, students developed their projects in more tangible forms.

CONVERSATION

NINA RAPPAPORT

When you started your firm all(zone) in Bangkok, did you intend to work first on smaller installations and then on larger projects? You seem to enjoy these smaller urban insertions.

RACHAPORN CHOOCHUEY

Before I went to study at Columbia University, I was working at a very big architecture firm in Bangkok, and I went to school with the idea that I was not going to be an architect. I thought, "No, I'm not going to become like all these boring archi-tects." But I like architecture very much and everything around it. So after my master's, I got a PhD at the University of Tokyo with the intention of doing everything around architecture while not being an architect. In Tokyo there were a few opportunities, so I worked on small installations and architectural exhibitions, which were quite fun. I thought that I didn't need to produce buildings. Then, after I came back to Bangkok, a good friend said, "These projects are getting a bit serious; let's make a small studio so that at least we have someone to pick up the phone when we receive projects." It started as just the two of us, and then two others joined. But then my friend left, and I had people relying on me, so I had to carry on.

NR

One of the things I have noticed about your work is that some of the projects provide solutions for issues that are overlooked by city officials in Bangkok, who are focused on major redevelopments. How did an interest in working on smaller commissions, like the marketplaces and pavilions, promote alternative ways of looking at urbanism?

RC

The open-air market from 15 years ago is a good example since it came to us when they couldn't find any architects to do it because it was almost too simple. It was interesting because there were issues that involved how the local economy worked in the city. Merchants can rent a 1.5-by-1 meter space for $500 per month and make a lot of money because they do three shifts— morning, afternoon, and evening. At the beginning we didn't under-stand why they wanted to hire us and spend half a million euros on a local market in the suburbs of Bangkok. But then, little by little, we realized that each merchant would earn the money back in one and a half years. So there was a clear economic logic that architects usually don't see in the same way the city does in terms of designing a high-rise, shopping mall, or condominium building.

Open air farmers market, Bangkok, 2012

Lighthouse project in all(zone) studio space, Bangkok, 2015

Another forgotten typology in Bangkok, and in many Asian cities, is the "shophouse," a model for mixed-use residential and retail. You took on the challenge of redesigning one for yourself. How did you make it an impactful catalyst for regenerating a neighborhood?

RC

Well, for me it was pure necessity. After I returned to Bangkok from my studies, I lived with my family. But their house is near the university, and the traffic is always bad. After six months I thought, "No, I cannot live like this." In 2007 I moved into the city and rented a shophouse, which was an obsolete type, and then I bought one after realizing that, even with refurbishments, it would cost one-third that of a more popular condominium. I live on one floor, the office occupies two others, and the other two floors are rented out. Little by little ten shophouses on this small street have been renovated, and three years ago we all put in money to repave the street. As architects we want to do something that has an impact on a bigger scale, and sometimes you just need to show an example; if it is good, people will follow.

NR

Another topic that I think is really important to you is the idea of adaptive reuse and transformation in both small and large projects, such as MAIIAM Contemporary Art Museum, in Chiang Mai, and the warehouse for the Duriflex furniture company. Are you focused on this approach because you love old buildings or because you feel it's a sustainable way to save materials and embodied energy?

RC

Actually our history is very short, and a 50-year-old building is already old here, so for me it's not about history but that it is a pity to throw things away, especially since after tearing down walls the construction debris is just taken to a landfill. It is more work to renovate than to build new buildings here, and it is a job that no one wants to do. That's why we are always able to do interesting things.

NR

Some of that involves maintaining or highlighting the existing urban fabric, in terms of the historical aura?

RC

Yes, the memory of a place and how people relate to an area of the city is important because that can transform a lot. New condominiums are required to have setbacks from the street, which leaves a hollow space in front of the building. It creates an extremely inhuman space because you cannot walk there. Usually there is a three- or five-meter-high wall, which changes the way people use the street. I have been writing articles complaining about this lack of public space.

NR

That is a great way to express your ideas too. What else have you been writing about?

All(zone), MAIIAM Contemporary Art Museum,
Chiang Mai, Thailand, 2015–16

All(zone), Set Controls to the Heart of the Sun, 2019, Sharjah

THE PARTICULAR AND THE PUBLIC

I have written about the spaces and rooms that are missing for service people, such as housekeepers and security guards, in large buildings. There are no lunchrooms, and sometimes they eat lunch in bathrooms, which is unacceptable. A building can be rated LEED Platinum while the workers have no place to take a break, so they sit on the street.

NR

Even delivery workers have no place to wait for their next orders. Were you able to implement your ideas?

RC

For MAIIAM Contemporary Art Museum, we asked the owners to supply a break room for workers with lockers and toilets. We really had to fight, but we got it! I think the client didn't like it so much at the beginning.

NR

You work with many different local and everyday household building supplies —from plastics, metal mesh, mirrors, and fabrics to concrete blocks—and adapt them for contemporary use. Do you have a strategy for selecting your materials, or are some of them so integral to the culture that you want to reuse them in new ways?

RC

Materials are related not only to our culture but also to the tropical climate. We still have a lot of small industries producing concrete blocks, plastics, and fabric, and owners are willing to produce small custom projects. I love visiting the factories to see how things are made. The nonstandard materials often give me a headache because sometimes you have to send them to a test lab to get them rated. We have been improving on concrete block since it is something that nobody wants to use. For the museum, we used the small mirror tiles used to decorate temples and experimented with the installation method, and now everybody is using them.

NR

Is there another material that you're developing and repurposing for a project?

RC

Yes, we are developing a fishing net with a company that makes all types of colorful nets. I asked them, "Why do you have all these colors for fish?" They said, "Different seas require different colors because the light is different, and it also depends on what type of fish you want to catch, because different fish see different colors."

NR

Looking back on your Light House project, commissioned for the 2015 Chicago Architecture Biennial and also installed in your office and a parking garage, do you feel that the idea of this flexible nomadic dwelling could be an inspirational provocation or a project to realize?

RC

That project was inspired by a real lack of affordable housing even for architects, but it is a bit extreme. We rented an abandoned parking space for one week, filmed two people living there, and showed the film at the biennial. The most interesting comments were from the security guard, who told us he would love to live like this because "you can see the light. But I have a little comment—we have to do something about privacy." We did find issues that we needed to solve. We constructed a second version in our office and rented it out as an Airbnb, and people came to sleep there.

NR

In a way it is a plug-and-play house, like an inflatable from the 1960s, and you used the idea as a basis for the project in the exhibition *Vulnerable Critters*, at La Casa Encendida, in Madrid. How did you develop it further there?

RC

The curators, Andrea Bagnato and Ivan Munuera, were dealing with issues of contamination before COVID-19. I was working with the faculty of public health at Mahidol University in Bangkok because people got COVID-19 from the hospital staff, not from patients. The staff live in very bad conditions and informal settlements next to the hospital. So we were called in to see if we could provide quick solutions to improving their living conditions. We recommended more ventilation, new lighting, and improved hygiene. But you really must tear down everything. For the exhibition, we proposed an idea developed from the Light House but more serious, with toilets, kitchens, and better organization as a midterm solution—temporary housing for ten

All(zone), Marmalade Sky, Wonderfruit Festival, 2017

All(zone) renovation of shophouse, Bangkok, 2014

THE **PARTICULAR AND THE PUBLIC**

years. If you don't do anything it's like sitting on a ticking time bomb, and it exploded when the pandemic arrived.

NR

What is the essence of the design of the MPavilion, in Melbourne, and how did you envision its use?

RC

The MPavilion was up for five months and hosted a few events every day for the citizens of the city. They had all kinds of activities, such as talks, screenings, fashion shows, kids' workshops, and music. After being in isolation during COVID-19 it was time to celebrate being together in public outdoors. Our pavilion was made for that. It was a place for people to see each other again in a casual, relaxed setting—like being under a big tree with slightly moving light and shadows.

NR

What is the subject of your studio at Yale?

RC

We are focusing on housing issues in Bangkok because the city has everything except affordable housing. We will explore and prototype innovative solutions in terms of architecture, ownership, and perhaps technology. Architectural solutions can be more open, more casual, and lighter in a tropical climate.

STUDENT WORK

THE PARTICULAR AND THE PUBLIC

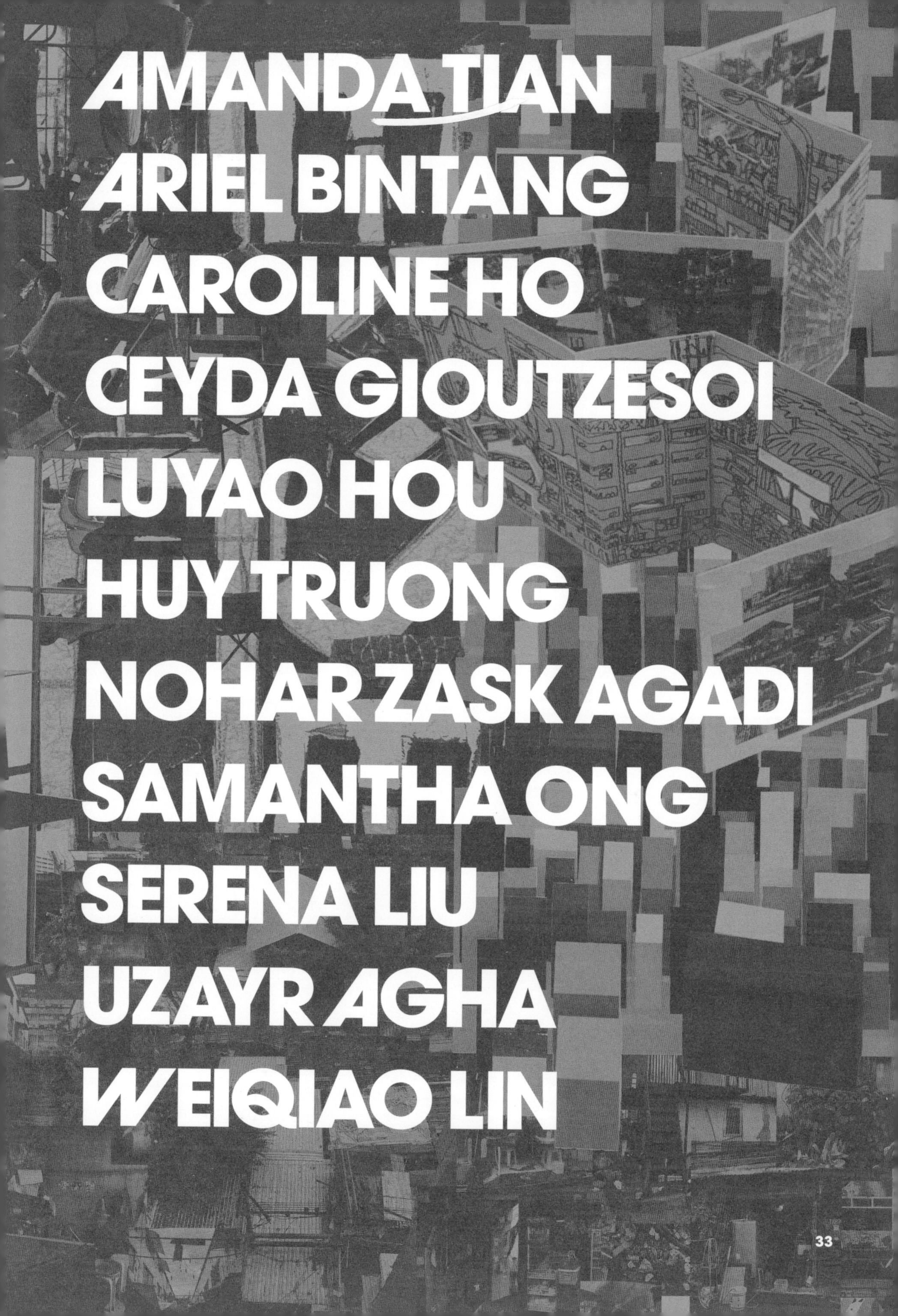

AMANDA TIAN

ARIEL BINTANG

CAROLINE HO

CEYDA GIOUTZESOI

LUYAO HOU

HUY TRUONG

NOHAR ZASK AGADI

SAMANTHA ONG

SERENA LIU

UZAYR AGHA

WEIQIAO LIN

AMANDA TIAN

RE-MEMBER TO REMEMBER

I believe in a vision of home as a metaphorical collector of memories. Past experiences are remembered through figural objects, becoming the creators of human social life and novel spatial experience. Central to this process is the question of individual perception: the emotional experience of domestic space is different for everyone. Like a mirrored surface that reflects distinct images at various angles, an experience of the home links past, present, and future.

During my time on and around our site in Bangkok, I paid particular attention to the many canopies and partitions. These shading elements serve to enclose and divide otherwise public spaces, even as they blur the line between individual properties. The rain canopies, roofs, and umbrellas create narrow, dim circulation spaces between homes. My design intervention responds to this context by introducing a large common sculptural form to house fifteen individual dwelling units, reflecting Bangkok's living memory as casual, borderless, and fluid.

Located at the intersection of Sanam Khil and Phra Chen Alleys in central Bangkok, the form interlocks with the existing urban fabric. Smooth spaces foster shared collective space, while more rigid gridded edges define private zones, creating an ever-shifting pattern of privacy and openness. Two systems—figure and ground—begin to overlap, blurring the line between order and hierarchy. Rooms are carved from solid mass, and boundaries are left incomplete, inviting residents to imagine their own domestic story's conclusion. Instead of locating traditional public spaces outside the project's more private core, collective programs are embedded deep within. Meanwhile each unit gains a private outdoor space.

A marriage of sculptural form to gridded ephemerality, the project adapts to its context, creating public gathering areas, "islands" for street vendors, and shaded spaces for massage stalls. Otherwise nomadic vendors might settle down to become part of the community, if only for a while. The continuous envelope—flowing seamlessly between wall, roof, door, and window—creates an illusion of motion and timelessness. With domestic spaces like kitchens, pools, and balconies located mostly out-of-doors, the design invites extended outdoor living and abundant daylight. Home, then, becomes not a fixed place but a shifting memory—felt, seen, and shared differently each day.

Urban aerial view

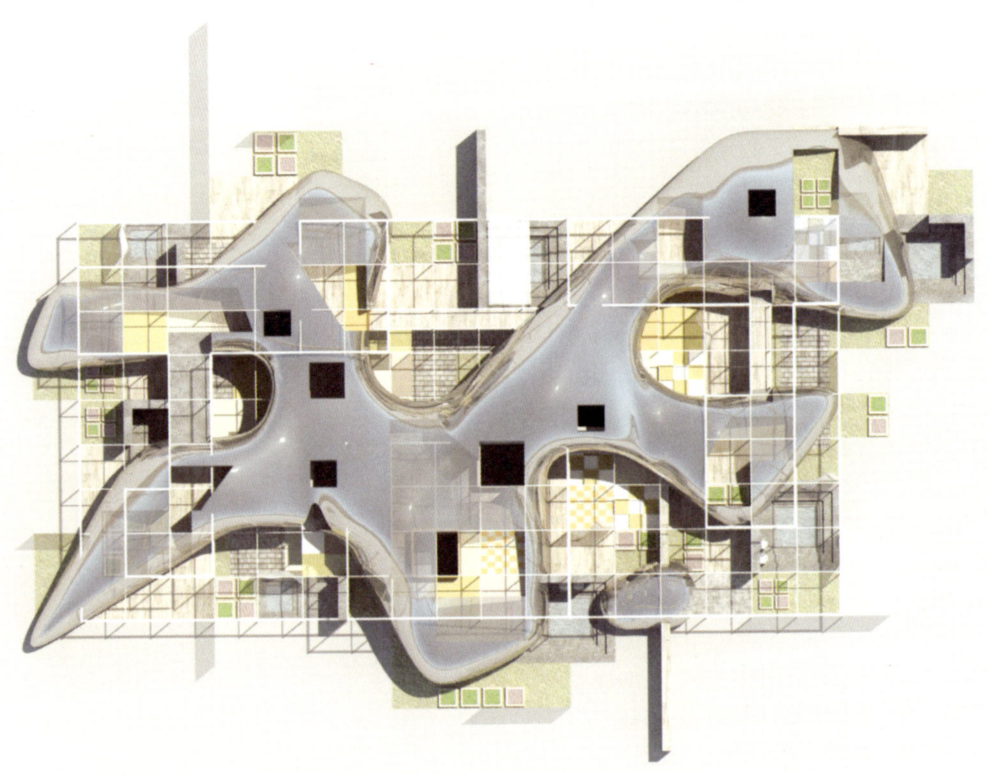

Plan

     THE PARTICULAR AND THE PUBLIC

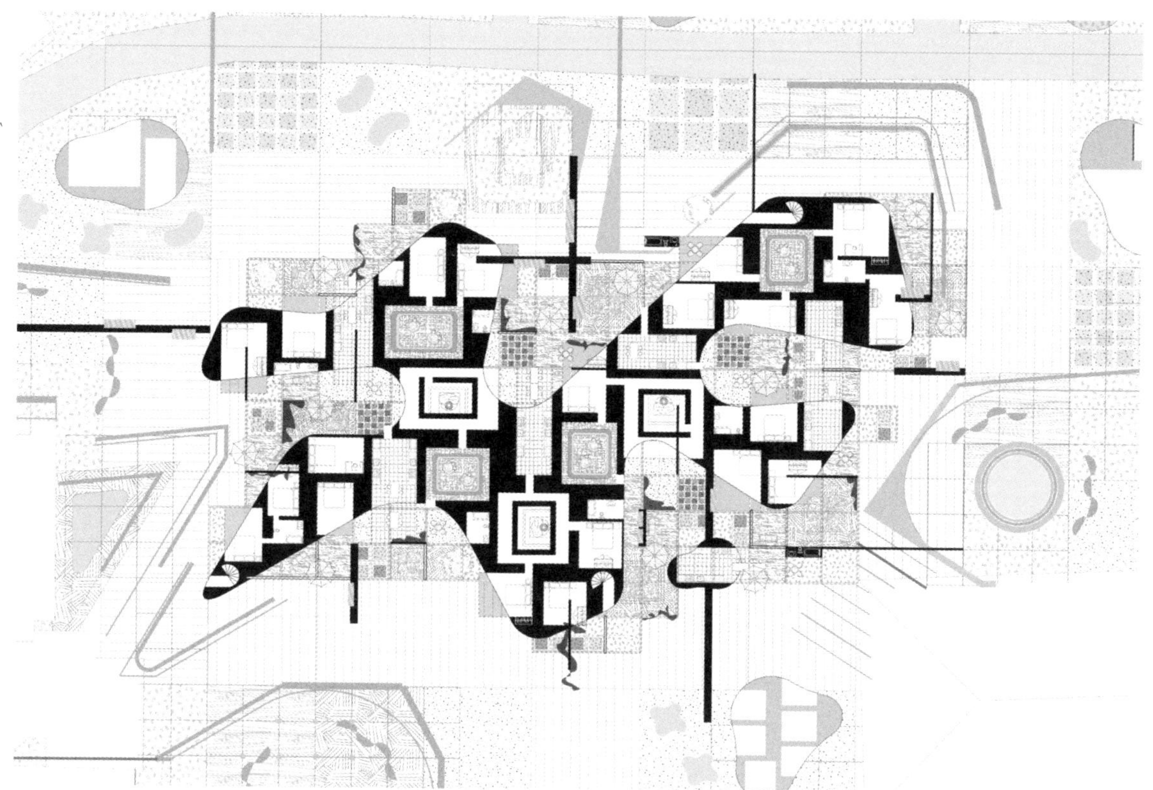

Ground-floor plan

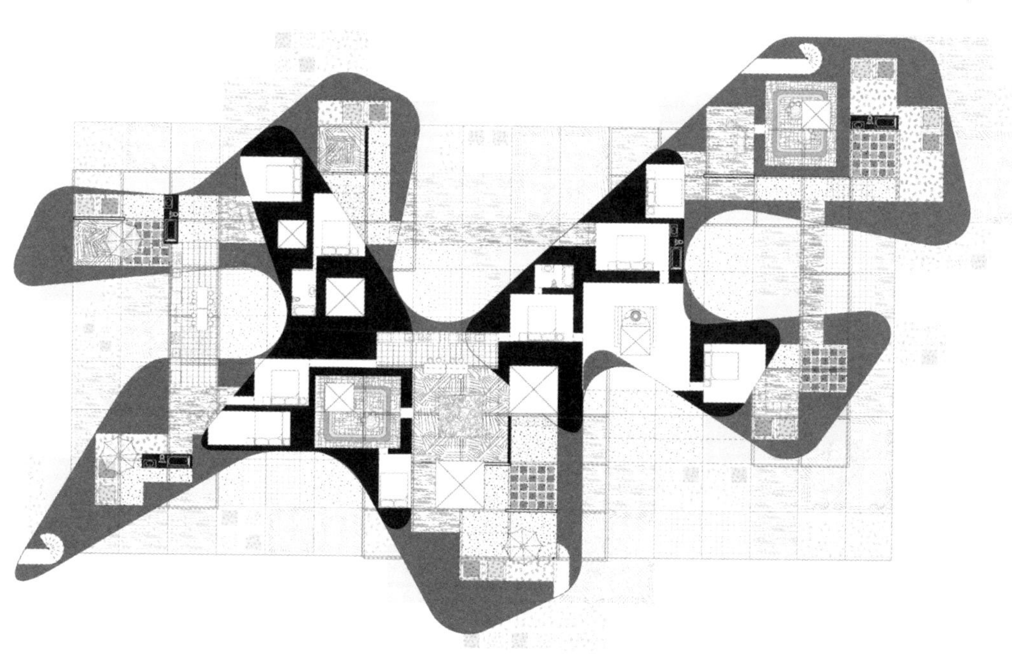

Upper-floor plan

New kitchen perspective

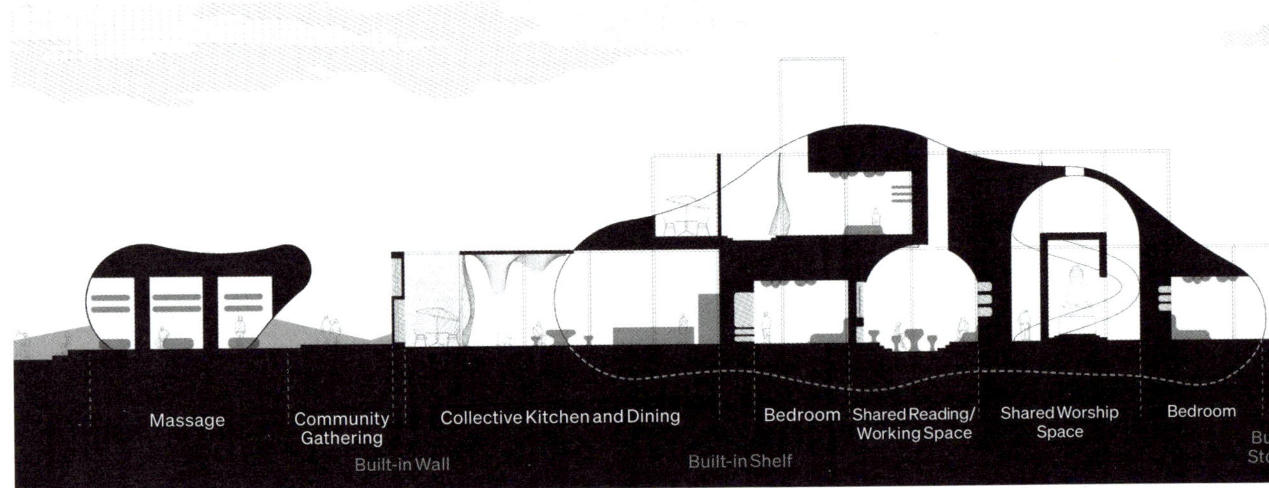

Section

Project elevation

     THE PARTICULAR AND THE PUBLIC

New rooftop perspective

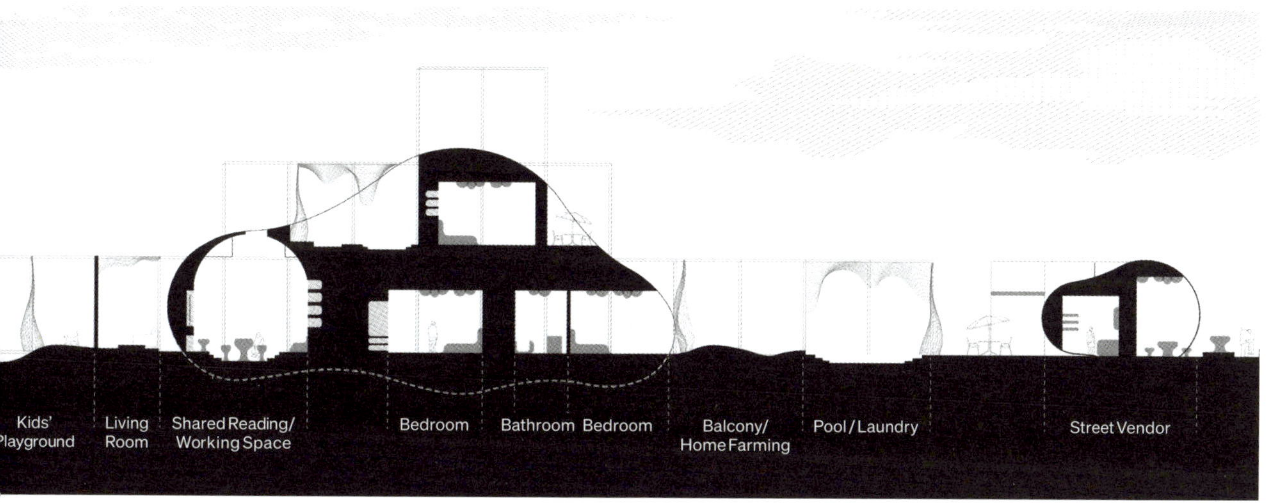

ARIEL BINTANG

FURNITURE QUA ARCHITECTURE

Between the permanence of Modernist ideals and the shifting boundaries of informal dwelling, the city of Bangkok continually negotiates its own evolving notion of contemporary domesticity. While formal architectural solutions are often imposed on informal housing conditions, Bangkok's residents frequently subvert these structures, adapting and reconfiguring them to accommodate their fluid, ephemeral routines. In doing so, they render architecture itself—understood as a static, finished object—unrecognizable, even irrelevant. What emerges instead is a living architecture, one in constant motion, shaped not by rigid form but by the rhythms of daily life.

This project begins with the premise that, in the context of modern urban domesticity, furniture and architecture are equally potent agents in shaping space and experience. Rather than positioning one as subordinate to the other, the project treats the two as interdependent. At the center of this investigation is the column—a fundamental architectural element that also becomes a piece of inhabitable furniture. It is reimagined here as a liminal device: part structure, part spatial apparatus, and part domestic object.

An unorchestrated field of furniture-integrated columns is proposed—elements that can be deployed or collapsed depending on the time of day and the needs of residents. In this model of social housing, individuals do not merely occupy private units but co-inhabit a shared domestic environment. The boundaries between the individual and the collective, as well as the formal and the informal, are blurred. Daily life unfolds as a choreography of reconfigurations, forming a domestic space that is adaptable, negotiated, and deeply human.

In rejecting fixed typologies, the project not only critiques the rigidity of Modernist frameworks but also proposes an alternative grounded in vernacular intelligence—a return to a collective and temporal sense of harmony.

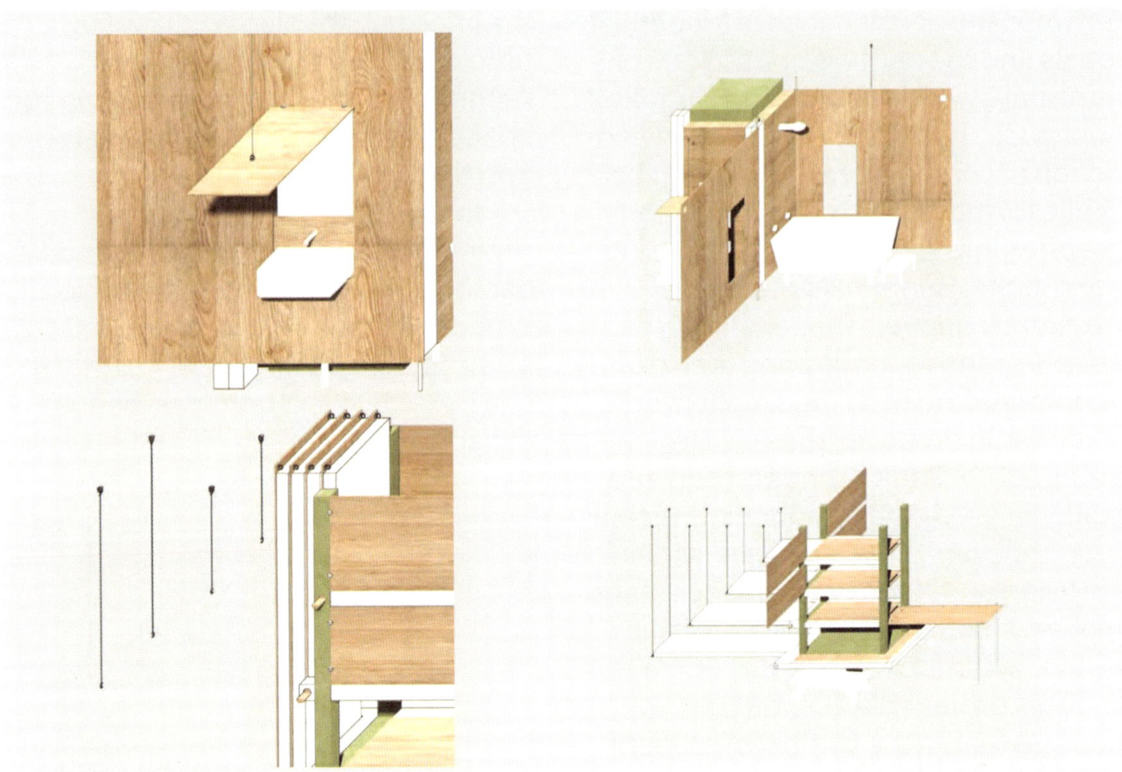

Axonometric details

Physical model

     THE PARTICULAR AND THE PUBLIC

Detail of domestic interior

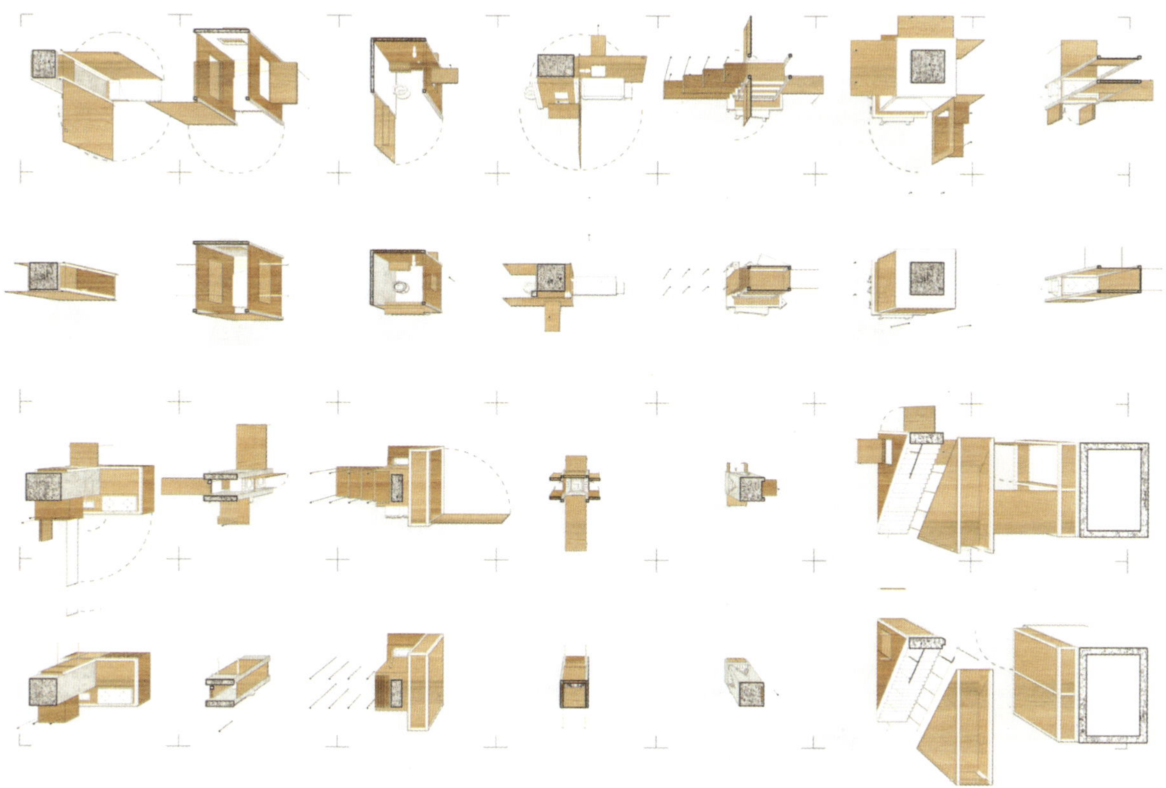

Plan diagram of domestic rituals

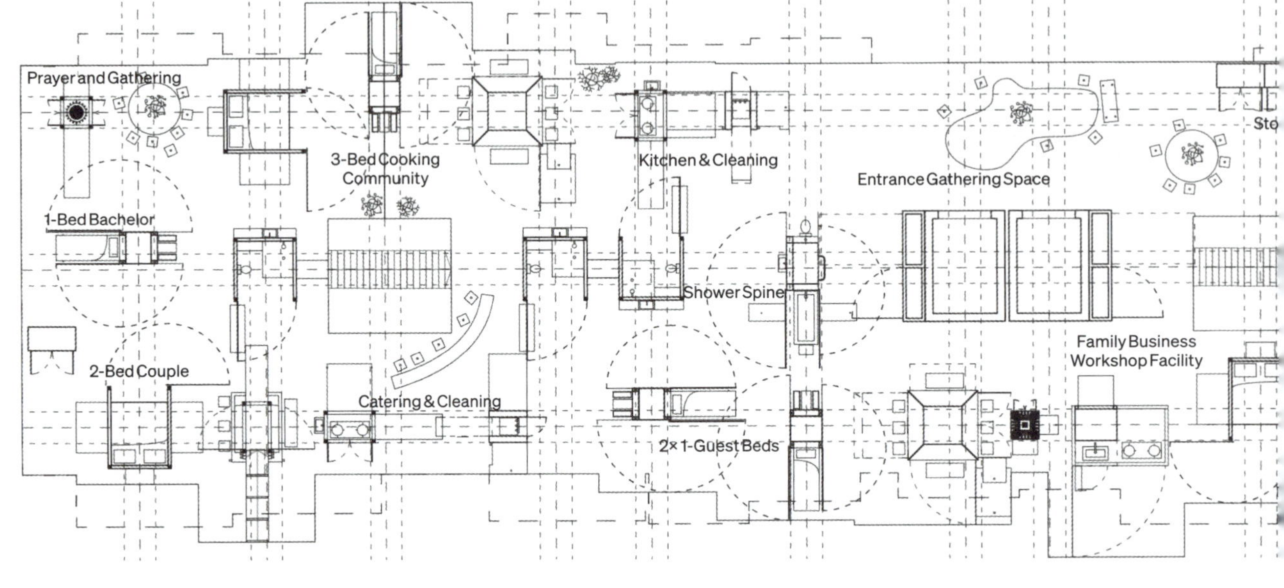

Project plan and elevation

Floor plan

   THE PARTICULAR AND THE PUBLIC

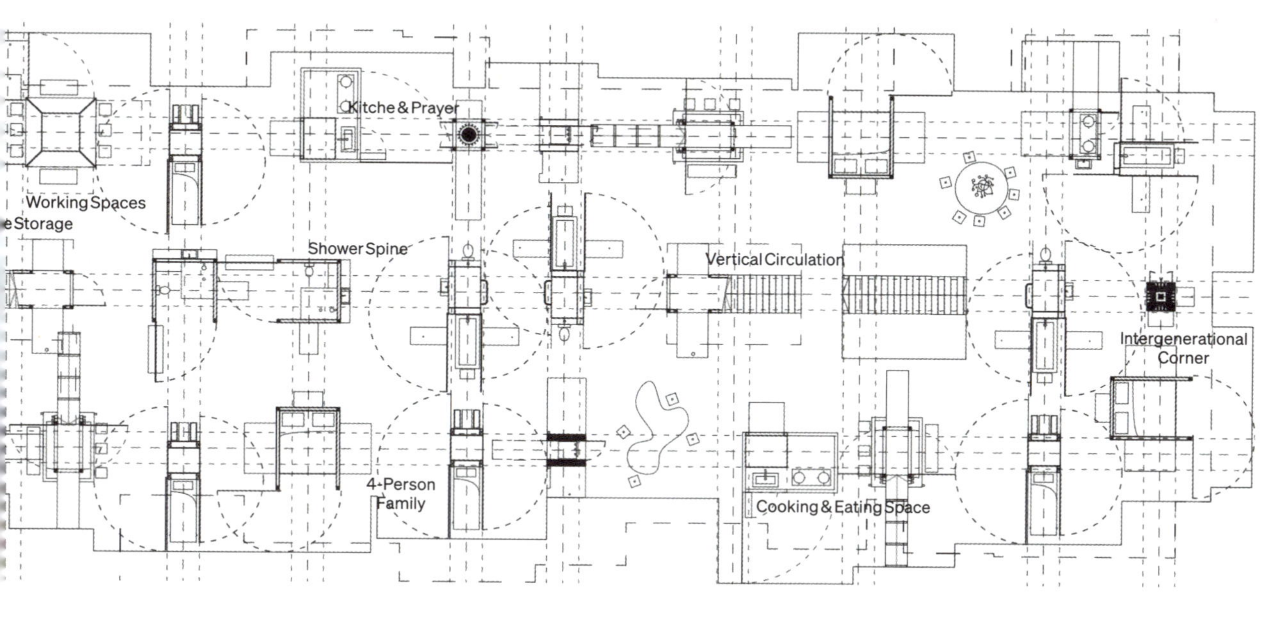

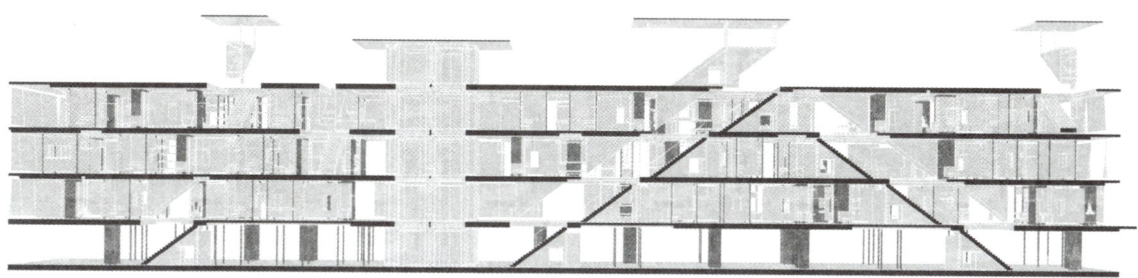

Project section

CAROLINE HO

A BODY OF WATER

Informality is produced by the convergence of contrasting formal orders and systems. Imagine the bowl. We understand the bowl as an object that can hold a volume of stuff—in this case, food. When we add the act of eating to the bowl, suddenly it can't perform perfectly anymore. The bowl is unable to accommodate the human action of scooping out portions of food unless the way it sits in space is manipulated. We must tilt and rotate the bowl to complete the act of eating.

Bangkok's landscape is topographically flat, with no major elevation changes. However, small moments that distort our experience of flatness can be found in the streetscape. High sidewalks, gutters, and thresholds are elements that produce consciousness in a body moving throughout the built environment. The body is aware of its position in space because of physical cues in the built environment. It is not only conscious of its location but also of the events happening around it. In Bangkok evidence of the conscious body extends far beyond the street, in the residents' response to the ever-changing weather conditions.

A future of severe flooding is already apparent and projected to worsen. The initial conception of the project brought elements of the street into the home. Where space is now defined not by walls but through gutters, thresholds, and sidewalks, the street is the most authentic place that embraces a coexistence with water. Replacing walls with these elements transforms the traditional shophouse into something that feels familiar yet is not. To be conscious of this feeling is to acknowledge its informality. Strategies are vertical too. Roofs and stairs are means by which water and people circulate through space.

Home is not limited to the house; it involves one's neighbors and community. The project is located in a lower-income region best characterized by its informal planning and development. The response toward water reflects the fluidity present in Thailand's attitude toward housing. Water is viscous; it is defined by its conditions, its containers, its boundaries, and in contrast, the home has no definite form. An exaggeration of strategies traditionally used to tame water and define spaces for living has, in turn, loosened conceptions of domesticity. Residents have become bodies that are conscious of their surroundings—of each other and the water around them. The project infiltrates the domestic space with elements from the outside. Roofs and gutters cut through its interior. It proposes a way of living with water through the tools we use to control it. The home becomes a machine for moving and storing water. It contains rather than repels.

Home evolves with the changes imposed on it by residents, through additions and demolitions. But here space changes in the presence of flooding. The project embraces flooding, and its aftereffects, as iterations of living. The home itself becomes a conscious body. Streets turn into canals; places to rest turn into docks. Places to play turn into workspaces. Domestic activities are not bound to the inside; they are fluid and responsive. The bizarre adjacencies of scenes of domestic life are brought together as we acknowledge one another. This project uses roofs and gutters to connect to the environment and surrounding buildings. In turn, these spaces become objects for local distribution in Bangkok's poorer districts. Home is fluid and adaptive. It is an ongoing negotiation that hosts the dynamic engagements that connect us. Home is a body of water.

Street elevation

Street section

THE PARTICULAR AND THE PUBLIC

Systems axonometric

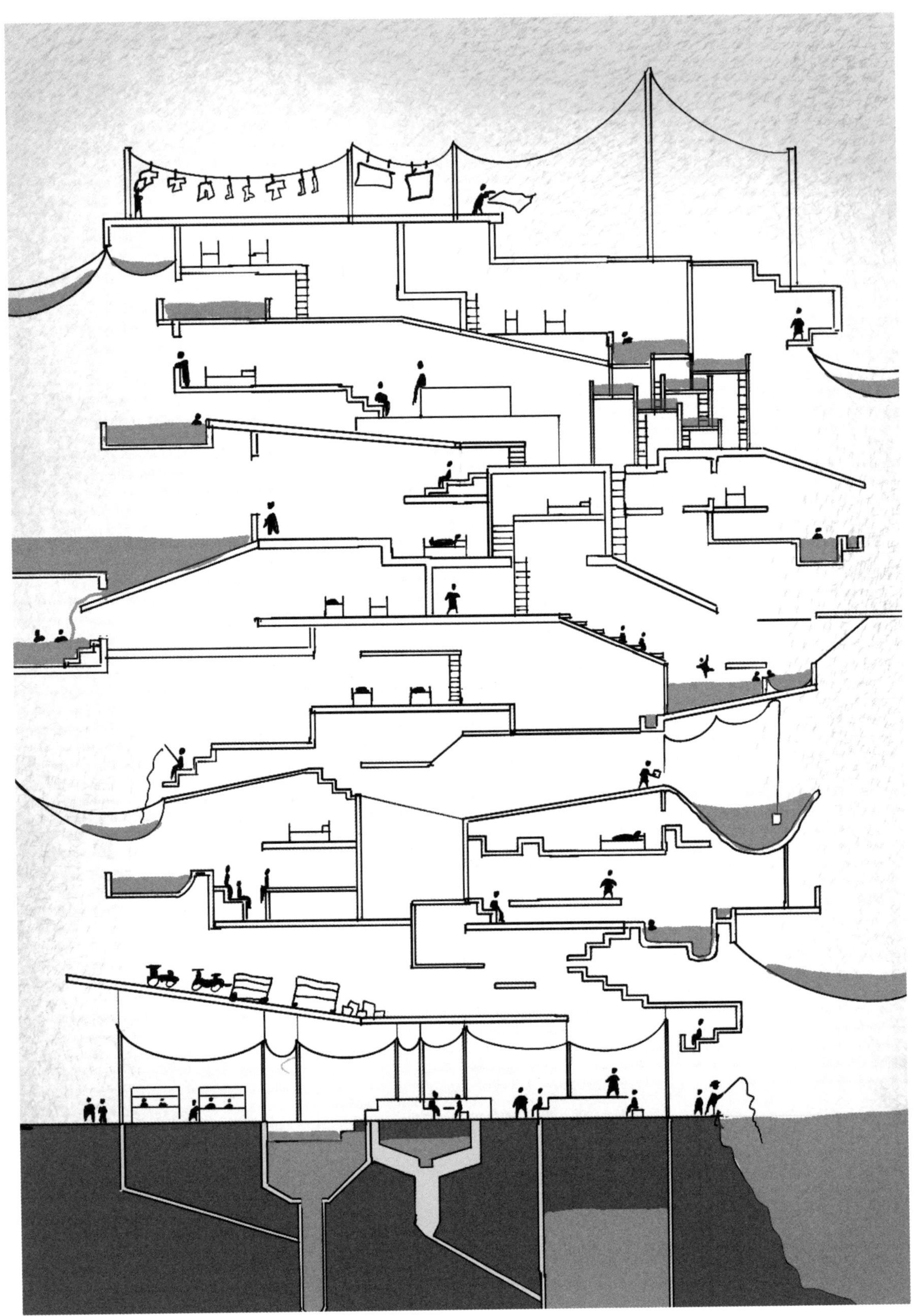

Concept section

          THE PARTICULAR AND THE PUBLIC

Concept physical models

Concept physical models

CEYDA GIOUTZESOI

GROWING INFORMALITY

ABSTRACT

This project explores how Bangkok's open and informal ways of living can be reimagined in a denser vertical housing typology. As cities grow taller, standardized and repetitive floor plans tend to limit spontaneous interactions between residents. These rigid arrangements, which support preconfigured and indefinitely repeatable daily routines, suppress the vibrant, interdependent, and fluid domestic life found in many of Bangkok's low- to middle-income neighborhoods. How can verticality in the urban environment—especially in housing—enhance rather than inhibit human connection?

PROCESS

At the threshold between order and chaos lies a vast gray area that defines the boundary between the formal and the informal. This project examines these soft edges—where boundaries become borders and vice versa—as potential spaces of social interaction. Using wax as a formal and spatial metaphor, we explore how materials behave differently under varying conditions. Wax poured into a mold and cooled becomes a rigid form, but exposed to unexpected forces like ice or water, it transforms—intertwining, melting, accumulating—into more ambiguous informal states. These transitions suggest that formality, as such, is often contingent on immediate context and individual perception, much like the interaction of color in the visual field.

In Bangkok, underutilized spaces—under bridges, near construction sites, and along rivers—are readily appropriated for domestic or communal use. The city's tropical climate fosters an unusual openness; slums and squatter communities evolve rapidly, often using improvised structures made from diverse reused materials. Interiors blur with exteriors, kitchens spill onto balconies, and fabric or glass bottles substitute for walls. Space and function are fluid, negotiated through use rather than prescription. Participation in construction is direct and communal, with pieces evolving from one use to another.

PROJECT

The proposed housing model embraces this adaptability. It allows for growth and intervention, with collective ownership distributed across a range of repeating modular building elements. Loose boundaries and undefined zones encourage spatial negotiation. Individual homes interlock, enabling residents to shape their environments —even as the boundaries dissolve and spill over into those of their neighbors. Verticality becomes a catalyst for community interaction rather than a barrier to active social life. A central void promotes internal dialogue, while the fragmented structure interrupts conventional plans, inviting alternative forms of living rooted in participation, flexibility, and mutual trust.

Ground-floor plan

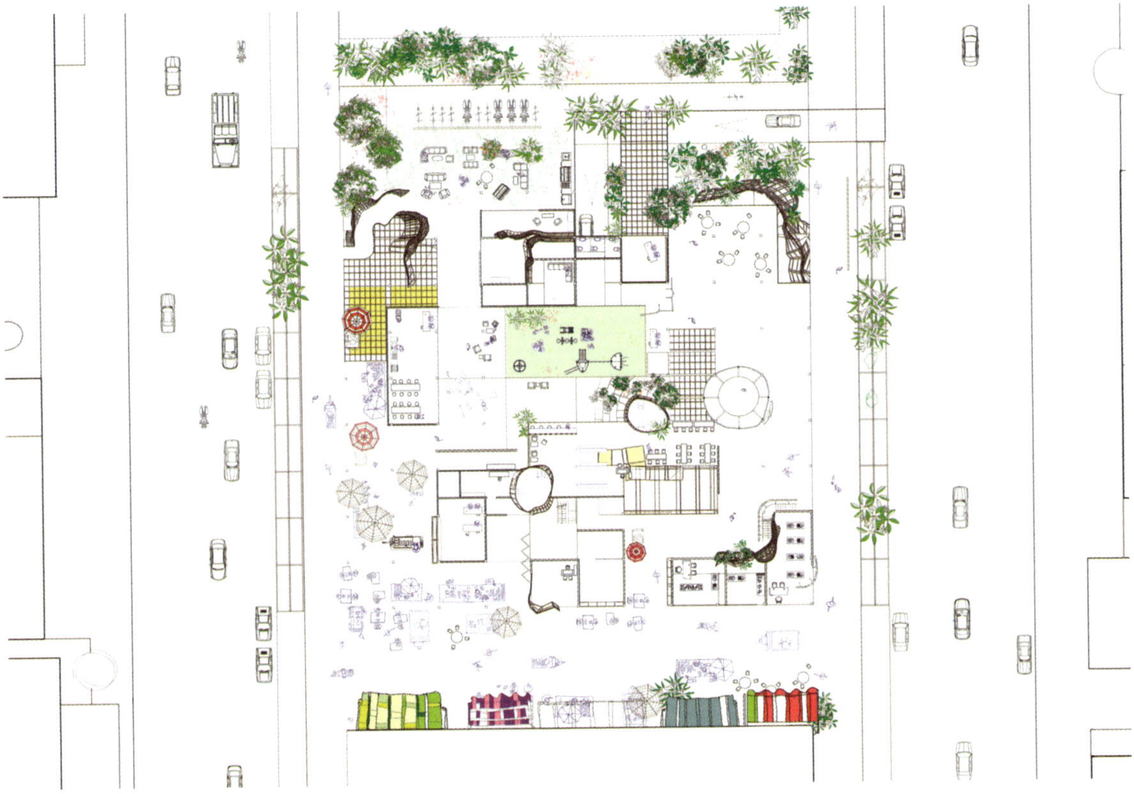

Upper-floor plan

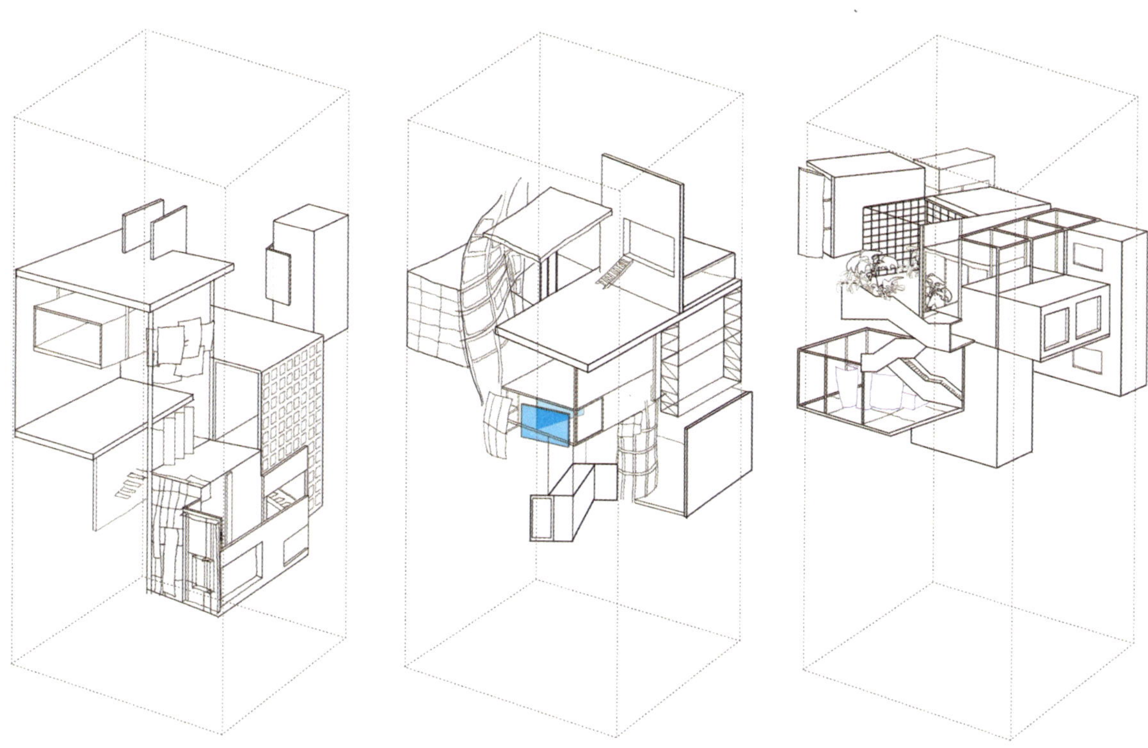

Concept diagram

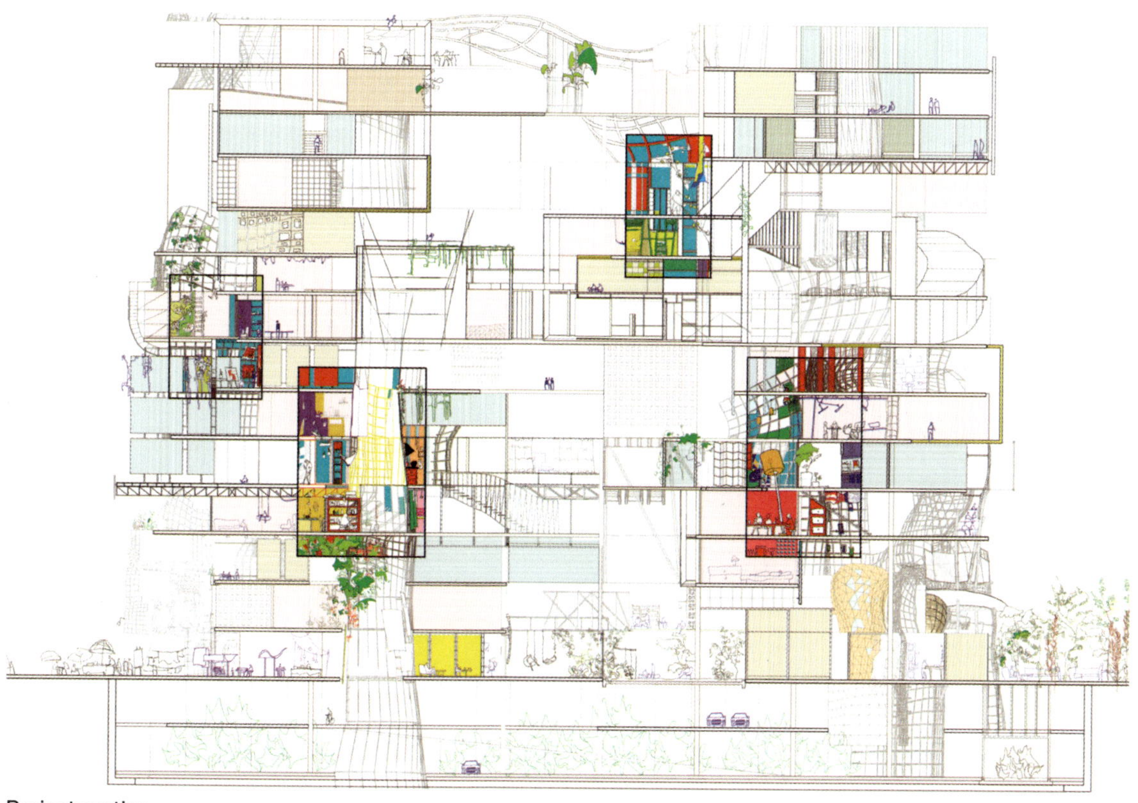

Project section

Narrative section and perspectives

Family 1

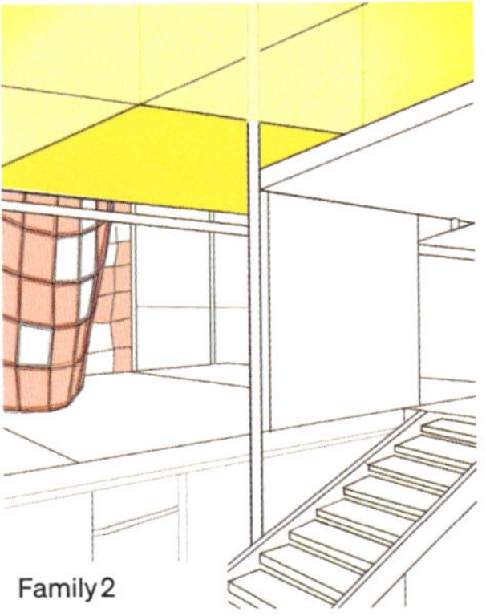
Family 2

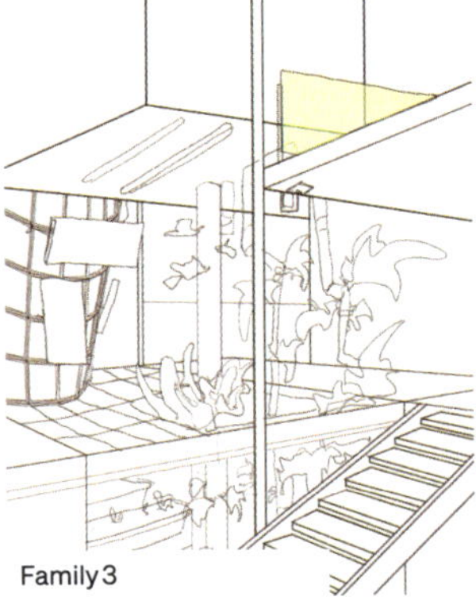
Family 3

Detail perspectives

Physical model

LUYAO HOU

THE *WORLD* OF THINGS BETWEEN US

More than a technical tool or a fixed ground, architectural drawing can serve as a collective instrument of speculative imagination. Inspired by the mutable appearances of things and the fluid definitions of space in Bangkok, where meanings often exceed their labels, this project explores the inherent ambiguity of architectural representation and the misreading of plans as a generative act. It reinterprets the floor plans of three Modernist visions of domestic living —Philip Johnson's Glass House and Mies van der Rohe's Brick Country House and Core House, each impactful, self-contained, and consistent according to its individual logic—to challenge and expand the boundaries of conventional modern housing.

The formality of the original drawings becomes a frame through which my informal interpretations unfold. This project suggests that when the architect steps back from the authoritative role of imposing persuasive forms, planning becomes a shared ground. Informal, everyday ideas are liberated through the tangible labor of construction and the materials of the real world. Home exists in the space between what is imagined and what is drawn. Both hand rubbings and digital 3D meshes abstract the dismembered object, offering different readings of the same thing—yet they appear visually similar. Where formality implies an order in place, informality disrupts that expectation.

Bangkok is a city of formal rigidity and spatial slipperiness. Here domesticity often transcends the divide between inside and outside: people cook on balconies, corridors, and sidewalks; plant gardens in wine glasses and along jogging tracks; and sleep between structural columns and during a street-side massage. Echoes of home appear around every corner. One doesn't need to be at home to feel at home. The word *home* itself becomes a slippery term, shaped by individual imagination.

This spatial informality allows objects and spaces to become mutable in both form and function. A circle in plan may be more than a column—it might be a satellite dish, a tree, a street umbrella, an electric pole, a perforated stool, a lotus-shaped lamp, a fan, a staircase, a pond, a twelve-seat round table, or even a disco ball.

The architectural plan—the most basic medium of the discipline—carries embedded ideas about units, domesticity, family, and home. Yet it is precisely through formal rigidity that we gain the freedom to draw, project, and reimagine. Even a boring, ordinary plan can provoke new understandings of what "home" means. Thus the three Modernist floor plans are reappropriated in the final exercise. Their formal abstraction and spatial fluidity offer fertile ground for reimagining domestic life, both personally and in the context of Bangkok.

As an (im)mutable mobile, the architectural plan becomes the first site of negotiation in the question of collective living. A thickened line in plan may be more than a wall or glass panel—it could be a water channel, a bench, a ceiling light, a kitchenette, a bamboo screen, a closet, a planter, a massage mat, or a poché for worshipping the Buddha. A square in plan may be more than Mies's iconic glass coffee table. It's an elevator.

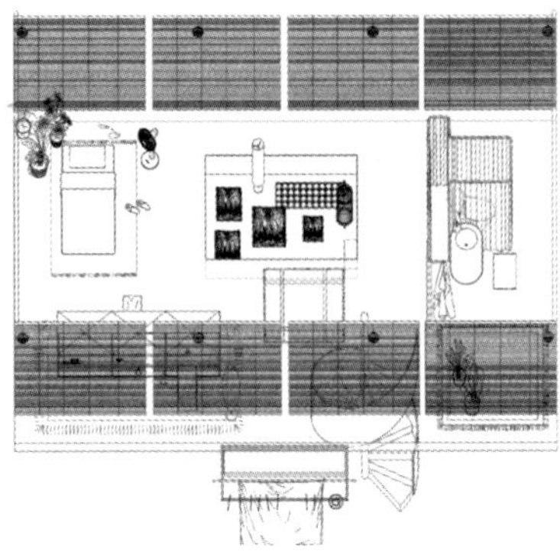

Glass House part one

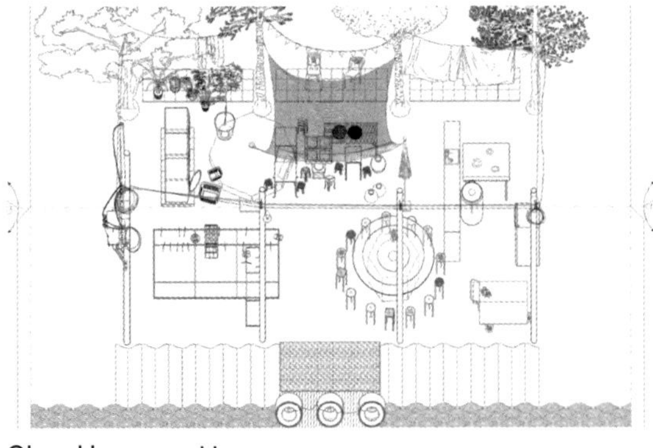

Glass House part two

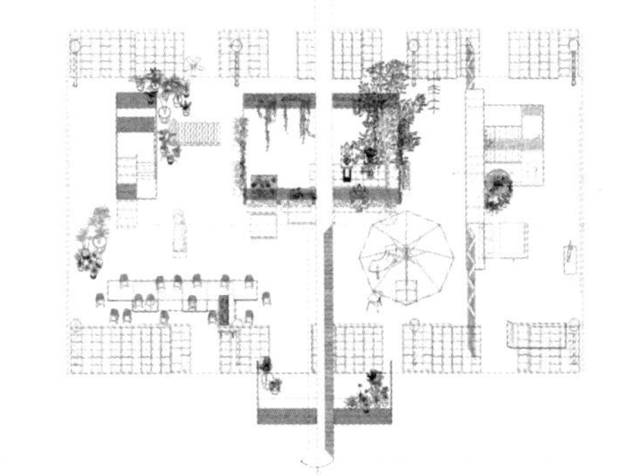

Glass House part three

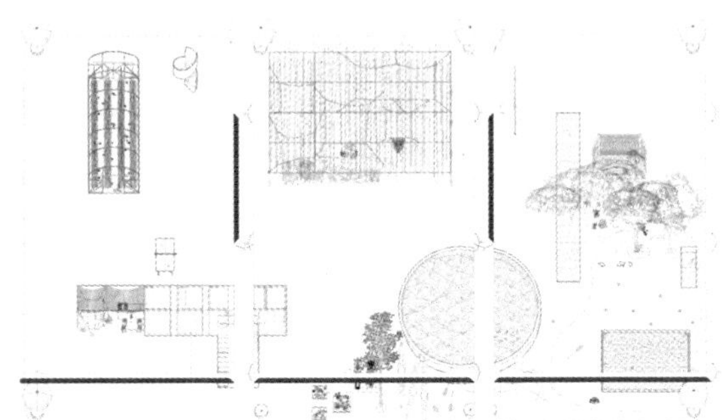

Glass House part four

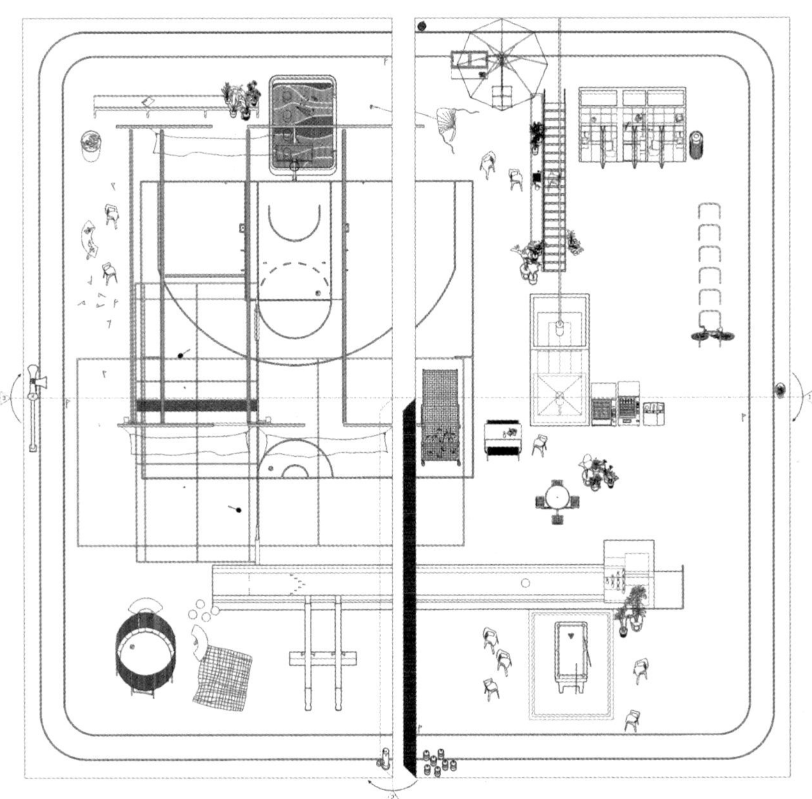

Core House

THE PARTICULAR AND THE PUBLIC

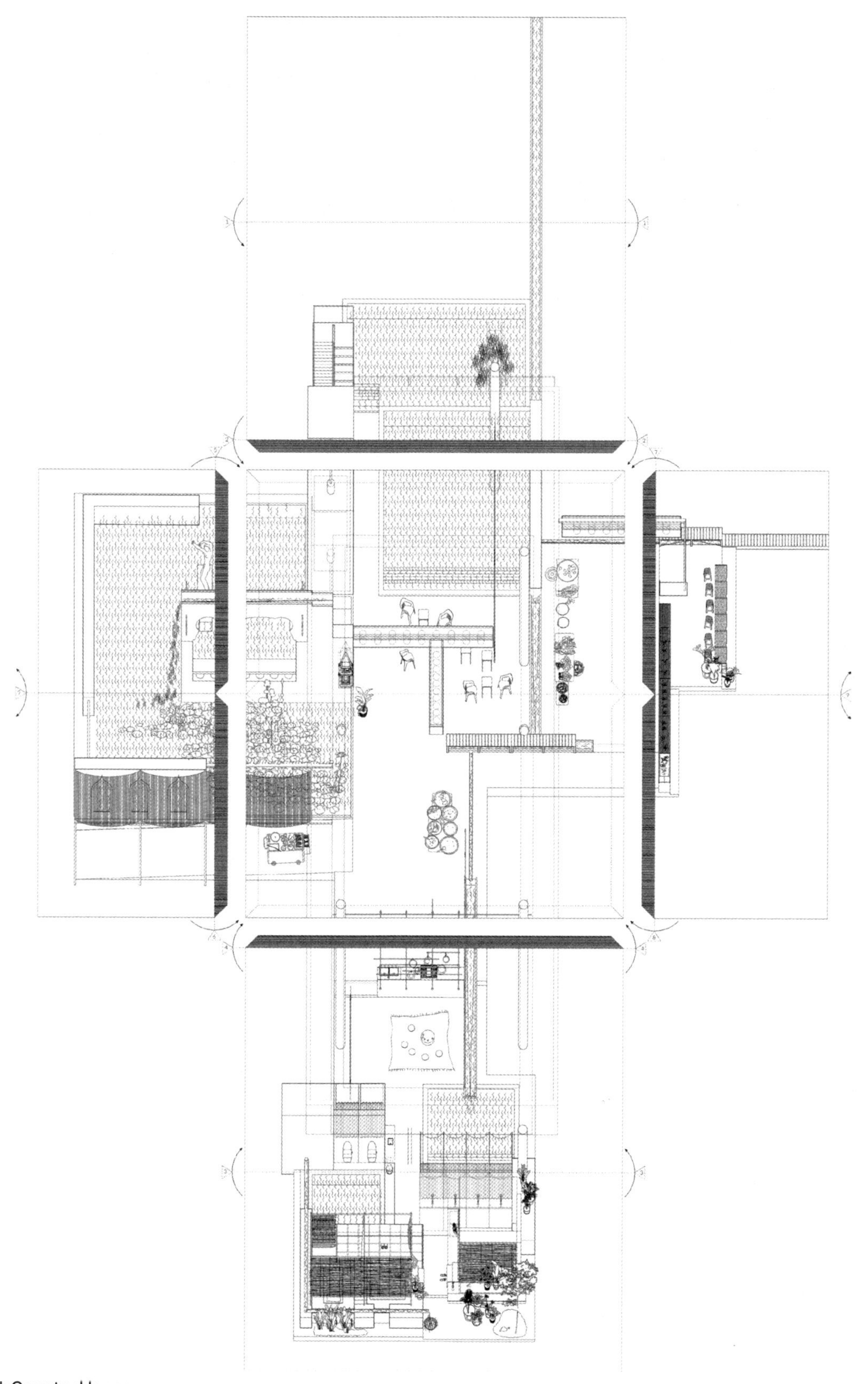

Brick Country House

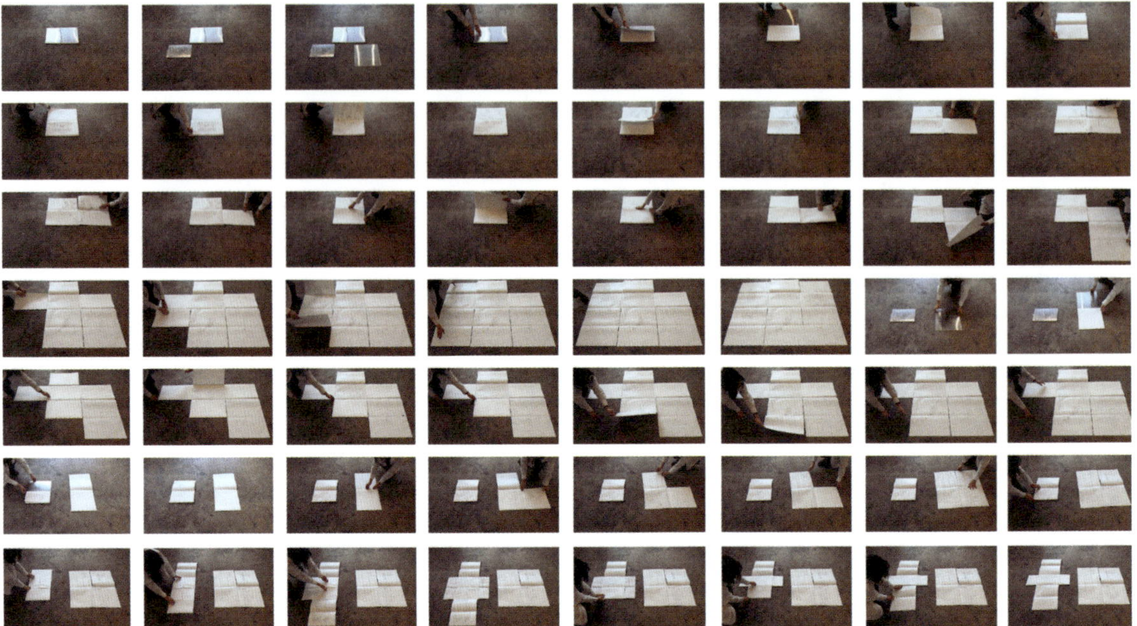

Manuscript unfolding

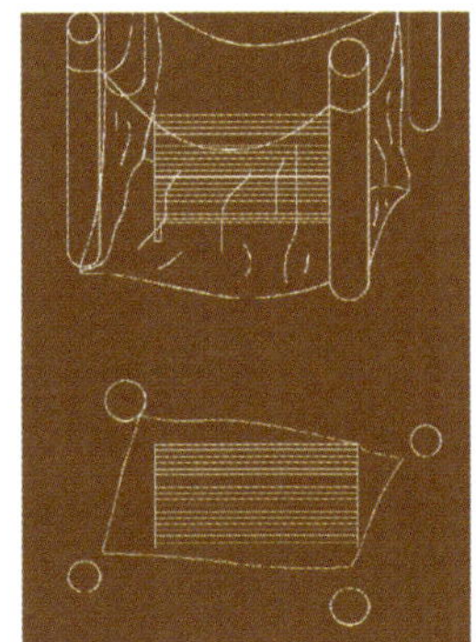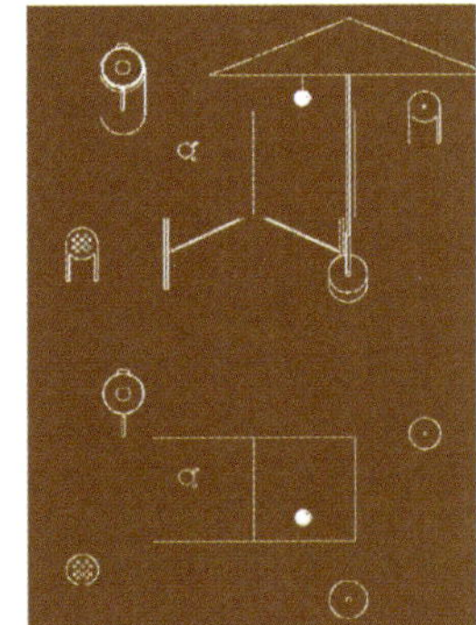

Postcards

Physical model

THE PARTICULAR AND THE PUBLIC

Physical models and manuscript

HUY TRUONG

FOUR ELEMENTS OF BANGKOK

This project reformulates Gottfried Semper's four elements of architecture —the mound, the wall, the roof, and the hearth—through the lens of contemporary (and possible future) Bangkok.

How are these elements redefined informally by the city's daily rituals? How does the collective authorship of urban life cultivate a shared sense of belonging? How might a renewed understanding of these elements help navigate the city's evolving landscapes?

Through a cast of allegorical architectural characters, the project explores and synthesizes new assemblies of Bangkok's architectural elements.

What if a foundation were the wheels of a motorbike?

What if a roof were an expanding tarp choreographed by those bikes?

How many kinds of rooms might come and go as needed?

What if a wall were the drying laundry of home?

What if a hearth were the breeze of a rotating fan?

How might domesticity itself generate new space?

What if the elements of architecture were not fixed objects but urban rituals— dynamic processes that shape the city continuously?

Between them all—foundation swiveling, wall storing, roof unfolding, hearth cooling—is a formalized joinery of informal scaffolding.

ARCHITECTURAL CHARACTERS

House of the Tree
Alone, it is a refuge in the water. Clustered, it becomes a floating park.

House of the Spirit House
Once present at every building site in Bangkok, the spirit house now collects offerings while adrift. Past spirits must seek its new location each day.

House of the Hugging Seeds
Stacked planter walls support herbs and vegetables. The house forms an intimate enclosure around drifting boats.

House of the Flying Laundry
Public form curves around private enclosures, catching maximum sun and wind. Laundry opens and closes rooms for bathing and lounging.

House of the Sizzling Sea
Buoyant bowls float below. Walls support tables, water jugs, and propane tanks. Tent roofs expand and contract above.

The Docks
The most collective character, the docks are a site of exchange: where fishermen sell their catch, vendors cook and serve, and neighbors gather to eat, drink, and talk.

A reinterpreted mural, late-twenty-first century, Bangkok, Thailand

What if a roof was an expanding tarp?

House of the Sizzling Sea: bowls act as buoys; walls hold tables, water jugs, and propane tanks; tent roofs expand and contract above.

Mural exploring informal bamboo assemblies

House of the Drifting Dreams: modular storage bunk beds and alcoves; collective scheming, reading, and lounging

The Docks: a site of collective exchange where fishermen share their catch, vendors cook and serve, and neighbors gather to eat, drink, and talk

House of the Wayfarer, late-twenty-first century, Bangkok, Thailand. A new climate reality defines the flooded landscapes of the Chao Praya Delta.

NOHAR ZASK AGADI

TWO BANGKOK

Contemporary urban forces often reflect postindustrial patterns. Traditional design strategies and preindustrial craftsmanship have gradually given way to the functional logic of the grid. Basketry, dating back to the early Neolithic era, exemplifies human adaptation over time—from twined weaving to modern caning, it reflects responses to political, climatic, and cultural shifts.

The urban grid reveals fluctuating spatial dialogues that shape daily life. This project explores two parallel urban dynamics in Bangkok: life within the grid and beyond it.

Bangkok's layered grid supports contradictory social activities. On the project site, there are upscale developments like One Bangkok next to low-income housing, highlighting discrepancies in spatial policy. State-led globalization has redefined social hierarchies and spatial management, marginalizing some, while bottom-up community-making embraces unofficial space-making principles.

Informal politics in low-income communities transform spatial logic at various scales, adding a "slippery" layer to the rigid grid. Public hallways and courtyards become living rooms or laundry areas; parking lots and sidewalks turn into food stalls or temporary retail. Infrastructure—power, light, shelter—guides nomadic urban navigation.

TWO BANGKOKS

This proposal offers a continuous utility network and shared resources, enabling flexible, unorthodox use of space and new types of domestic relationships within the formal grid. During the pandemic, digital communication became vital for forming publics, and temporary contracts emerged to sustain trade.

"Two Bangkoks" envisions a virtual and physical interdependence as a soft public infrastructure to regulate unofficial practices, maximizing the use of official spaces.

Power and data access across a virtual grid allow urban nomads and residents to connect, trade space, and meet various needs. Ephemeral light structures ease negotiation with authorities and access to the urban fabric. This system opens streets for recreation, supports urban expansion, and redefines housing logic by enabling adaptable, temporary spatial programs.

2 Bangkoks public living

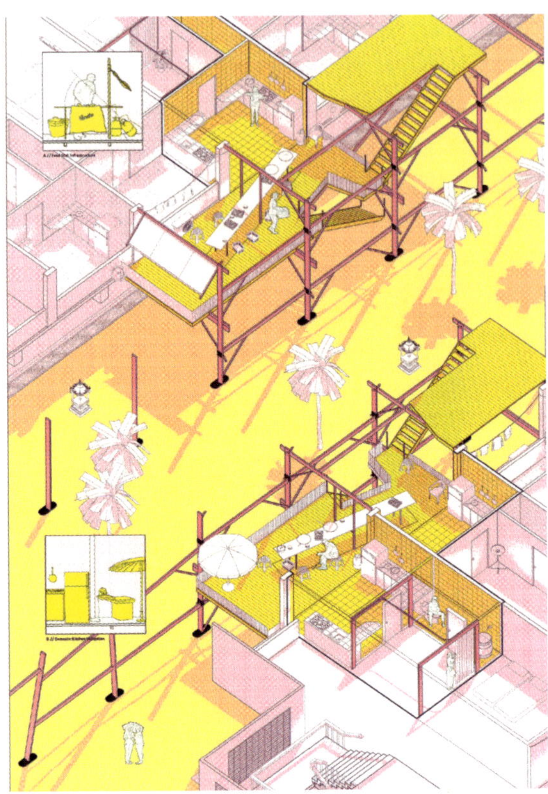

2 Bangkoks legitimized commerce

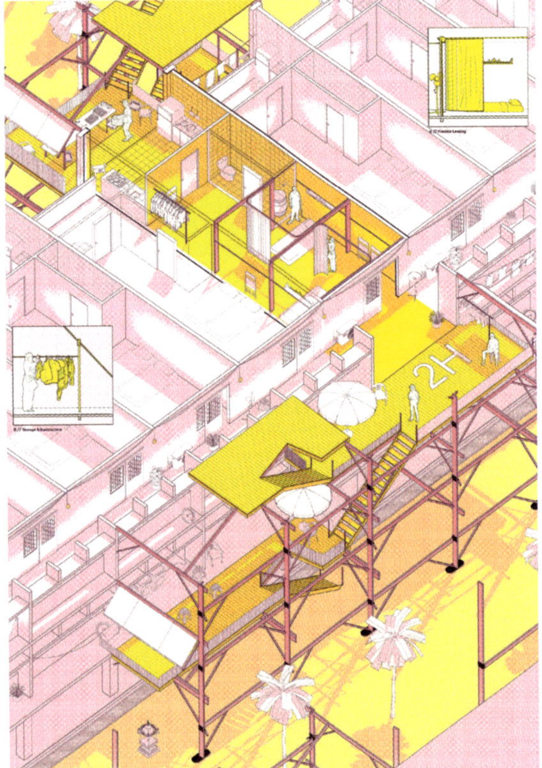

2 Bangkoks urban nomads

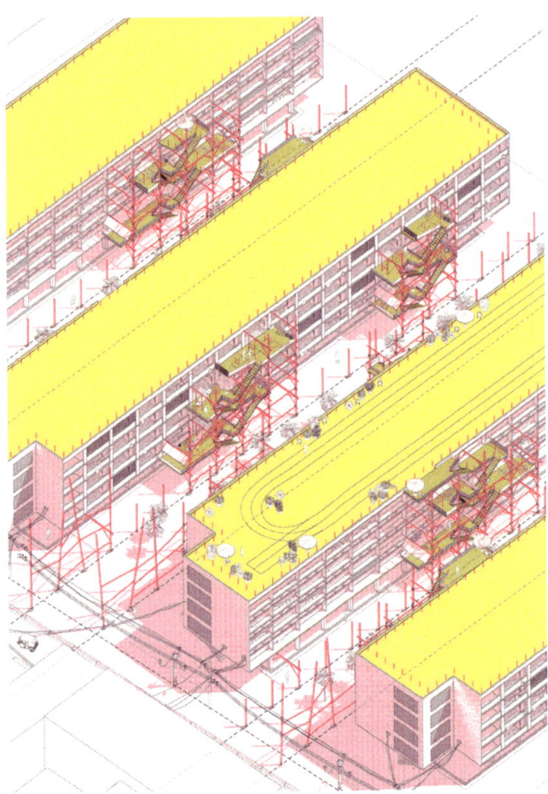

2 Bangkoks public legislation of informal urban policy

THE PARTICULAR AND THE PUBLIC

Lumphini-Benchakitti Park

Ayutthaya Ordination Hall

Physical model

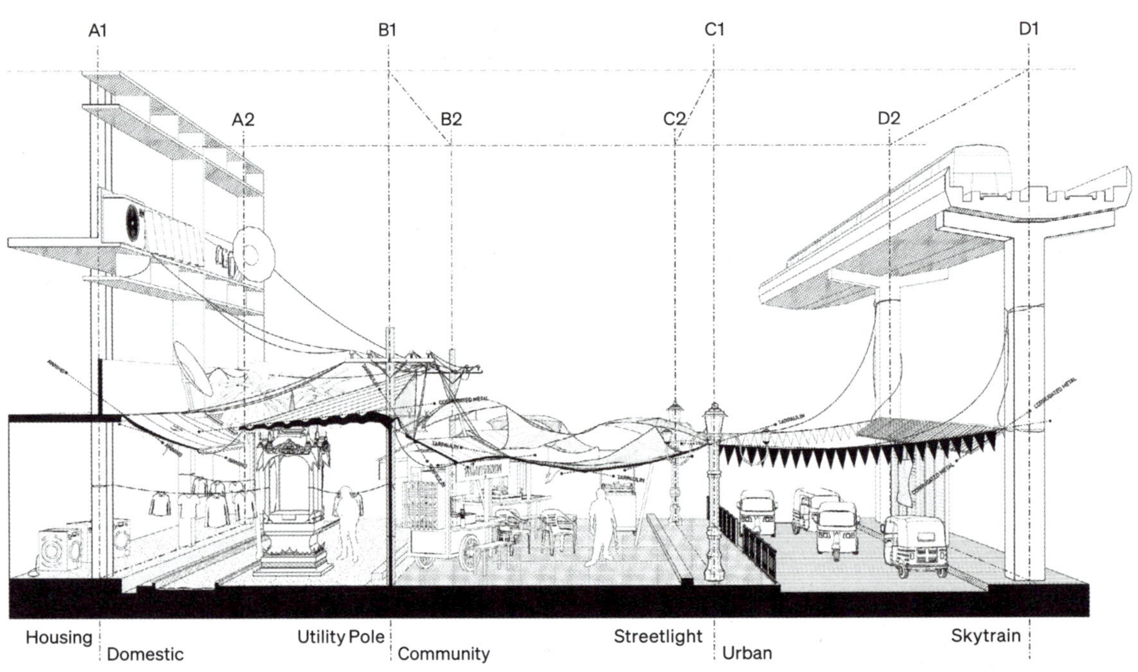

Section detail

Scaffolding physical model

SAMANTHA ONG

MY HOUSE GOES ON FOREVER

"My House Goes on Forever" explores the fluid boundaries of belonging and the creation of home. In Bangkok the urban and the domestic are inseparable, merging so completely that clear distinctions between spaces blur. Within the home these boundaries are defined by objects of belonging and interventions of residents—what they keep, discard, or cherish—revealing an overlapping and malleable sense of home. This flexibility reflects a communal spirit of trust, extending the idea of home beyond physical limits and blurring edges, if they exist at all.

NEWSPAPER

The newspaper arrives with a fixed, rigid order—from article layout to physical form. Yet through cutting and folding, the formal grid is disrupted and the composition is transformed into something informal and dynamic.

BANGKOK SLIPPAGES MATRIX

A collage captures the collision of formality and informality, domestic and urban life, while the accompanying drawings show various household activities. The voids in these compositions emphasize how activities domesticate space, allowing context to evolve. These collages form an operating matrix, enabling users to mix different contexts with activities and creating unexpected "slippages" or overlaps.

MY HOUSE AS IT SLIPS

Building on this matrix, imagined sections combine diverse activities with varying degrees of privacy and overlap, allowing for surprising interactions within the home.

HOW TO GROW A HOUSE

By sharing communal spaces and objects of belonging, individual homes expand beyond their physical boundaries and the idea of home shifts from a single building to a network of interconnected spaces throughout the neighborhood.

THE NEWSPAPER THROUGH TIME

Inspired by the newspaper's incremental folding and cutting, the density of articles and sheets changes over time, reflecting the fluidity of information and space.

MY HOUSE AS A FIELD AND SPRAWL

Rearranging spaces by activity and privacy, homes transcend traditional physical limits, embracing collective living with overlapping and exclusionary zones. As clusters of homes form, varied materials and openings create porous communities that adapt to diverse urban conditions—from large open lots to small leftover pockets.

The house goes on forever.

     THE PARTICULAR AND THE PUBLIC

Bangkok Slippages accordion collage

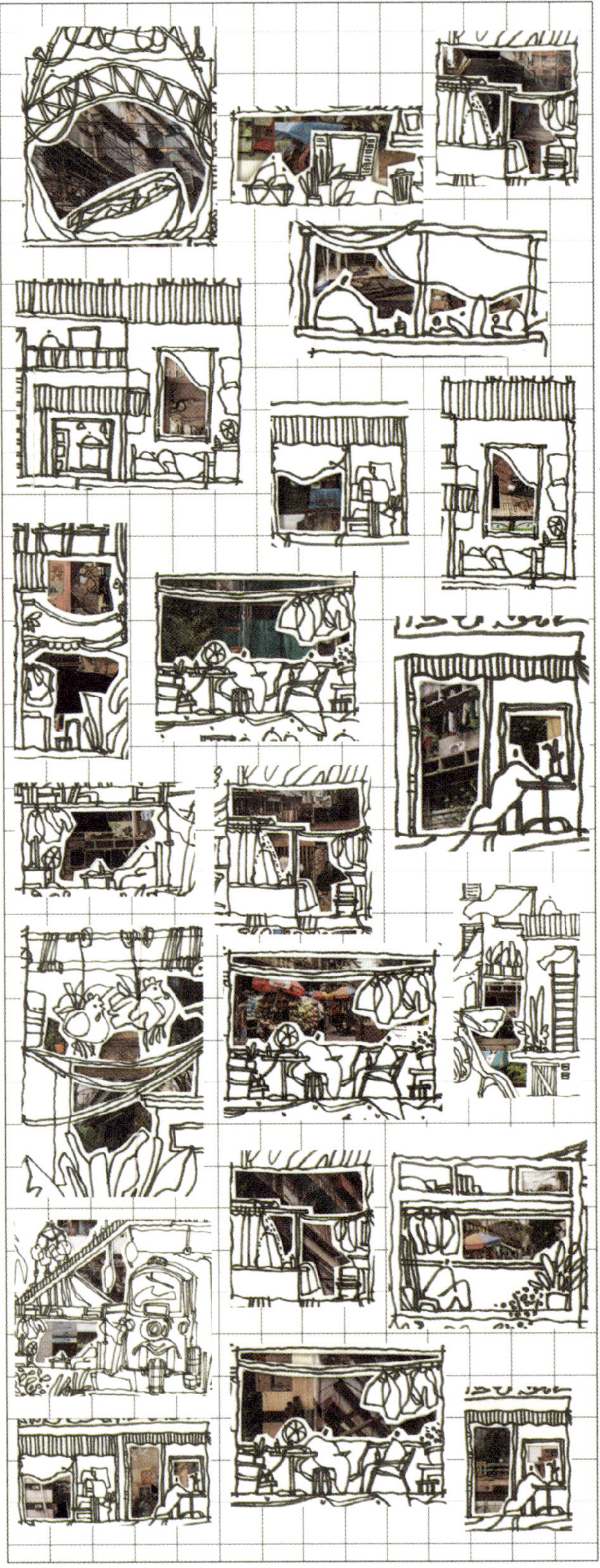

Two collages are assembled together, allowing users to mix and match different contexts to various activities to create unusual combinations, or "slippages."

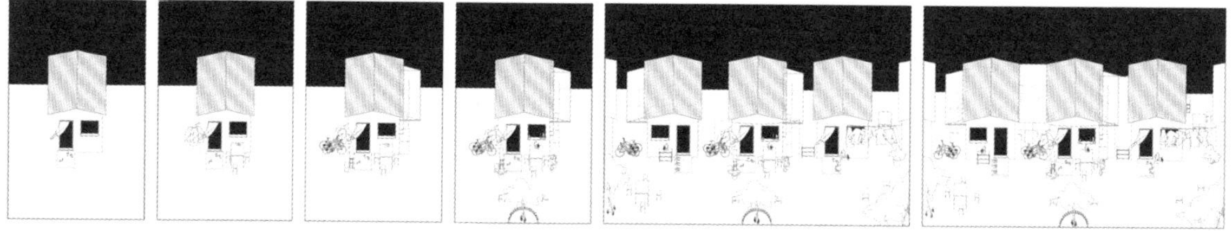

Diagram showing how the house grows

Site plan

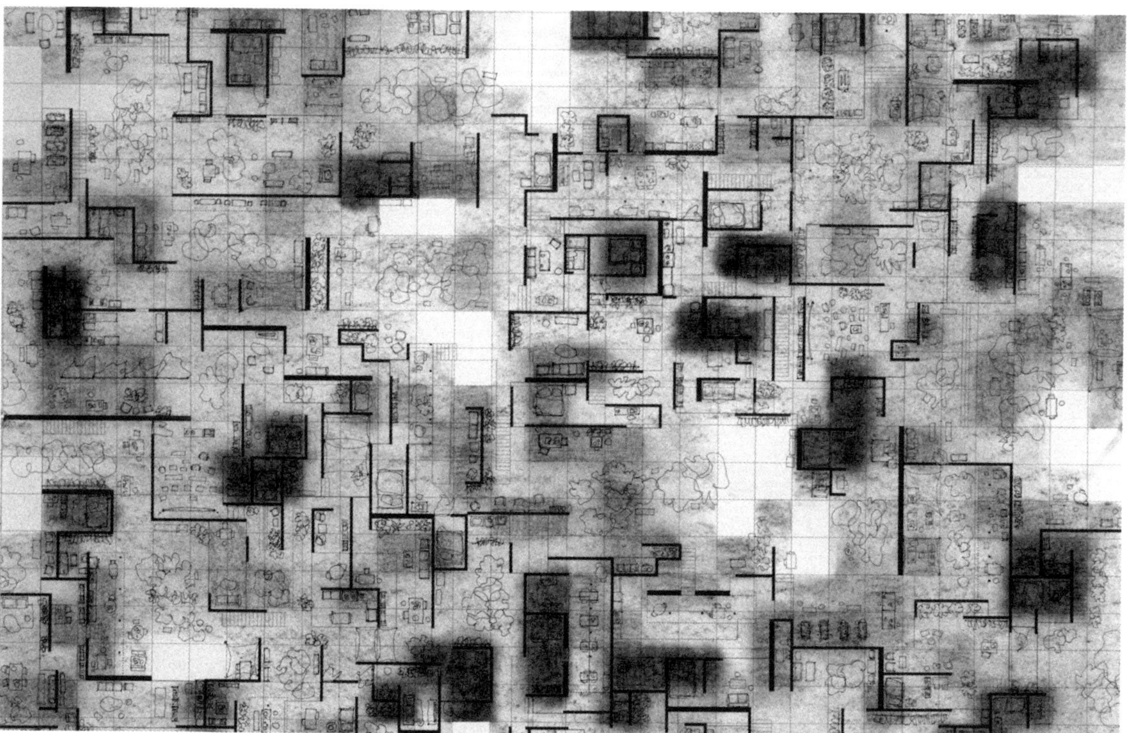

Project floor plan

SERENA LIU

KNOTTED HOMES

The first part of this assignment explored the (in)formality of an everyday object through the transformation of a wine bottle. Using the bottle as a mold, I shaped cardboard pulp to replicate its form. This process involved breaking down "formal" cardboard boxes into a soft, "formless" pulp, then reassembling that pulp back into the precise shape of the wine bottle. The transformation highlights a fascinating reversal — rigid, structured materials dissolving into amorphous matter, only to regain a defined, recognizable form. To complement this, related drawings focused on the role of line types in architectural notation, using varying line weights and styles to document and communicate the changing material qualities of the cardboard throughout its transformation.

As the project progressed, the design process shifted toward envisioning a linear, chronological narrative of domestic and urban life, which I termed the "linear community." This narrative materialized as a freestanding sculptural element resembling a filmstrip. However, the strip did not remain linear: it was folded, looped, and threaded through itself, creating a complex spatial configuration. This manipulation introduced a series of unexpected and unpredictable relationships between programmatic elements, reflecting the multifaceted nature of urban living.

Experientially, the project maintains a balance between linear progression and spatial complexity. It offers a clear sense of movement from one point to another — an understandable sequence from point A to point B. Yet the knotted, intertwined formal character of the architecture disrupts straightforward navigation, inviting users to embrace choice, distraction, and open-ended exploration. Through this interplay, the design challenges predictability and fosters a dynamic, playful environment that reflects the fluidity and ambiguity of everyday life.

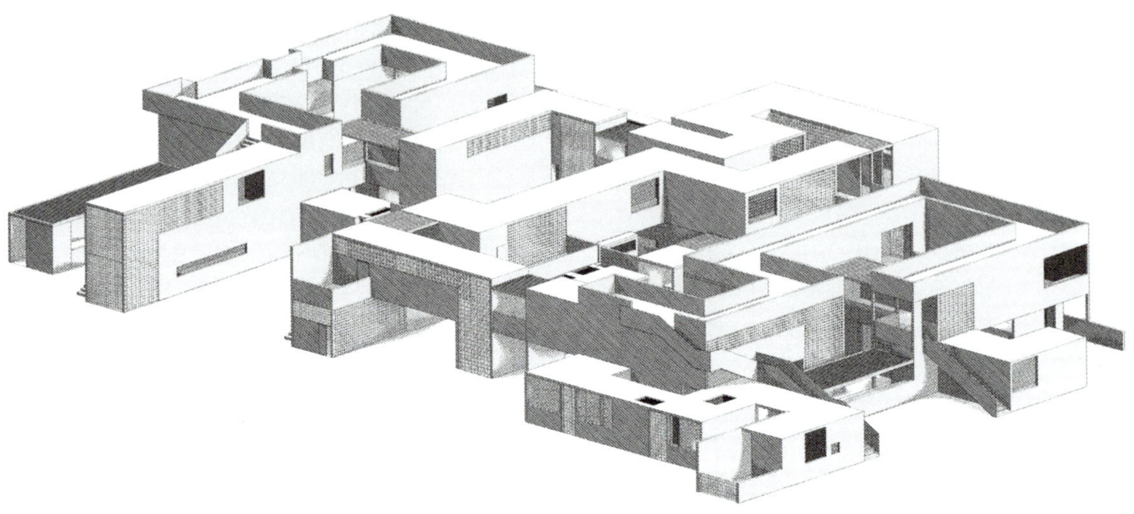

Project axonometric

Courtyard perspective

Inner courtyard

THE PARTICULAR AND THE PUBLIC

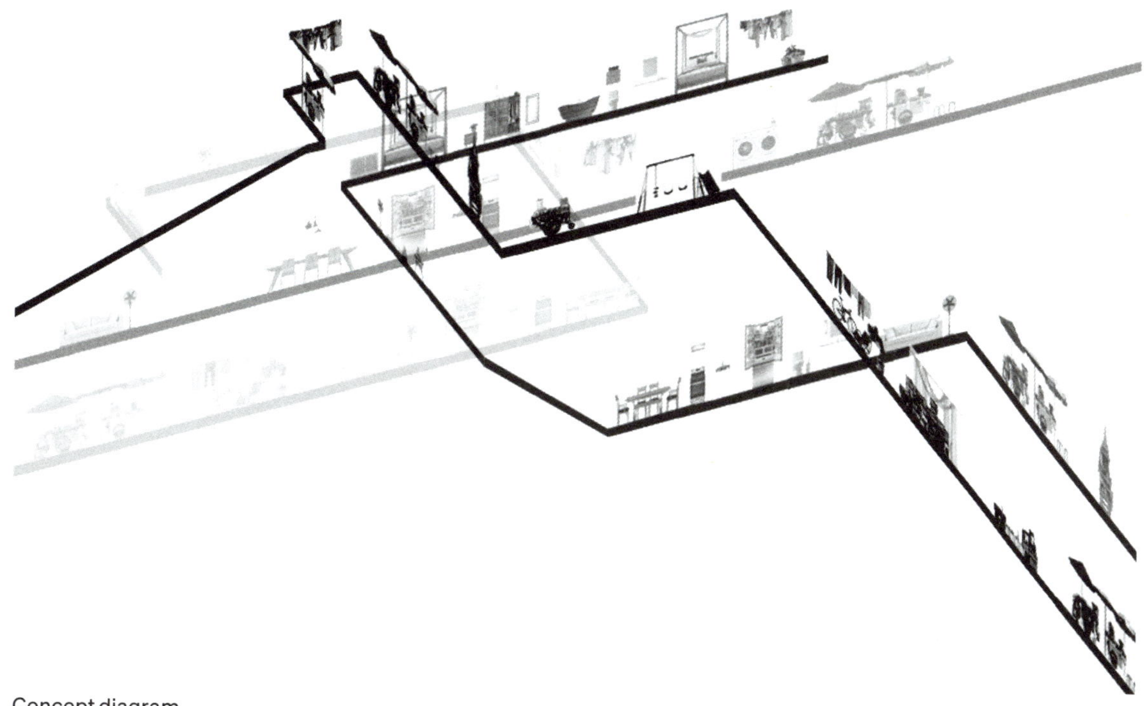

Concept diagram

Project site plan

Section through conceptual model of Knotted Home

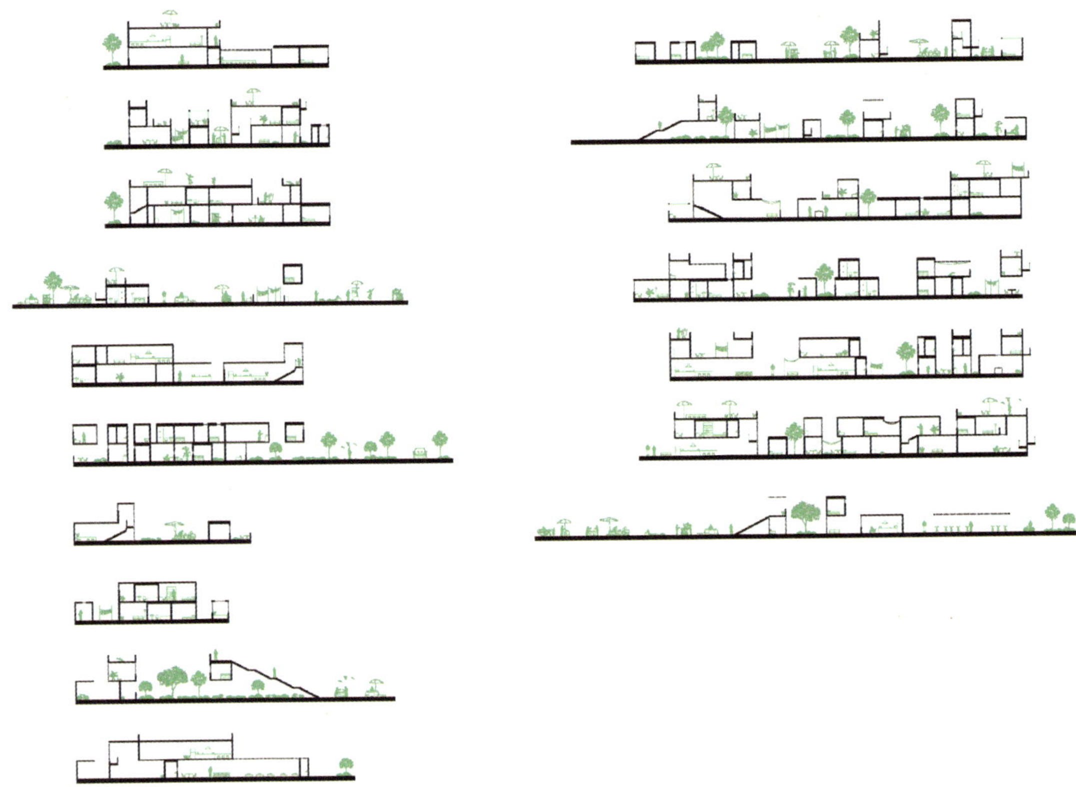

Section collection

   THE PARTICULAR AND THE PUBLIC

Conceptual model of Knotted Home

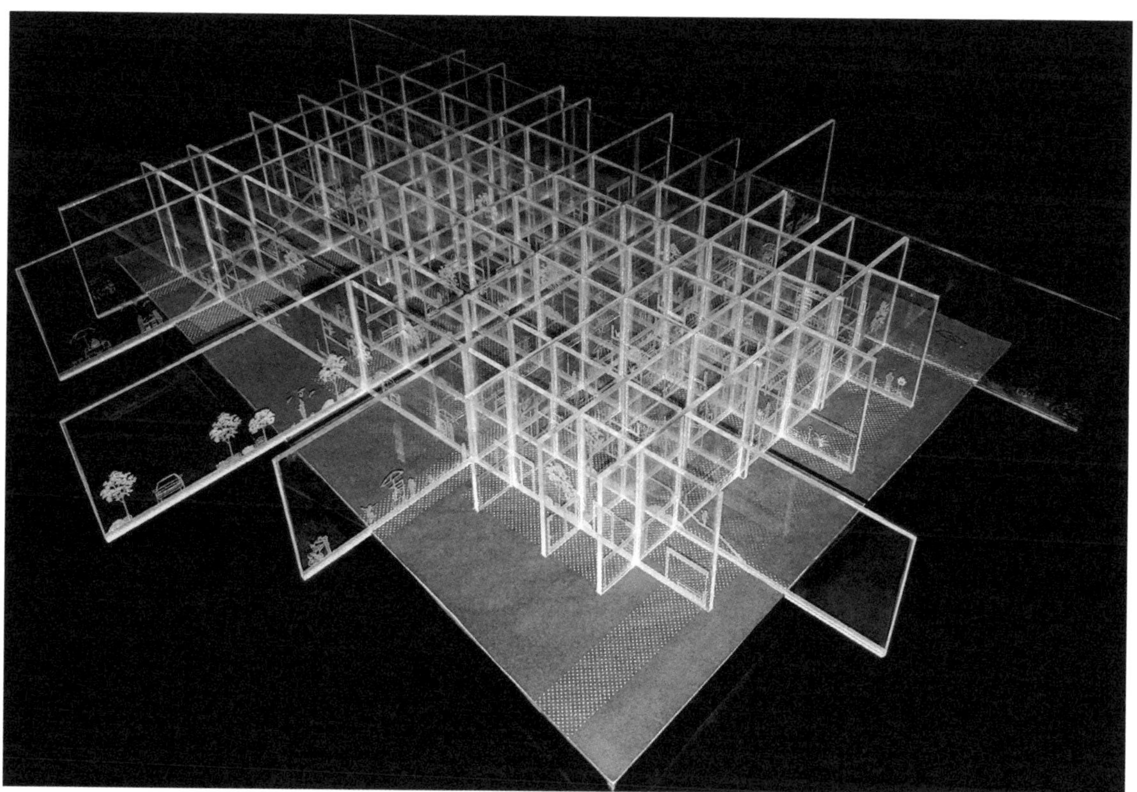

Physical model of project proposal

UZAYR AGHA

REIMAGINING DOMESTICITY

This project interrogates the conventional image of the home as a private sanctuary for the nuclear family, proposing instead a model of domestic life that is flexible, porous, and deeply embedded in its urban, cultural, and environmental context. Grounded in research on housing in Bangkok—one of the world's densest and most climate-vulnerable cities—the proposal explores how spatial practices drawn from traditional Thai homes can offer new ways to live together in the face of rising temperatures, flooding, and shifting social patterns.

Historic Thai domestic architecture, characterized by lightweight construction, open-air decks, modular panels, and adaptable platforms, inspires the project's architectural language. These homes were not static or singular but multigenerational, reconfigurable, and layered with shared rituals and communal labor. I draw a critical comparison between this precedent and the rigid, compartentalized housing models offered today—particularly the five-story walk-up apartments common in Bangkok's public-housing sector. Despite their limited space and prescriptive layouts, these apartments still host small moments of informality, suggesting an ongoing desire for fluid collective living.

Using scaffolding as both a structural and a conceptual framework, the project embodies a new domestic condition that privileges circulation, improvisation, and gradations of privacy. It draws from oblique projection and axonometric drawing techniques not just as representational tools but as generative devices that enable ambiguity, layering, and negotiation between private and communal realms. The resulting spatial system avoids fixed boundaries, instead proposing rooms that are interconnected yet distinct—where domestic life can be shared, reconfigured, and adapted over time.

Rather than suggesting a return to the past, this proposal critiques the trajectory of modern housing and asks what lessons can be learned from preindustrial and vernacular models. In doing so it advocates for housing that is more socially responsive, environmentally attuned, and open to multiple modes of living—offering a resilient and inclusive vision of domesticity in a rapidly changing world.

Project axonometric

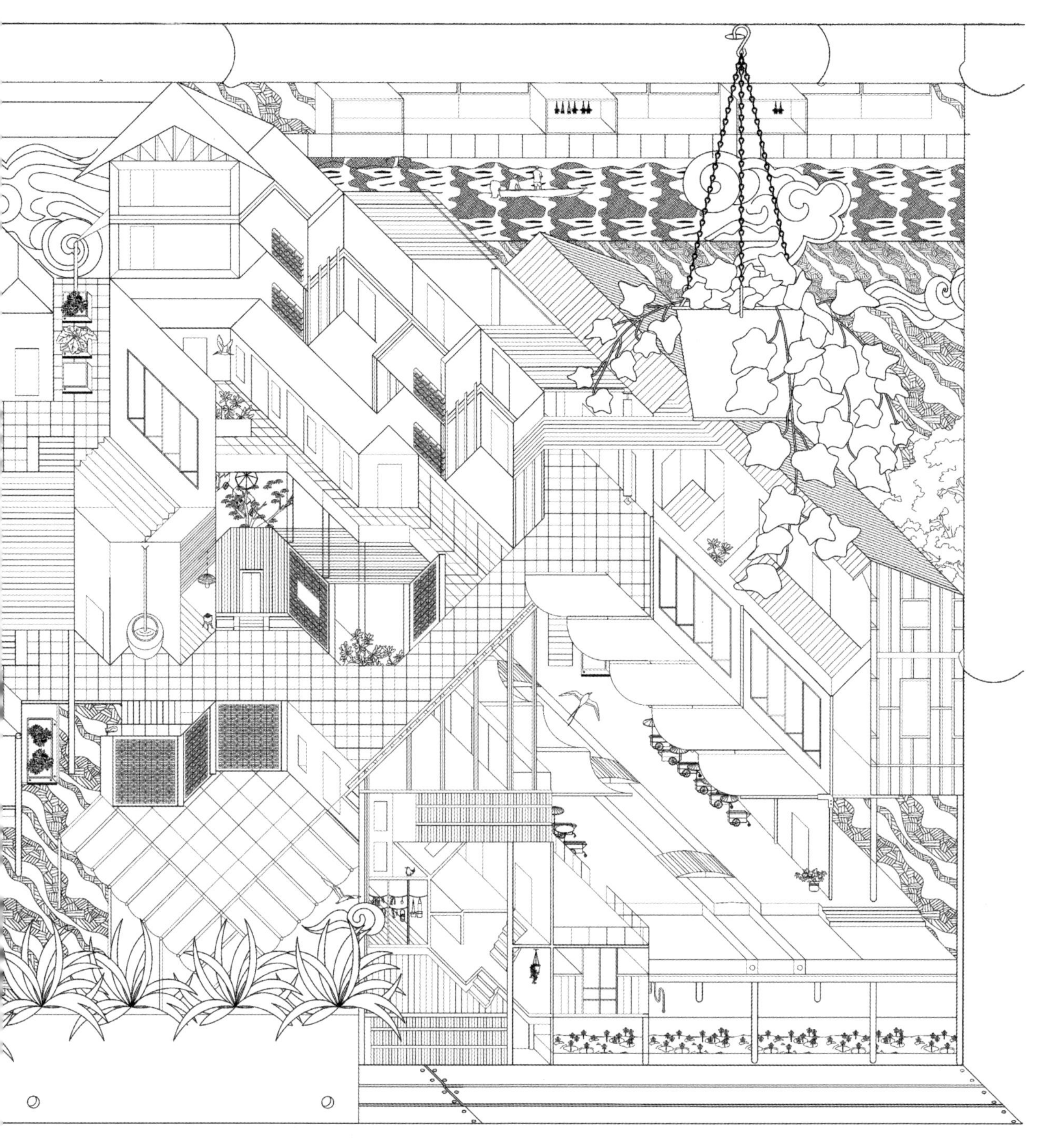

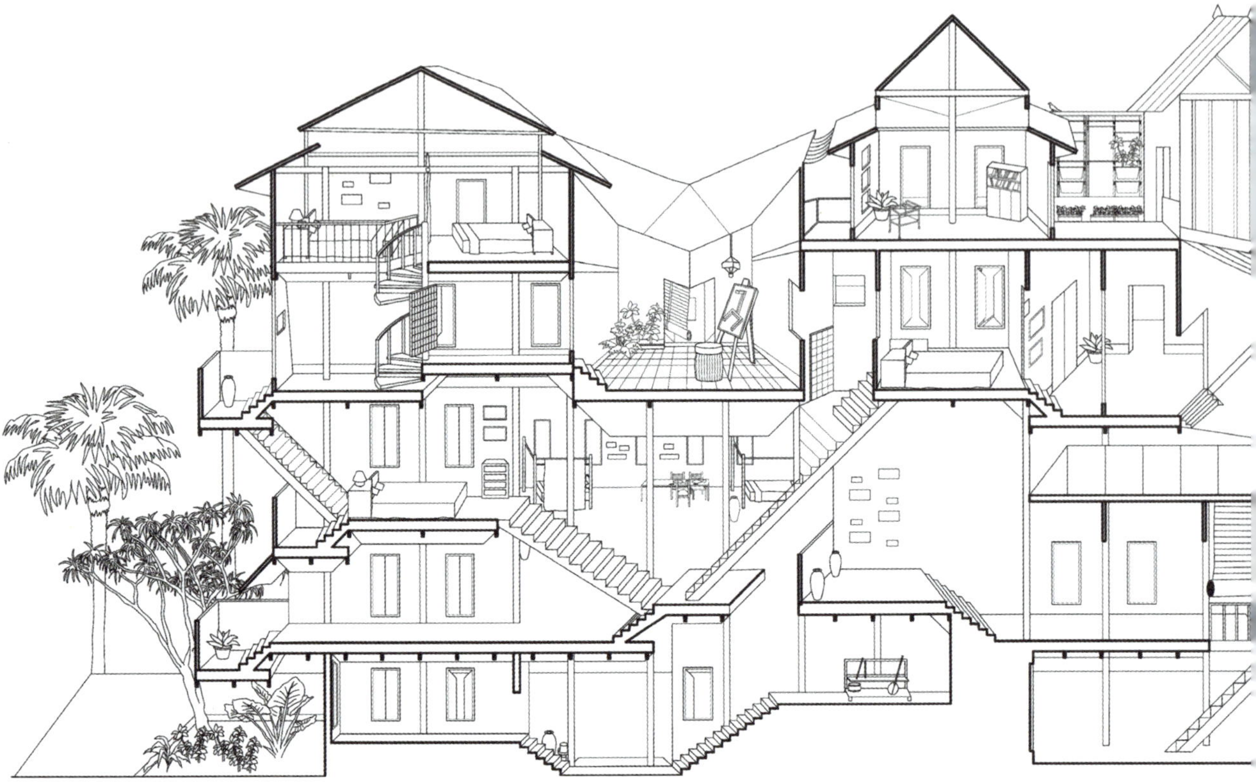

Project section

Object painting

Scaffold painting

Drawdel

WEIQIAO LIN

CORRIDOR AND BALCONY

CORRIDOR AND BALCONY

This project focuses on two architectural elements: the corridor and the balcony. In contemporary urban housing, corridors and balconies are often situated on the periphery between public and private and urban and domestic. Regardless of their essentiality, they have often been overlooked in the spatial design of domestic interiors. However, the ways corridors and balconies are occupied by Bangkok's low-income communities suggest spatial potentials that resist the monofunctional classification of urban domestication. Besides acting as the organizer of traffic and individual units, the corridors in the low-income housing of Bangkok play multiple roles — shared kitchen, dining area, living room, laundry facility, retail shop, storage, and so on. The various uses of spaces reveal the common interest of the local community and the spatial potential of corridors. While corridors may disappear in cases like high-end housing, where residents have private traffic routes connected to their apartments, balconies are present in every housing type. It's not only a border between interior and exterior but also a kitchen, garden, storage room, and laundry, as well as a projection of individualism in the increasingly homogenized face of the metropolis. This project portrays activities in the corridors and balconies of Bangkok as a criticism of the monochromatic design of spaces and reexamines their roles in both domestic and urban contexts through spatial configuration.

SPECULATIVE INTERVENTION: THE BRIDGE

The project takes shape in an urban-scale housing design situated on the pedestrian bridge in the urban center of Bangkok. The 1.3-kilometer bridge was built in 1999 and connected two central parks that had been under renovation. It was intended as a symbol of new urban development in the city and painted green to convey its symbolic meaning. However, even though the bridge has provided a walkway and bike lane above major traffic routes and the canal, the elevated condition lacks connections to the existing urban fabric. In fact it doesn't benefit the people who live around it; it serves temporary users, such as joggers, bikers, and visitors.

A portion of the bridge was selected for design intervention. The design focused on three existing conditions: the sidewalk, the ground-level canal, and the elevated green bridge. After setting up the grid-proportion configuration, the design begins by developing six different communities, each with twelve living units and six bathrooms in different spatial configurations and unit types. After combining and spreading them across the bridge, it consists of 468 living units and 234 bathroom units. The rest of the space has been defined as the corridor and balcony. The corridor acts as the shared living space, and the balcony acts as the mediating zone between domestic and urban spaces. By transforming the green bridge into a balcony for the social housing, the original bridge becomes a platform for urban activities, which often take place informally in the context of Bangkok.

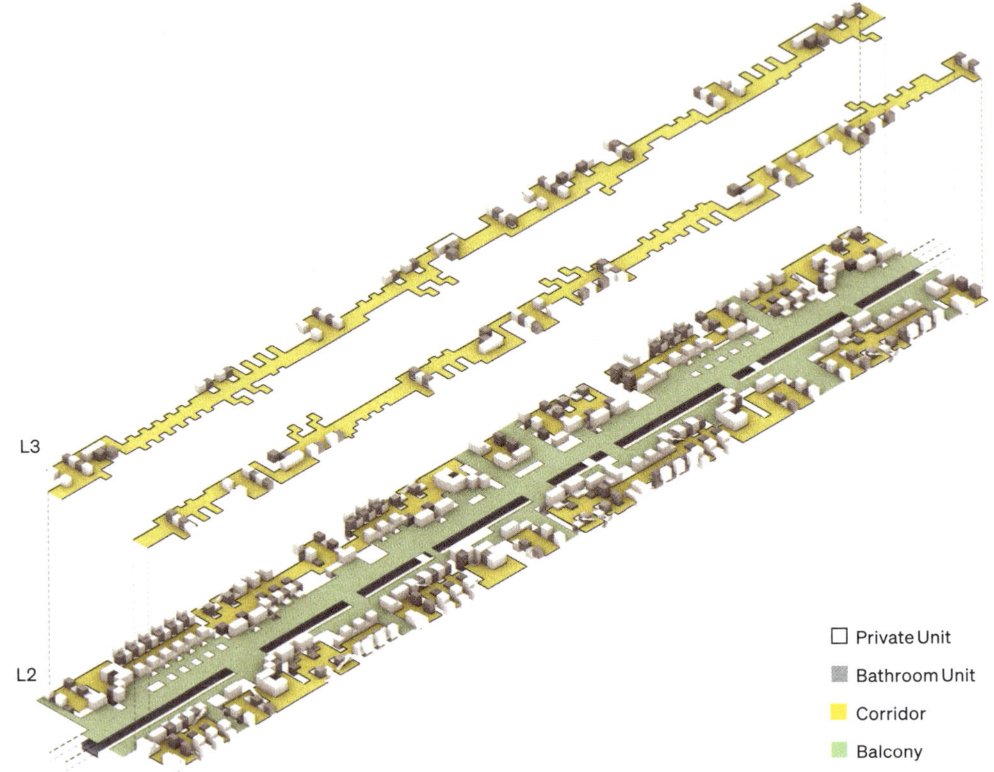

Diagram of formal formation

Project isometric

THE PARTICULAR AND THE PUBLIC

Perspective of balcony

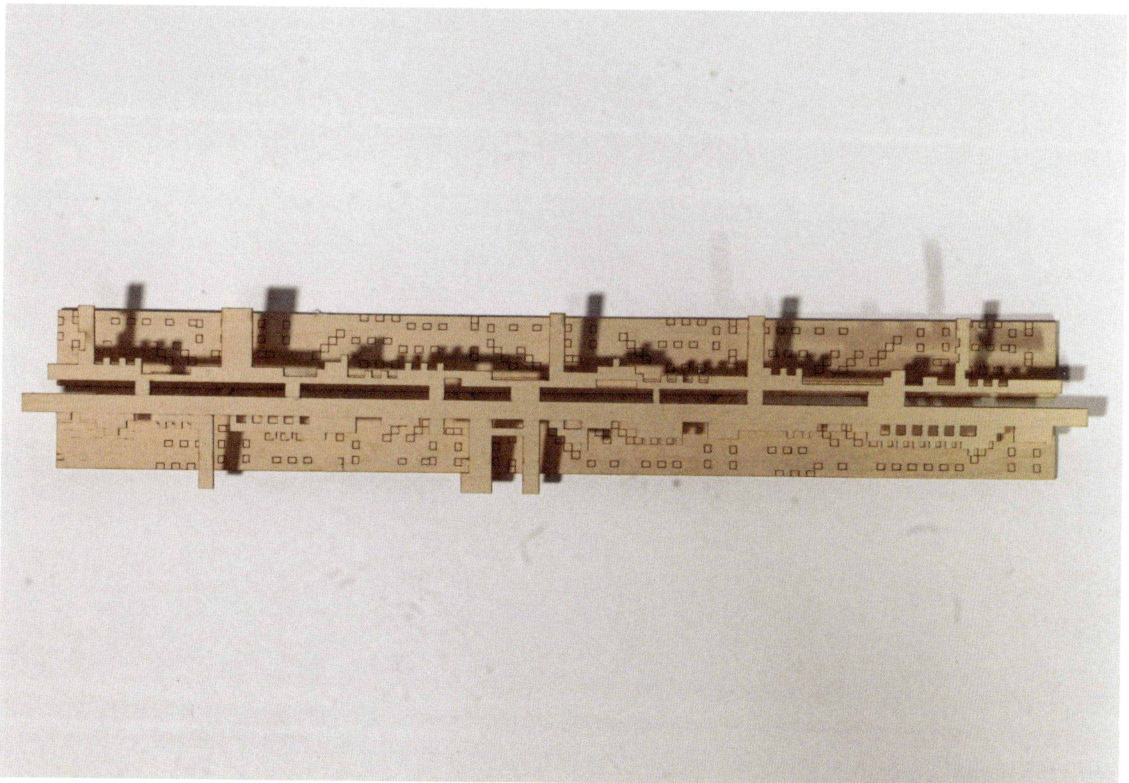

Physical model

Ground-floor plan

Second-floor Plan

Upper-level plan

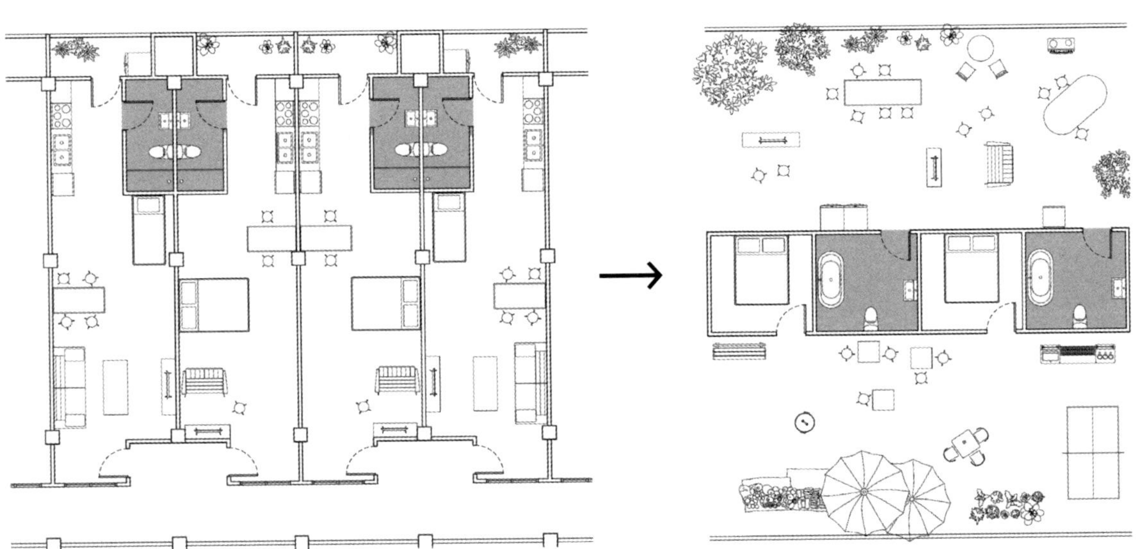

Concept diagram of corridor and balcony

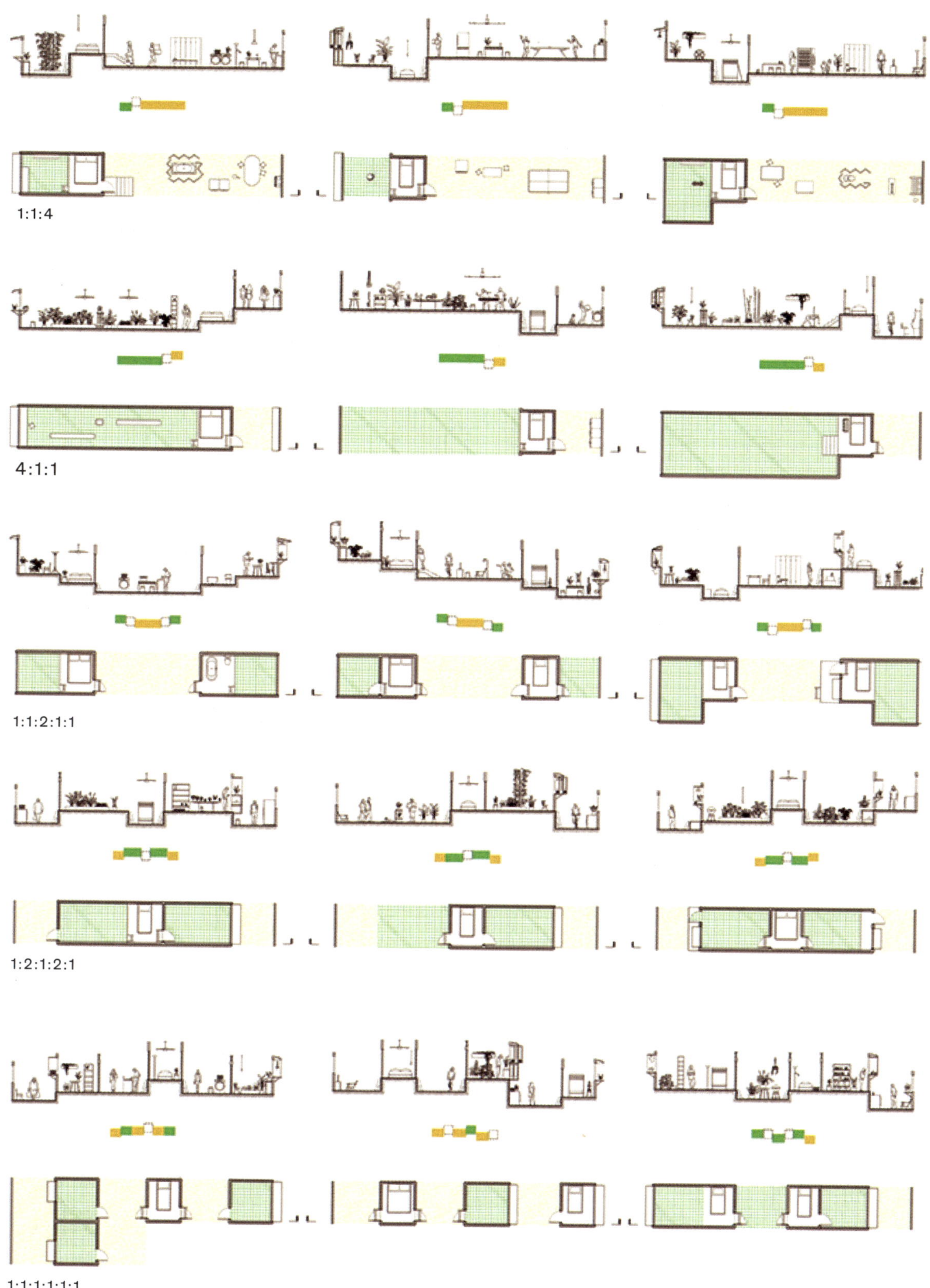

Project section catalog

A PARTI (New Engla B

CARRIE NORMAN
THOMAS KELLEY
VIOLETTE DE LA SELLE

CULAR
nd)
UILDING

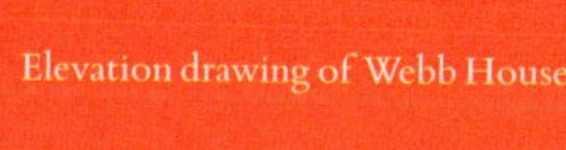
Elevation drawing of Webb House

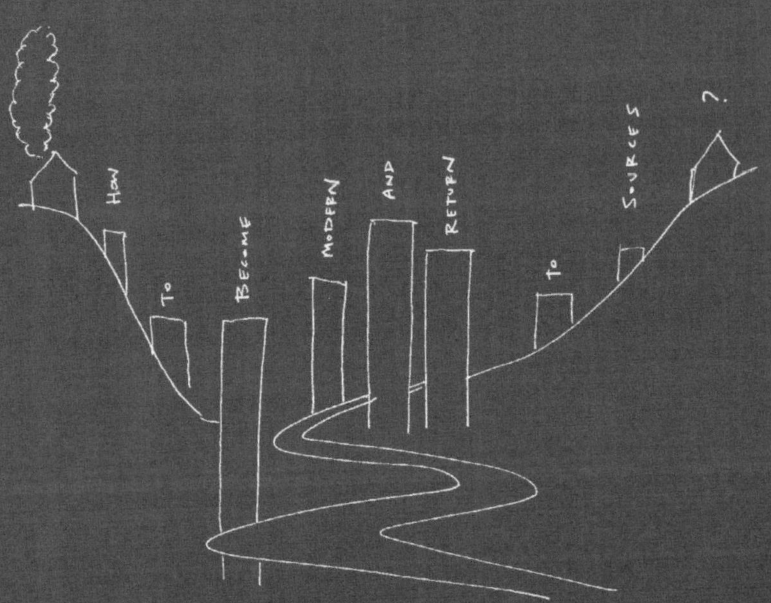

1 CULTURE AND CIVILIZATION

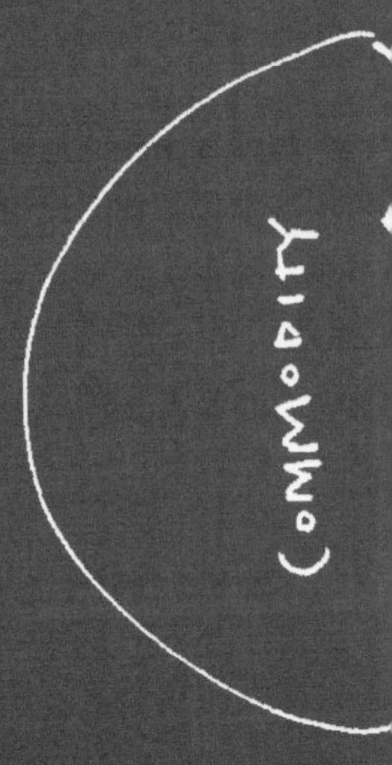

2 THE RISE AND [...]
AVAN[...]

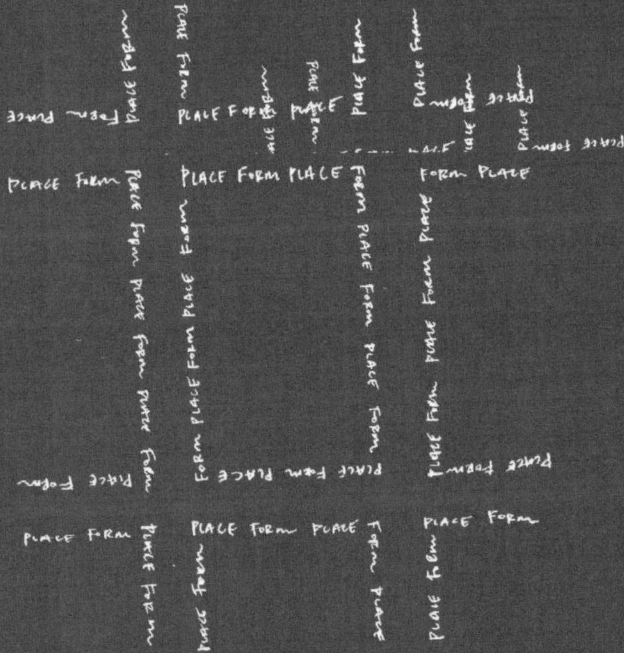

4 THE RESISTANCE OF THE
PLACE-FORM

5 CULTURE VE[...]
TOPOGRAPHY, CONT[...]
AND TECTO[...]

THE PARTICULAR AND THE PUBLIC

ALL OF THE
GARDE

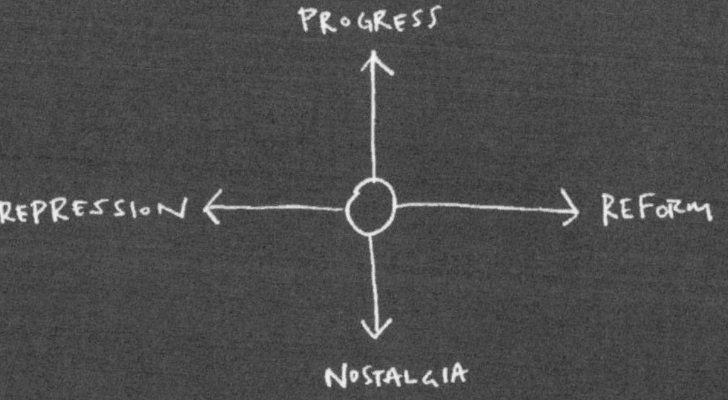

3 CRITICAL REGIONALISM AND
WORLD CULTURE

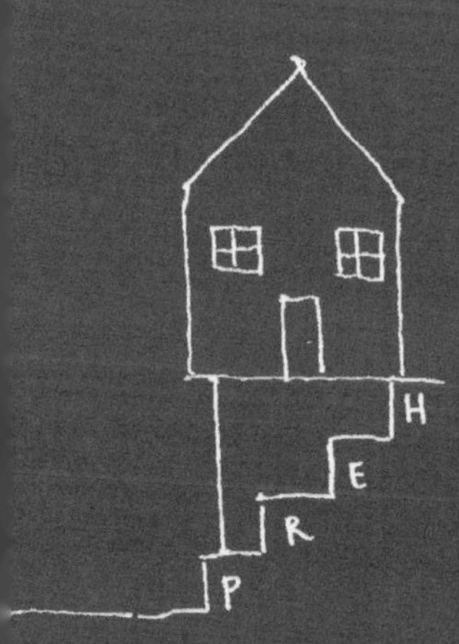

US NATURE:
T, CLIMATE, LIGHT,
C FORM

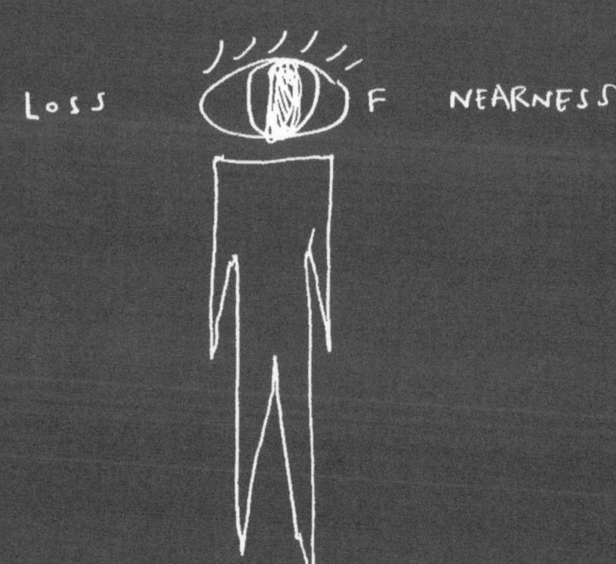

6 THE VISUAL VERSUS
THE TACTILE

NORMAN KELLEY

PROCESS

Forty years ago Kenneth Frampton's essay "Towards a Critical Regionalism: Six Points for an Architecture of Resistance" outlined a process for building that poised reason with expression—two elements that he believed were either too saturated or too absent within the Modern and Post-Modern movements. What the essay does not do is describe an actual regional building. Reading beyond paradigmatic building examples of Mario Botta, Jørn Utzon, or Luis Barragán, you're left with a maddening argument that is too binary, too paradoxical, and too resistant—and yet exquisitely positioned to question issues of globalization, attention, and reform in our contemporary moment. Lewis Mumford, in *The South in Architecture*, noted that "regionalism is not a matter of using the most available local material, or of copying some simple form of construction that our ancestors used, for want of anything better, a century or two ago. … Regional forms are those which most closely meet the actual conditions of life and which most fully succeed in making a people feel at home in their environment."[1]

Frampton's essay reads as an exercise in contextual ambiguity. We like to think of it as the death of the grand tour, or an expanded balance between Modernist tendencies to abstract tradition, with vernacular tendencies to reflect it. We are not saying that architects should replace a trip to Rome with a scavenger hunt through their own backyards, but we have found that the meaning we sought in this Yale advanced studio was to recontextualize something immediate and tangible. The challenge with this kind of practice is finding ways of looking that promote discovery with a degree of hindsight, or as Frampton quotes Paul Ricoeur, "How to become modern and to return to sources."[2] It is important to stress that the Yale studio practiced Frampton's text not as doctrine but as predicament. Students were encouraged to question the text in all its forms by analyzing the critiques of others. In Keith Eggener's "Placing Resistance," he appraises the essay as a "general theory of the particular."[3] In "A not so Critical Theory," Carmen Popescu describes critical regionalism's "intended particularization" as cultural marketing.[4] In most post-critique the particular tends to arise as a denigration of Frampton's thesis. So we positioned the studio in a more literal format: we begin with a particular building as our site.

The extant structure related to this architecture course has a complicated history. The building is located 40 minutes from New Haven in Wethersfield, Connecticut, a town founded in 1633 that claims to be the oldest in the state, with a population of 26,000. The building is a three-and-a-half-story Georgian-style house with two chimneys. The house was framed in wood and clad in clapboard siding and slate shingles by Judah Wright in 1752 for merchant Joseph Webb following his marriage to Mehitable Nott. The massive gambrel roof provided upper-floor storage for Webb's trade goods and sleeping quarters for the household's enslaved people. Today it is referred to as the Joseph Webb House and is painted white with green shutters on the Main Street side. According to historical records, the house also served as George Washington's headquarters in May 1781. Washington met with French commander Comte de Rochambeau in the first-floor parlors to finalize the joint military campaign that led to the victory at Yorktown, ending the American Revolution. The fact that "George was here" is what has likely kept an otherwise unexceptional house intact until now.

Following Webb's death, the house's ownership changed hands several times—going first to Webb's son, Joseph Jr., then to a local judge and his grandson, and then to a group of businessmen, who attempted to convert the house into a library—until 1916, when antiquarian Wallace Nutting purchased the house. This is when the house stopped being a residence. After extensive renovations and the installation of painted murals in the hallway and front parlors, Nutting opened it to the public on July 4, 1916, for tours as well as a sales area and studio. The Joseph Webb house was one of several historically significant sites in the Nutting's "Chain of Colonial Picture Houses." He liked to use his buildings to stage female models dressed in colonial garments set amid reproduced furniture. Thomas Denenberg writes about Nutting's brand of colonial revivalism in *Wallace Nutting and the Invention of Old America* (Yale University Press, 2003). The book quotes Nutting as saying, "Not all the old is good but all the new is bad." Unfortunately, the travel restrictions created by World War I caused Nutting to lose money on the venture. In 1919 the Connecticut chapter of the National Society of the Colonial Dames of America (NSCDA) bought the building to be preserved as a house museum and headquarters.

Under the Provisions of the Historic Sites Act of August 21, 1935, the house was designated a National Historic Landmark in 1961. The inscription on its marker reads: "This site possesses exceptional value in commemorating and illustrating the history of the United States." The current interior has been restored to an eighteenth-century appearance and stands as part of the tripartite Webb-Deane-Stevens Museum, operated by the NSCDA.

BACKGROUND

The students began by producing a set of survey drawings using the standards and guidelines of the Historic American Building Survey (HABS). Students visited the house twice and recorded everything, photographing and measuring with great care, without the use of any laser equipment. The aim was to examine the home closely. Its status as a second-tier house museum in a forgotten town allowed us an all-access pass to get as close to the structure as possible. The 1.5-acre lot includes a garden and a barn. To the north and south are two other landmarked houses, the Silas Deane House (1769) and the Isaac Stevens House (1789). There is also a visitor's center that was added recently to the south elevation.

The main entrance to the house faces east, and that is where its Georgian affectations—multipaned sash windows, stately symmetry, and neoclassical portal—are most clear. The west elevation of the house includes an ell, or an additional wing, with a small gambrel roof perpendicular to the length of the main house. The ell dates to 1765 and was likely added by Joseph Webb's son. The first and second floors of the house are the most decadent, featuring wood paneling and an ornate central staircase. The attic, which includes a partial raised floor and roof hatch, exposes the house's timber frame. The original house is a foursquare organized around a central corridor with an off-center staircase. Flanking the corridor are two chimneys that subdivide the adjacent four rooms. The house does not currently contain a kitchen, but one would likely have existed on the first floor. George Washington's room was on the second floor. The survey also included interior elevations, as well as careful documentation of furniture and door hardware. The students were encouraged to draw together and document as much as they could during the two site visits, aided by a structural report provided by the house museum director.

FOREGROUND

The next assignment tasked the students with producing a set of exacting as-found drawings—or a closer, more idiosyncratic revision of their recently completed survey. Like for Alison and Peter Smithson, the "as-found" is something physical or historical, such as a brick or a worn foundation. The results included plan revisions based on Wallace Nutting's photography, hand-drawn overlays that highlight the structure's deteriorating timber frame, literal depictions of the house's unsettling features, and enlarged details of craftwork in wood. Following the survey and as-found drawings, we embarked on a five-day bus tour to visit the six states of New England.

Travel Week

To confront Frampton's theories directly, we considered the context through an expanded historical, geographical, and cultural lens. By disciplining our contextual boundaries to a region as specific as New England and focusing on First Period architecture, we hoped to discover new ways to assimilate its derivative traditions, as well as its missteps. We typically arrived at a new place by nightfall, and it would reveal itself by morning. The tour began with a conversation around precontact building traditions: What did a precolonial house look like?

In Connecticut we explored a reconstructed Long House that a group of high schoolers made from local trees. In Massachusetts we toured the Hancock Shaker Village, near Stockbridge, discovering that disciplined social and religious constructs often resulted in forms of rationalism that grew out of gender bias and labor practices rather than order. We also met with the stewards of archival ephemera at Historic New England's warehouse in Haverhill. A tour of MASS MoCA introduced us to contemporary adaptive reuse in art installations. Vermont offered the opportunity to explore a region with harsh climate and topography and consider Frampton's principle "building the site" head-on. Some students visited the design-build school Yestermorrow, while others took a snowshoe hike along the trails

     THE PARTICULAR AND THE PUBLIC

of the ski resort Mad River Glen. On our way out of Vermont we checked in with George Sawyer, a second-generation Windsor chair maker, to learn about his family's craft. Our introduction to the New England coastline was in Portland, Maine, where we visited an iconic lighthouse. In Portsmouth, New Hampshire, we toured the Strawbery Banke Museum, an uncannily preserved colonial village staged with actors in period costume, where we learned the distinctions between preservation, restoration, reconstruction, and rehabilitation.

One of the most exquisite examples of colonial architecture was the "stone ender," an early American building imported from Britain, found mostly in Rhode Island, where one wall of the house was stone, including a fireplace and chimney, and the remainder was constructed of wood. In Providence we toured the Nightingale-Brown House with historian Ron Potvin, who reminded us that George Washington was not a deity and believes that we have enough house museums, particularly those commemorating the first American president. He teaches classes in which students are asked to propose alternative tour programs around alternative histories critical to understanding the house anew through aspects such as labor and pleasure.

Index and Studio Program

Once we returned from our trip, the students began work on an index, or a set of proposal drawings, for converting the Joseph Webb House into a space for public programming, based on the concept of an Athenaeum. Historically the Athenaeum has had many interpretations. The name comes from Athena, the goddess of wisdom, and in ancient Greece it was a place of engaged learning with a literary or scientific emphasis.

Bus

Clemence-Irons House

Historic New England Archive

Institute for American Indian Studios Wigwam

Nicholas Brown House

Point Lighthouse

George Sawyer Workshop

Hancock Shaker Village

Mad River Glen Ski Resort

MASS MoCA

Strawberry Banke

Site Survey

It could be thought of as a loud library where public discourse is encouraged. The exercise aimed to inspire the students to replace the function of domestic privacy with a public use. We provided the students with a deliberately vague direction and scope, including only a basic size restriction of no more than 5,000 square feet—approximately the same size as the existing house—and the requirement that historical landmark restrictions be strictly enforced.

The idea of the index is a reflexive device used to redirect attention to the subject; the presumption is that all future meaning hinges on the source. The index drawings are produced using a similar graphic standard—black delineates existing structure, red new structure, and yellow demolished structure. The idea was for each student to propose a syntax for how an architecture is conceived from something found—or in our studio's case, how an architecture is formed from an early American house in New England.

The index drawings were deliberately binary and encouraged students to wrestle with many of critical regionalism's flaws. As Eggener writes, "Critical regionalism is, at heart, a postcolonial concept. ... Like postcolonialist discourse in general, critical regionalist writing regularly engages in monumental binary oppositions: East/West, traditional/modern, natural/cultural, core/periphery, self/other, space/place. Like the postcolonialist project Ricoeur described, Frampton's version of critical regionalism revolved around a central paradox, a binary opposition: "how to become modern and to return to sources; how to revive an old dormant civilization and take part in universal civilization." It is the tension arising from this problem—the struggle to resolve it, more than its eventual resolution—that fuels critical regionalist discourse.[5] This fact underlies Frampton's emphasis on issues of resistance and process over product. Though the representation exacerbated the binary condition of old versus new,

          THE PARTICULAR AND THE PUBLIC

many of the student proposals transcended this categorization through one, or multiple, categories that include contradiction, an expressionist contrast to the supposed historical faults of the house; therapy, fixing a problem in the original house's framing construction; or critical intervention, turning the house into a series of installations as commentary. It should be noted that building alterations are not able to mend or improve all histories. When new buildings are formed from old ones, architecture has the opportunity to sidestep the aesthetics of restoration, reframe questionable histories, and project future forms of optimism.

REFINEMENT

In the third and final part of the studio, the students further examined the particularities of the context to produce a greater sense of authorship and loosen the direct contrast of their alterations to the existing house. In addition to addressing issues of regionalism, preservation, and history, they were tasked with refining their index proposals to meet a minimum set of building requirements in terms of the studio's general alteration guidelines. The guidelines included specifying program and construction type, adhering to ADA and local egress codes, and maintaining high levels of indoor environmental quality. For this final phase we also introduced a new medium of representation: a static frame animation in which the camera holds a single frame while ephemeral qualities of light, sound, and movement complicate the image. We aimed to confront Frampton's critique of the purely visual, or scenographic, and posit a novel sensory alternative. In addition, the final drawings no longer read as binary as before. Any distinction between new and old may be highlighted only by a nuanced gray tone. The proposals allowed the scale of the site to expand and collapse, extant materials to be further examined, forms to be inflected with renewed meaning, and social environments to be observed and multiply. And, of course, in the spirit of a studio that was inspired by an essay, writing was featured as a supplement to drawing.

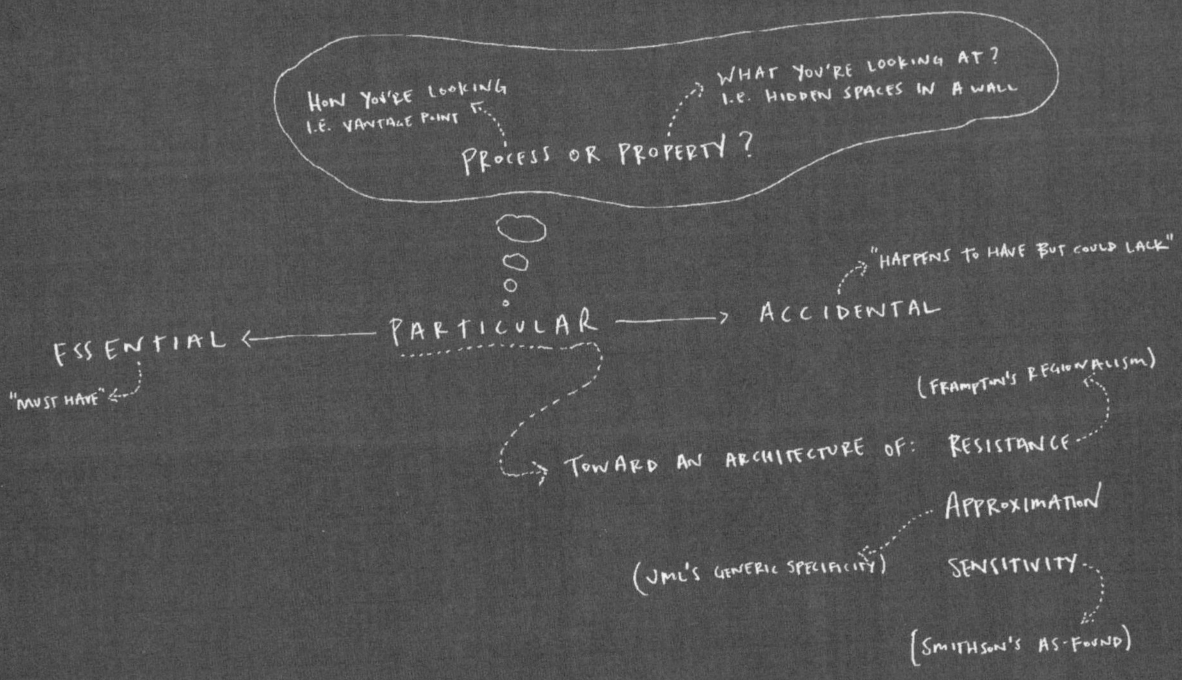

By focusing on the first places of Western colonization, the studio entangles a sensitive political context with a questionable vernacular building tradition. The hope is that this entangled process will reveal universal lessons on how to manage architecture's anxieties about context. When we take stock of how we are conditioned to comprehend people, places, and things, the particular serves to provoke a fundamental question: What is context? Context is everything, context is anything. Context includes and excludes. What is context but a bunch of stuff that one filters in or out based on individual predilections? Our desire to engage context head-on is not meant to replace authorship with refinement or promote a rearguard aesthetic movement as Frampton may have implied, but rather to incite an egalitarian way of interpreting the world around us. The result is not a question of how regional, or global, something might appear, but of how to make something public, or at least visually accessible, in a manner that completes something found without being too specious or populist. Consider the particular as being situated somewhere between the essential, a must-have, and the accidental, what one has but could lack. In a building project the essential task might be to reduce the form to suit local construction standards and egress requirements or add primitive containers that maximize FAR. The accidental might be a singular, fleeting observation about a specific material or a prosaic social encounter between users in a Harold Bloom-like swerve.

1

Lewis Mumford, "Lecture One: The Basis for American Form," in *The South In Architecture: The Dancy Lectures, Alabama College 1941* (New York: Harcourt Brace and Company, 1945), 30.

2

Paul Ricoeur, "Universal Civilization and Natural Cultures," in *History and Truth* (Evanston, Illinois: Northwestern University Press, 1965), 271.

3

Keith Eggener, "Placing Resistance: A Critique of Critical Regionalism," *Journal of Architectural Education* 55, no. 4 (2002): 228–37.

4

Carmen Popescu, "Critical Regionalism: A Not so Critical Theory," in *The Figure of Knowledge: Conditioning Architectural Theory, 1960s–1990s*, ed. Sebastiaan Loosen, Rajesh Heynickx, Hilde Heynen (Leuven, Belgium: Leuven University Press, 2020).

5

Eggener, 228–37.

STUDIO BRIEF

The studio examined how buildings manifest when your attention is fixed on your immediate surroundings. Frampton's essay "Towards a Critical Regionalism: Six Points for an Architecture of Resistance" (1983) argued that place, topography, climate, light, tectonics, and the tactile are concerns that should inform all buildings, regardless of the site. Whether his criteria are self-evident or disputed today, this studio practiced the text and others through a more literal and accidental format: the alteration of an existing First Period building in New England. Our attention oscillated between an extant building and an actual region. Situated among the first places of Western colonization, the studio engaged a sensitive political context to reveal how vernacular building traditions could offer universal lessons on managing architecture's anxieties of context. The ambition was for the studio to project an architecture of particularity by which as-found conditions are identified, sorted, and abstracted in a difficult whole that revalues the obscured, as well as banal, histories of place.

Building alterations cannot mend or improve all histories. When new buildings emerge from old buildings, architecture has the opportunity to sidestep the aesthetics of restoration, reframe questionable histories, and project future forms of optimism. Beyond the documentation of the immediate lot and building, the constellation of alteration practices prioritized the following: (a) renovation of parts or all of the existing interior, (b) conversion of all or parts of the existing program, and (c) addition to the existing structure. If an interior is renovated, a program is converted, and a space is enlarged, each alteration should serve new uses and users. More specifically, a private home was transformed into a public Athenaeum. This was our scope.

Dominated by rules and charters, the risk-averse discipline of historic preservation has never catalyzed a central position in the study of architectural design (yet). As the dialectic between tradition and modernity continues to confront the way history is wedded with contemporary practice, this studio was positioned within a complex bargain between the two. When building on a building in New England, how might architecture absorb the particularity of place, person, and activity? Together we aimed to find out. Organized into three parts, the studio privileged drawing as the primary mode to navigate the murky regions of as-found culture and its attendant architecture.

CONVERSATION

This discussion was published in *Constructs*.

NINA RAPPAPORT

How did you start working together, and where did each of you begin your architectural practice?

CARRIE NORMAN

We met nearly 20 years ago, when we were undergrads studying at the University of Virginia. During our time there we often collaborated with our professors, Jason Johnson and Nataly Gattegno, of Futureforms, on a number of competitions. Their office became a model practice for us, pairing teaching with professional work. Thomas and I met again in graduate school at Princeton. From there we followed different paths: Thomas went to Chicago and started teaching, and I went to New York to start a professional practice. We hoped another collaboration would bring us together again, and in 2012 we settled on a competition hosted by the Architectural League of New York. Like a lot of others starting out, we were both moonlighting and working on the competition nights and weekends. We didn't win, but I think we got an honorable mention. It was enough to give us the confidence to keep working together. We opened a bank account, started a website, and have been calling our collaboration Norman Kelley ever since.

THOMAS KELLEY

In 2012 I was awarded the Rome Prize at the American Academy and fled to Rome, where Carrie came to collaborate on one of our first wall drawings. A year later we completed "Wrong Chairs," a collection of alterations to seven American Windsor chairs. The project seeded intellectual themes centered around optics and alterations that our practice continues to wrestle with and consider.

NR

How does Chicago's legacy as an architectural city—with historical masters such as Sullivan, Burnham, Root, and Mies, as well as Tigerman and the new generation—play a part in your approach to architecture in both academia and professional practice?

TK

Bob Somol, Stanley Tigerman, and Margaret McCurry were early supporters of our practice. In many ways Chicago—unlike New York and Rome—had a linear history since the Great Fire. The tension between the first school of Burnham and Root and the second school of Mies is where our practice took off. Tigerman, Jeanne Gang, and John Ronan carved out what is being called a "third" Chicago School, to which we contribute. Stanley made it a point to promote younger architects, organizing salons at his apartment where all the young and eager would come to meet key figures in Chicago's cultural scene. While there were myths about him being a cantankerous, combative architect, we never saw that side; we saw him as a supporter with an amazing wit and critical eye.

View of the Arthur and Janet C. Ross Library

Norman Kelley, Notre, retail space, Chicago, 2019

Norman Kelley, Lobby with Amphitheater for Beacon Capital Partners, Chicago, 2022

THE PARTICULAR AND THE PUBLIC

We often shared plans with him before building them. We proudly used one of his quotations on the wall of the Aesop shop in Bucktown: "The grid is abstract as well as realistic."

CN

As an outsider I sometimes think of our status in Chicago as the most local non-local architects operating in the city, but I also hope that to be the case in every place we work. I hope our work treads carefully in all histories, major and minor. Sometimes the little-known or overlooked local histories offer as much or more to learn.

NR

Much of your work begins with the line and drawing things that then manifest in shapes or physical dimensions. What is particular to your idea of a "drawing on the wall" versus that of the mural as a concept for the American Academy in Rome?

TK

The project is inspired by the anamorphic tradition, which is tied to perspective drawing. It is constructed of space that we drafted digitally and translated to a two-dimensional surface that we then traced onto the wall. The drawing is more of an act than an artifact. We were interested in a one-to-one scale that was a superficial type of architecture and that, from a specific vantage point, corrected what we took note of as possibly an afterthought by the original architect.

CN

One of our shortcomings is that we studied only architecture. Unlike many graduate students who have studied other disciplines, we studied architecture and then architecture—specifically hand drawing. So drawing rather than mural making is in our vocabulary.

NR

For the 2015 Chicago Biennial you created drawings that were integrated with the building's windows. What was your interpretation of the space and the experience of the visitor?

TK

We refer to these vinyl window super-graphics as drawings. The way we worked with Sarah Herda and Irene Sunwoo was more of a curatorial method. The window dressings could move around to mitigate light or views based on the requirements of different exhibitions. The way it was delineated and the style of the graphic representation derive largely from how architects tend to draft window dressings. It elevates what is sometimes denigrated as an interior move to more of an envelope.

NR

It reminds me more of a scenography and the way you create settings for interactions when not working on a complete building. What is the difference between scenography and architecture, or even interior design, for projects such as lobbies and the choreography of objects?

CN

Scenography is one way to portray architecture as background. Our work often involves altering something that already exists, and we feel the need to look closely at the background. Our contexts can be historical, geographical, or even personal; they can also be direct and material. Our installation for the exhibition

Spaces without Drama, curated by LIGA at the Graham Foundation in spring 2017, comes to mind. The show's prompt involved tracing similarities between theatrical stage sets and architectural scale models. We designed a table whose horizontal surface served as the ground for restaging itself within its immediate context.

TK

Scenography is a loaded term for its connotations to Modernism and interior design. In earlier works, scenography comes out of our vision, designing from particular vantage points and curating the works around a specific way of looking at a project. It has been exciting to yield works that no longer require one to experience them from a specific vantage point to appreciate the vision. Sound is a component in a recent lobby project at 190 South LaSalle Street, and it doesn't require your eyes to be open at all to experience. But I think we use the image to analyze the work, so sometimes it gets packaged as being highly scenographic, as opposed to something more three-dimensional or experiential, which is something we are contending with as we grow.

NR

How do you view the conditions of working within an existing building as both a limitation and a liberation from the constraints of your designs? And what is your design process for the Notre stores and the lobbies that you've been working on?

CN

Some architects might enjoy the freedom of a blank page, but we prefer it when there is already a drawing on the sheet.

Most projects begin by looking closely at the existing conditions and then drawing them, even if we're given a set of as-built drawings. Observation takes work, and it's our job to find value in existing structures. Anne Lacaton has a great value proposition she calls "making do," and it refers to locating opportunity in what might readily be cast off. In the Notre project, the building's baggage included a three-foot grade change between street and interior. Making do introduced accessibility as a guiding motive, prompting a very gentle 1:20 stair ramp that has become one of the project's most successful features.

TK

I would say that the initial survey is not neutral; it's heavily biased. We get the most out of projects where our collaborators—owners, clients, and stakeholders—are open to thinking about an existing site in terms of both distant and immediate histories. For example, the Notre space was a confectionery factory and an art gallery for Rhona Hoffman. How do you synthesize these dueling histories in a way that challenges whatever the new typology might be? Building less is what we prefer.

NR

At the smaller scale, you design furniture with an ironic twist, creating critical art objects. Why do you decide to adapt or reorganize furniture elements that may have a historic value or context, and what are your goals in terms of the design interpretation of these pieces?

TK

Novelty is not interesting to us. At best, New England colonial furniture is just a synthesis of European trends. We would like an opportunity to participate in a form of historical revisionism to do something different. Fortunately the work coexists with what has already transpired. For our most recent Venice Biennale project, we started with the material, veered into DIY fabrication, and then found ourselves circling back to Enzo Mari drawing manuals and objects, regardless of whether we wanted to or not. In this case we had to figure out how to produce a set of instructions for yielding an object that could be made by a framer. We like to rethink colonial attitudes and how they may have misappropriated origins to produce what truly could have been an American sensibility. We are perhaps chasing a premodern sensibility that leans more toward regional sensibilities and particularities of place.

NR

What if you were to take George Washington's or Thomas Jefferson's furniture and imagine a project that relates to political and social reevaluations of history, as we are doing today?

TK

We take an apolitical stance on George Washington's collection of furniture. To us it is a diverse collection of objects. Perhaps the way our project has become more political is in rethinking what is wrong and trying to derive a narrative about altering what was previously there. We have just completed a lobby renovation in a building designed by Philip Johnson, who is a very charged author these days. One way to engage is by shifting attention toward other aspects of that building's history, not to forget but to elevate what is a more promising kind of future.

NR

What is the focus of your studio at Yale?

TK

It will take the form of what is happening in our practice now: conversions or alterations to existing buildings, a design drawn from the context to develop a theory of observation through a survey drawing that can manifest or project a proposal forward. We are excited to introduce this process to the students as a way of mobilizing the drawing or as-built survey from something that was typically a neutral or objective document into something specific and even highly biased, based on the way you see.

STUDENT WORK

THE PARTICULAR AND THE PUBLIC

TIANA KIMBALL
BENJAMIN FANN
JONATHAN CHU
ABBY REED
JERRY CHOW
IRIS YOU
JESSICA ZHOU
CALVIN LIANG
INGRID PELLETIER
BOBBY CHUN

TIANA KIMBALL

ALTERATION
1

 THE PARTICULAR AND THE PUBLIC

This Athenaeum focuses on the discipline of photography and its contested objectivity. In its infancy photography was regarded as a science, a true documentation of what is. This ideology is still alive, confronting us in the documentation and study of history. Photography began around 1839 with the invention of the daguerreotype process. Decades later, with Pictorialism, photography gained recognition as an art form. The idea that photographs could be more than an impartial indexing of reality came with the potential to craft particular messages through photography. Abundant examples of this craft are encased in the Joseph Webb House. The Athenaeum's photo archive and gallery are curated to juxtapose parallel histories told through photographs. A permanent installation showcases Wallace Nutting's Colonial Picture Houses alongside diverse work by early twentieth-century photographers.

To convey the development of photography as an art form, the Athenaeum's collection begins in 1839. Particular attention is given to the early twentieth century, when the modern assembly line was introduced for making cars and other everyday products. In 1917 the country entered the First World War, while on the domestic front women fought for their right to vote. It was during these years that Nutting built a business selling nostalgia for a "better" time through his hand-tinted photographs.

As a public place of learning, the Athenaeum should engage the street. Exterior alterations and additions invite visitors from Main Street to experience the Athenaeum's collection. Inside, bits of the original Webb house are preserved as staged elements of something new. Additional galleries in the new construction display the Athenaeum's extensive photography collection, organized chronologically in modest rooms echoing those of the original house.

Nutting used the fluidity of photography to establish a stance against American progress in the early twentieth century. While he photographed women in domestic roles typical to the colonial era—staged as props in the background, likened to the homeowner's other possessions—prominent female photographers captured themselves and other women dressed and posed to challenge gender and identity norms of the time. The Athenaeum recounts the many sides of these stories through a carefully curated collection of photographs. In *Perspecta* 22: "Paradigms of Architecture," Frampton wrote: "There is no such thing as an objective record in the positivistic sense. Indeed, even if such a record were possible, its cultural and critical value would be virtually nil."

Areas of new construction employ the principles of displaying and storing craft, in this case photography. Many have written about the underlying properties of a good photograph. In the early stages of Pictorialism, for example, H. P. Robinson established a set of rules including the balance of lines and composition within the frame. It is with these "rules" that the architecture is formed, from the plan to the elevation of a gallery wall and the details of a handrail. New construction and preserved structural elements are reconciled through a method of transposition; alterations and additions offer a background for the house's artifacts and relieve them of functional responsibilities. This allows the artifacts of the house to be staged within an image that reflects its history.

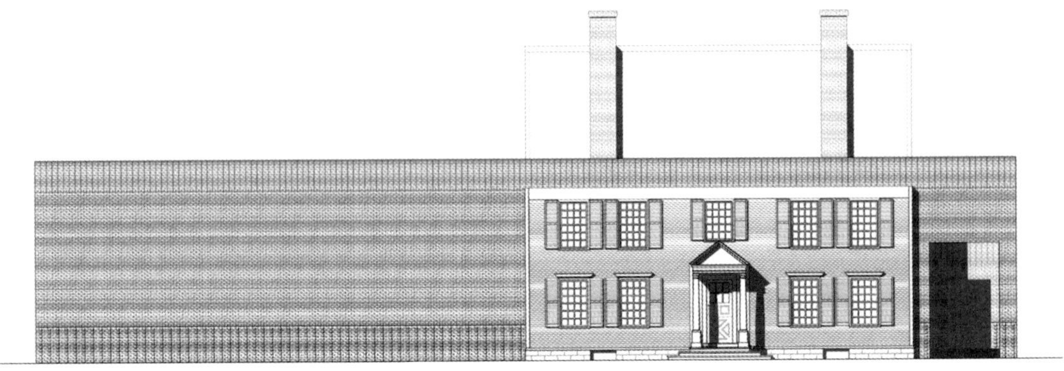

East elevation

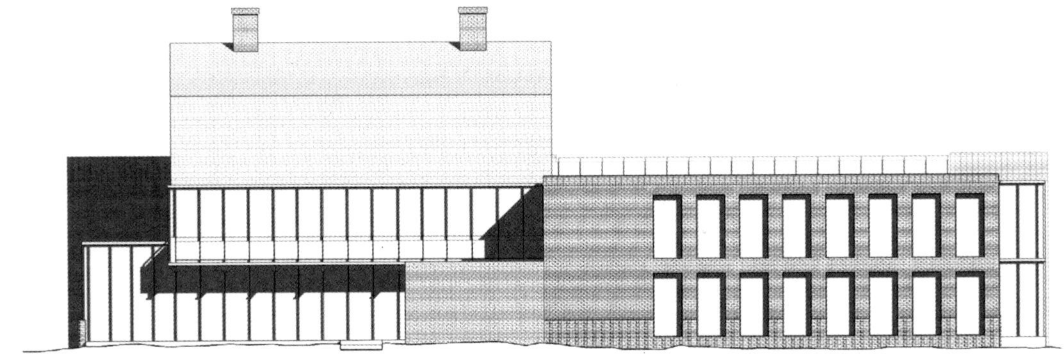

West elevation

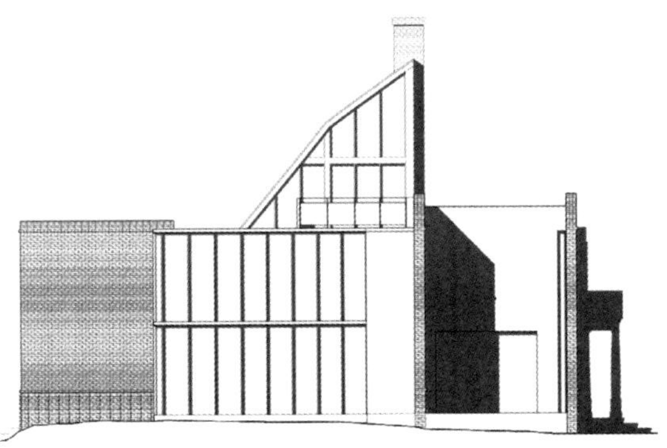

South elevation

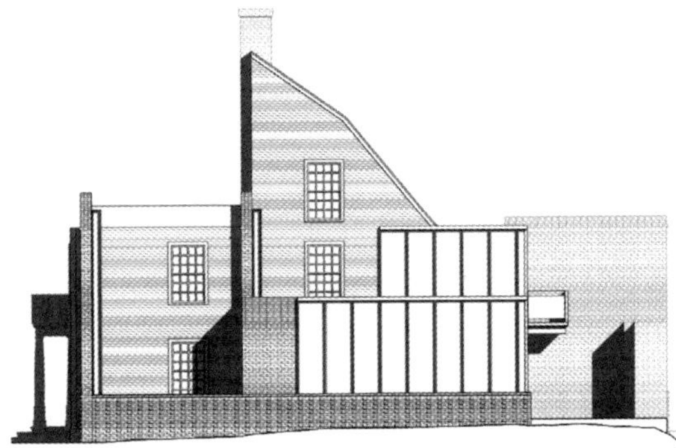

North elevation

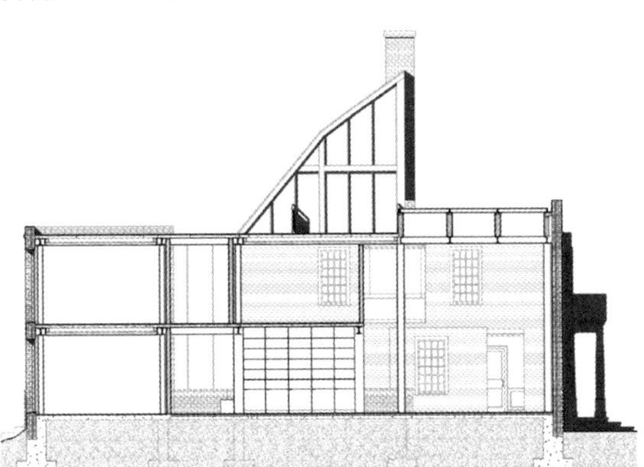

East-west section

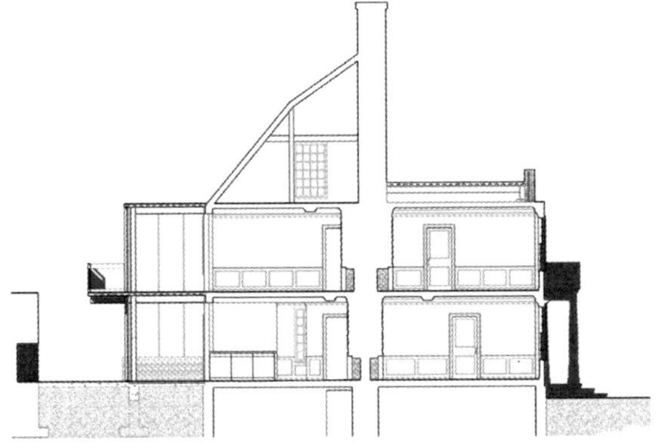

North-south section

THE PARTICULAR AND THE PUBLIC

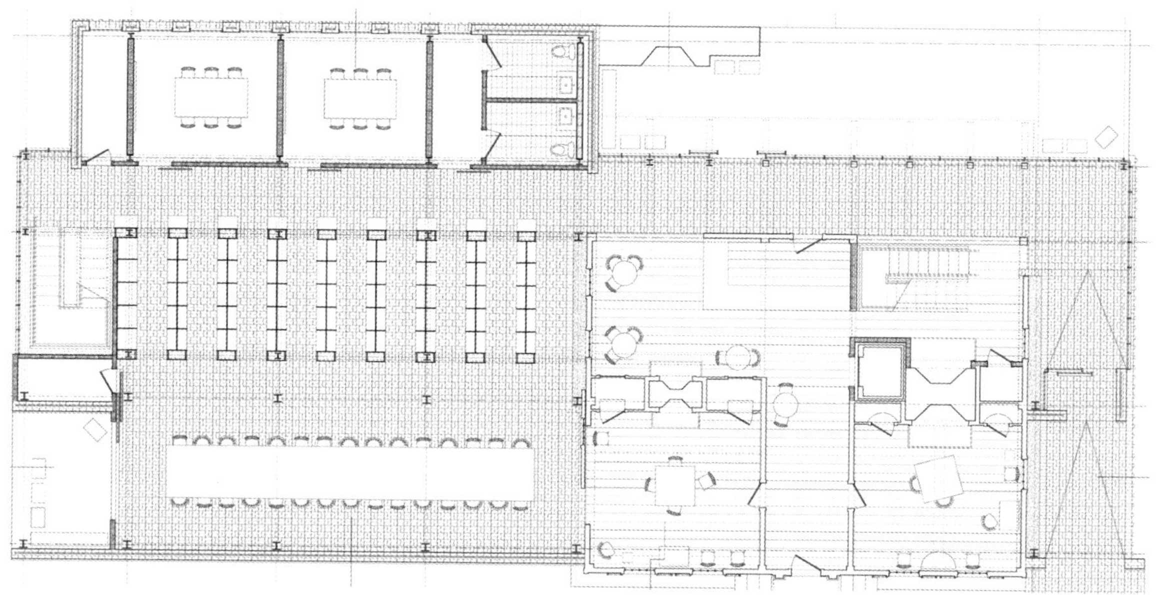

Ground-floor plan

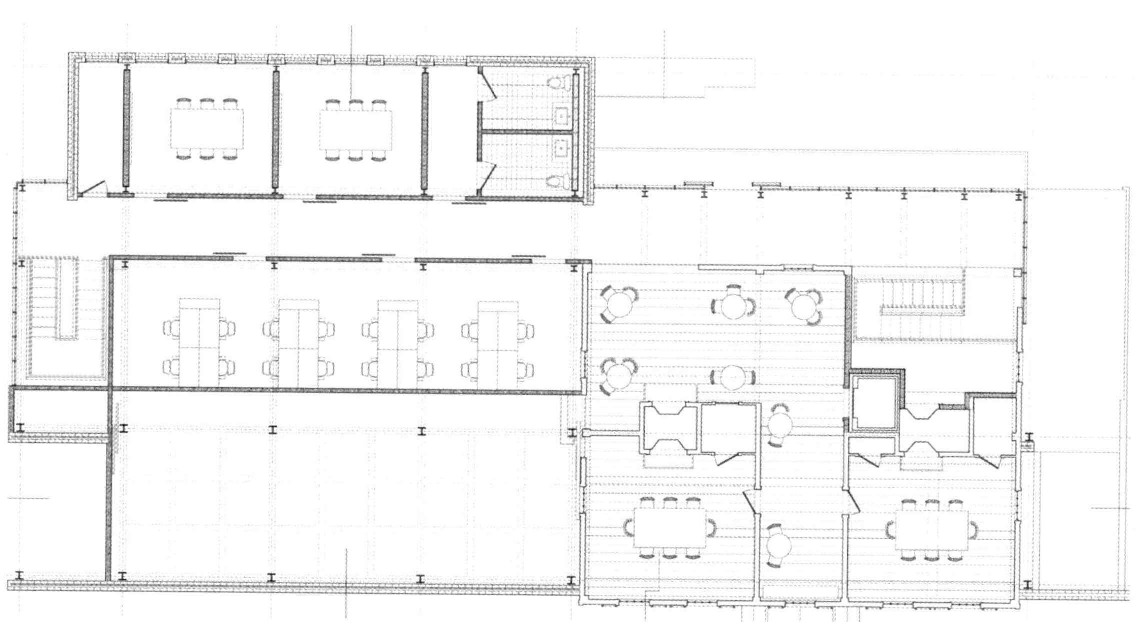

Second-floor plan

Model, north elevation

  THE PARTICULAR AND THE PUBLIC

BENJAMIN FANN

ALTERATION 2

Around the hearth the first groups formed: around the hearth the first groups assembled; around it the first alliances formed; around it the first rude religious concepts were put into the customs of a cult. ... Throughout all phases of society the hearth formed that sacred focus around which took order and shape.It is the first and most important element of architecture.

— *The Four Elements of Architecture*,
  Gottfried Semper

In New England the hearth was once the only source of warmth and light throughout the harsh winters. People would gather around for meals, company, conversation, and heat. For New England's historic houses, the physical hearth encompasses more than just the fireplace. Often fireplaces are adjacent to storage or circulation of adjoining spaces and culminate at the roof in a series of chimneys—a hearth condition. By examining the existing hearths of the house and introducing new hearths as part of an addition, the proposal reorients, reactivates, and renews the formal significance and social impact of public assembly in relation to the organizing element of the hearth.

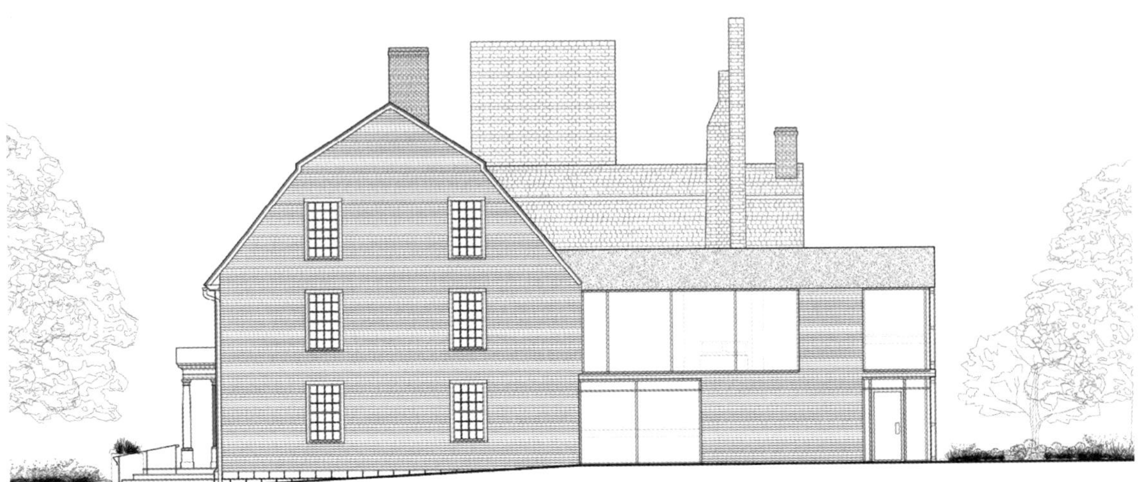

West elevation

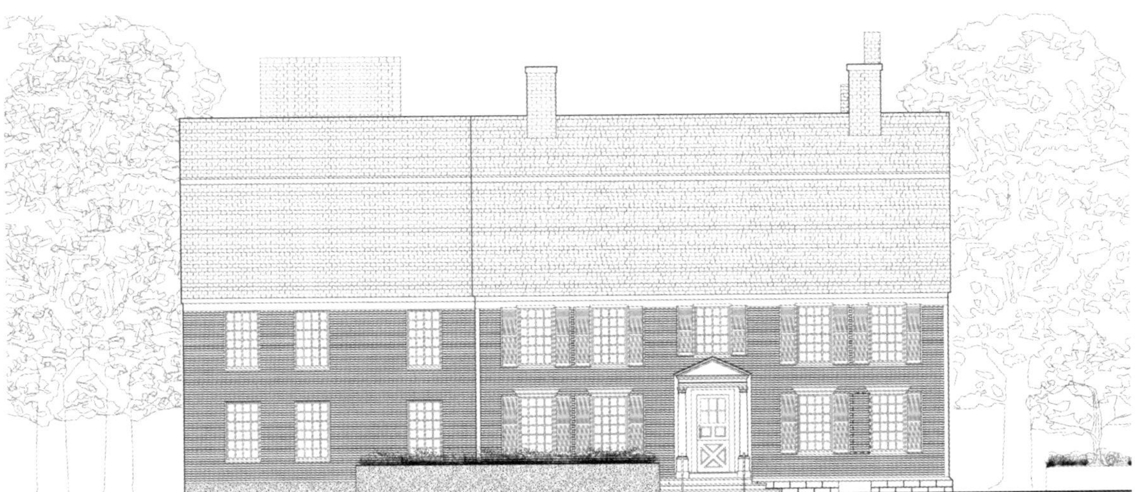

East elevation

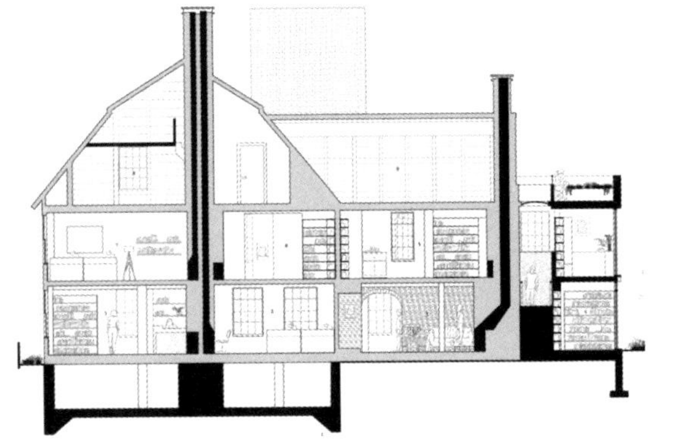

East-west section

North-south section

THE PARTICULAR AND THE PUBLIC

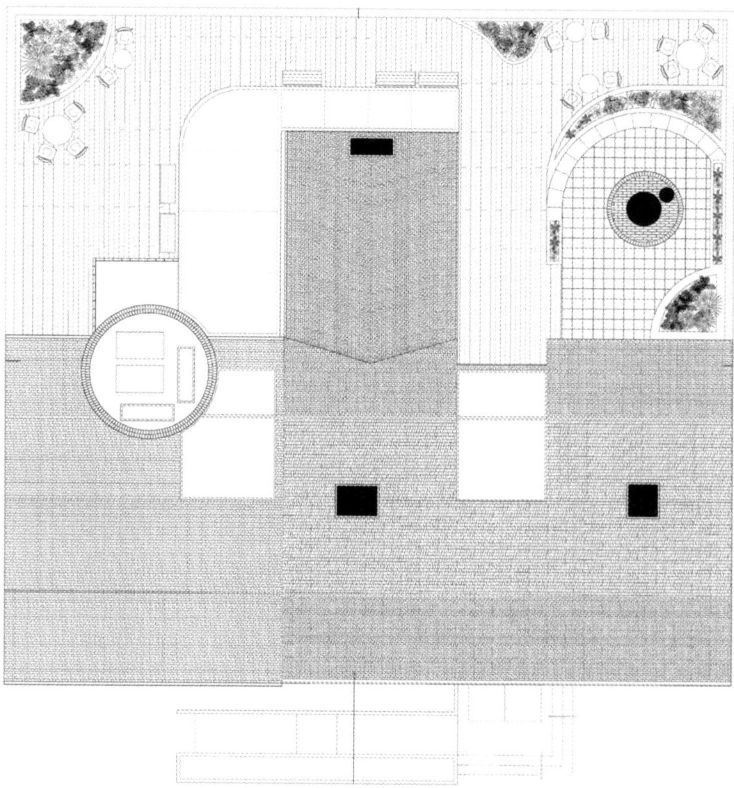

Ground-floor plan

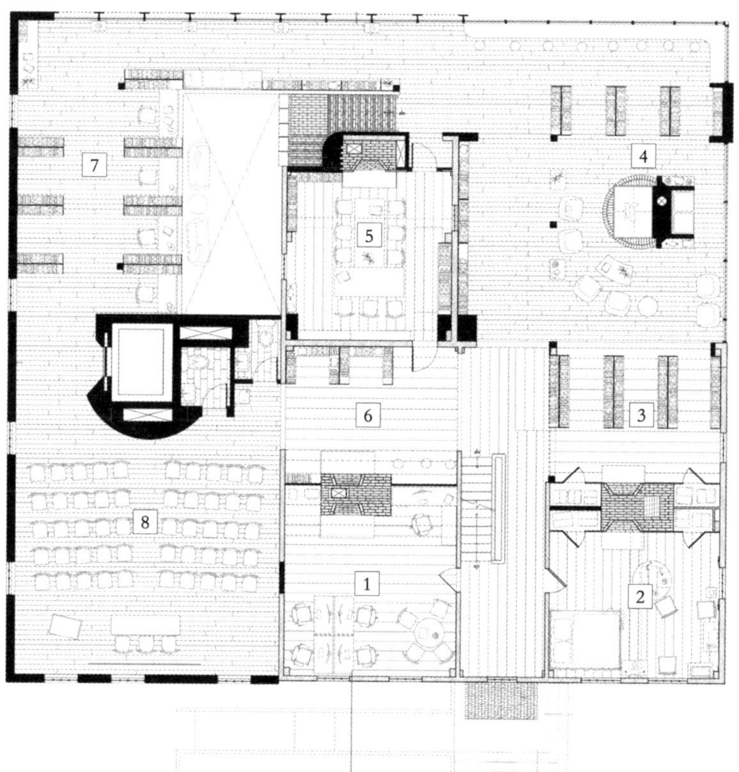

Second-floor plan

1 Office
2 Washington's Bedchanber
3 Book Stacks
4 Public Reading Room
5 Rare Books Archive
6 Curated Book Collection
7 Book Stacks / Study Carrels
8 Assembly Space

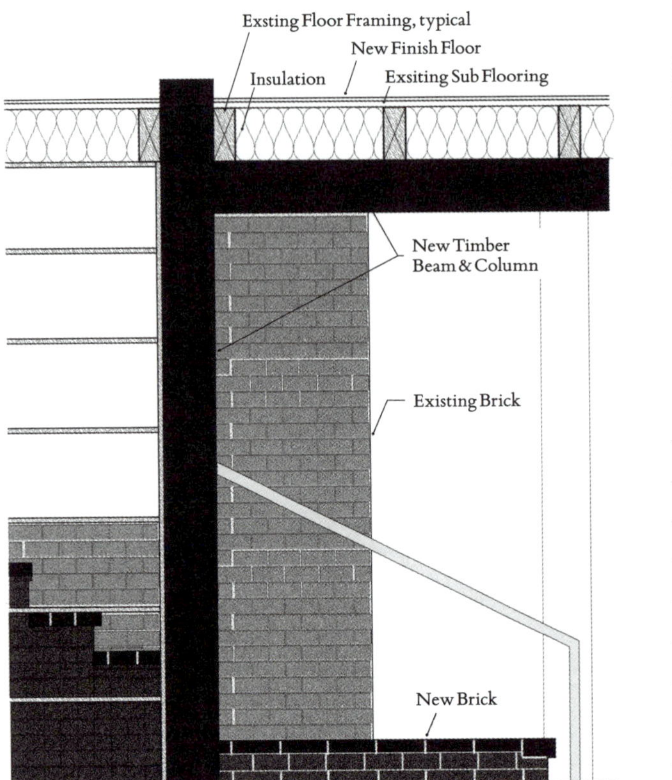

Typical hearth detail

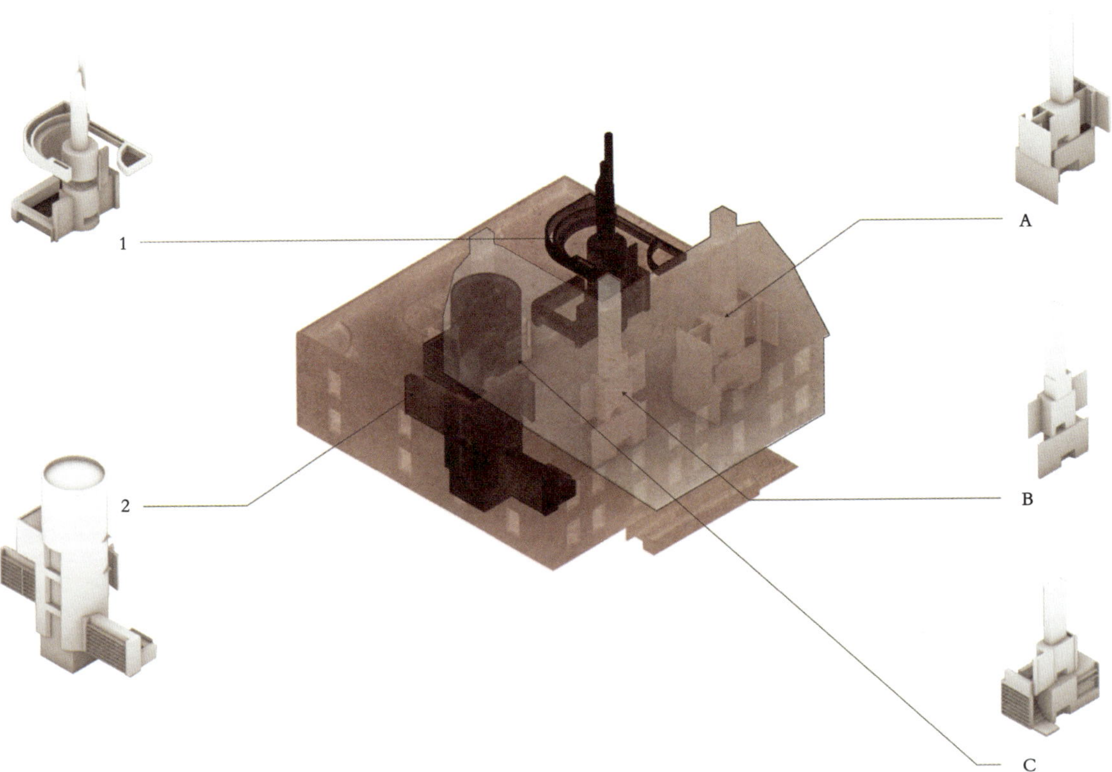

Axonometric, hearth details

THE PARTICULAR AND THE PUBLIC

Model, southwest corner

Model, east elevation

JONATHAN CHU

ALTERATION 3

The Joseph Webb House possesses an intimate character and does not appear on lists of the most famous or grand houses in America. Yet hidden away within its modest exterior are three layers, or scales, of history that suggest a narrative both broader and deeper than meets the eye: national, regional, and local. Each of these histories informs, in a kaleidoscopic way, the particulars of the space as it is found today.

Successful alteration of the house into an educational public program will involve integrating, expanding, and adapting these three scales of history. While this may be considered a theoretical underpinning of the project, it foregrounds architecturally specific interventions. A logical sequence of spaces will be choreographed, and significant existing spaces, such as the Washington parlor, may be altered minimally to become architecturally didactic by revealing layers of the original structure and its subsequent evolution to visitors. We may also adopt a critical framework for presenting history in a house museum that is relevant while providing a range of functions that cater to a diverse community.

Given the multiple house alterations already undertaken, our latest transformation is by no means terminal and is only one of many inflection points in its chronology. We will incorporate flexibility and modularity, both spatially and temporally, for future similar endeavors, anticipating changes in use or scale for new programs.

In one reading of the original house, the two-story hallway is the most architecturally significant space. It is at once singular and particular in its condition and can function as a central gathering and distribution hub. Anchored by the hallway, this alteration allows for converting the adjacent existing rooms or extending the hallway to an additional structure while introducing a horizontal/planar coherence that could be distinguished vertically/sectionally.

We may consider additions to the house in plan and section. The latter would involve employing underutilized attic space as a gallery to celebrate the formal and cultural qualities of the gambrel roof and experiment with openings and lighting. Alternatively there is the potential to expand and contract spaces, where the shifting of internal boundaries within the container of the original tartan grid—formed by rooms, fireplaces, and the hallway—may be explored. For the structure to facilitate an educational function focused on the complex layers of history, it must be carefully executed to combine acts of preservation, adaptation, and calibration. The Athenaeum presents an opportunity to connect locally grounded vernacular architecture with the broader discourse of culture and society in America's past and present.

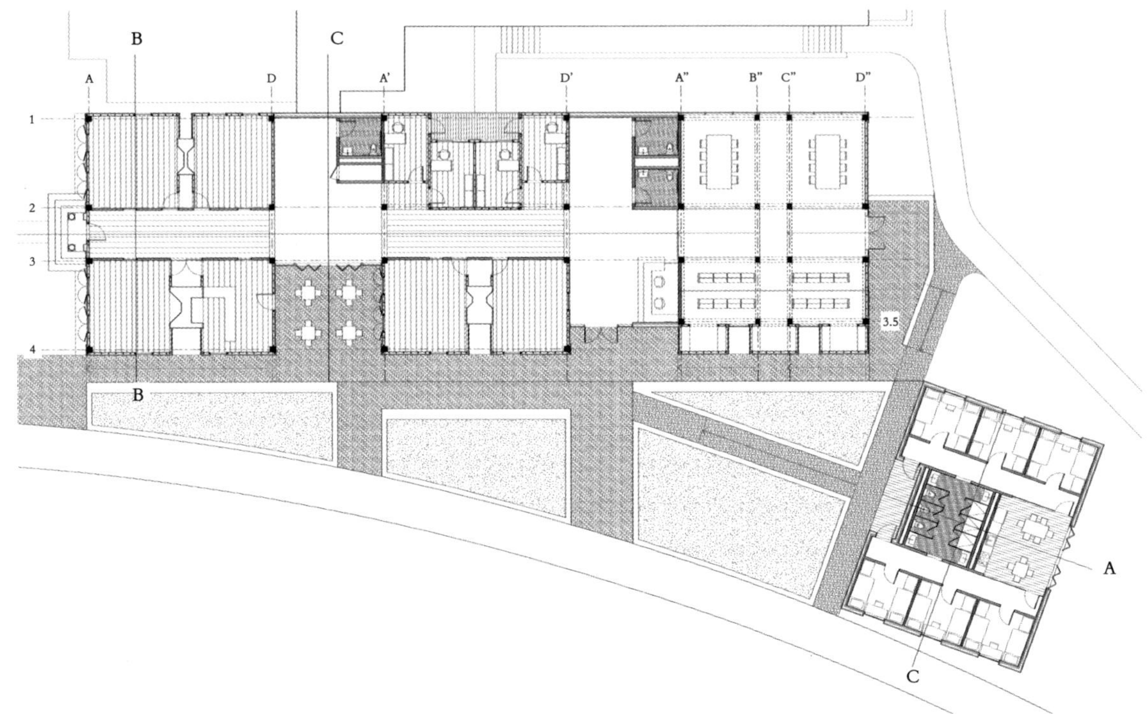

Ground-floor plan

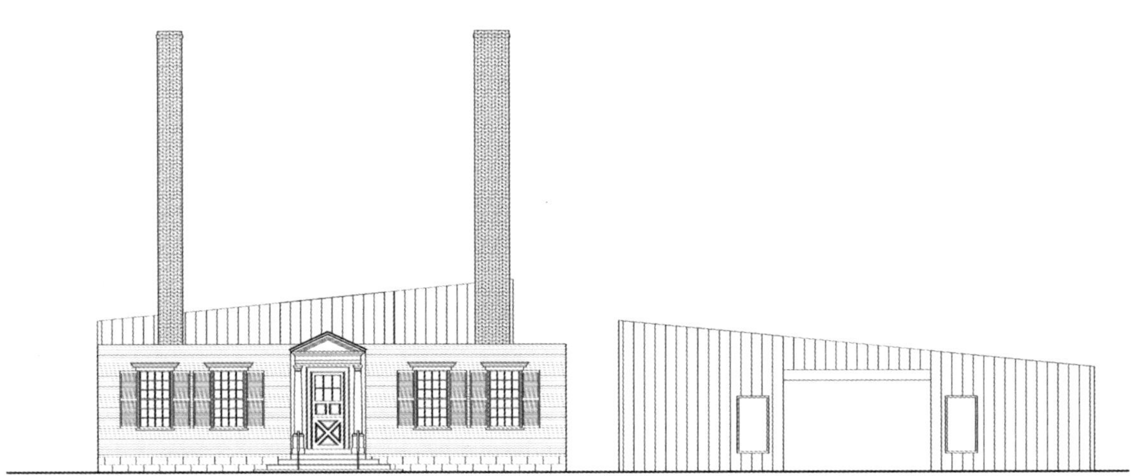

East elevation

     THE PARTICULAR AND THE PUBLIC

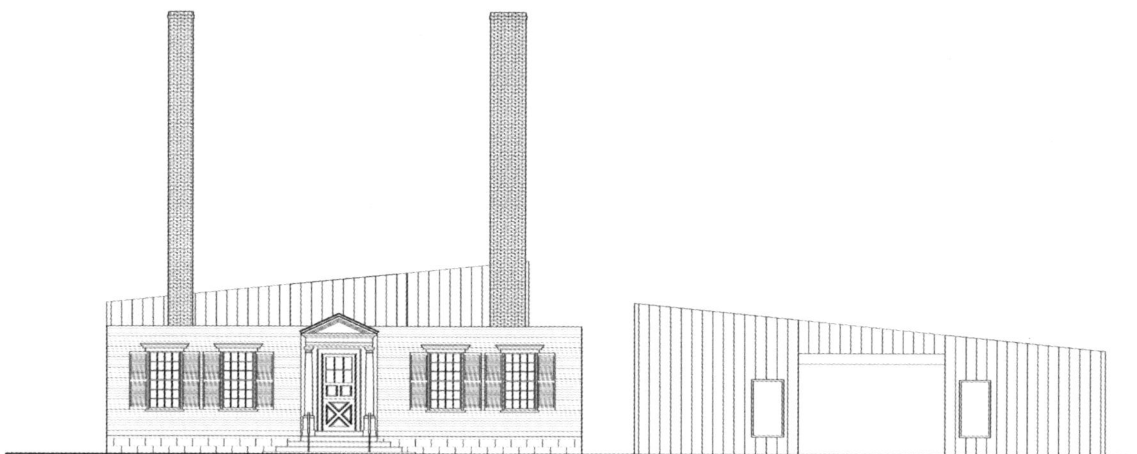

North-south section

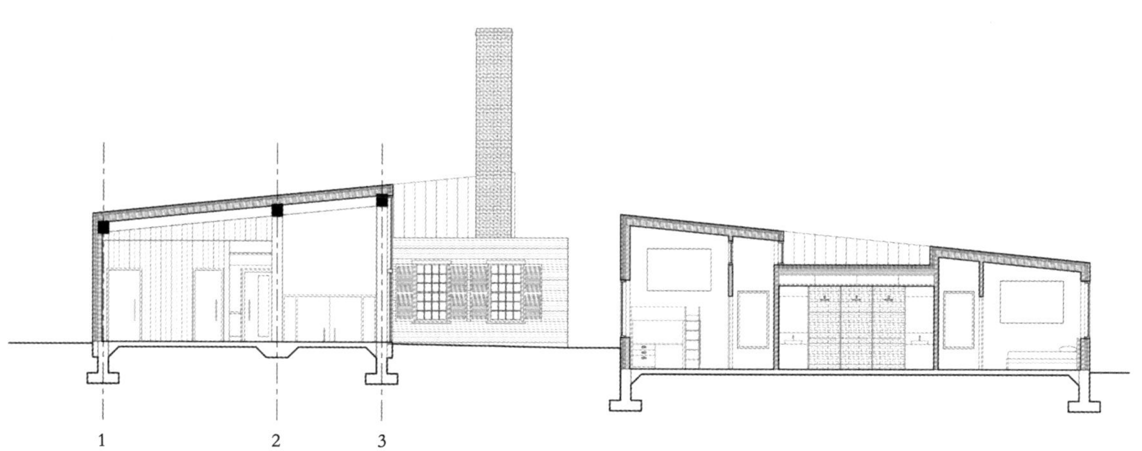

East-west section

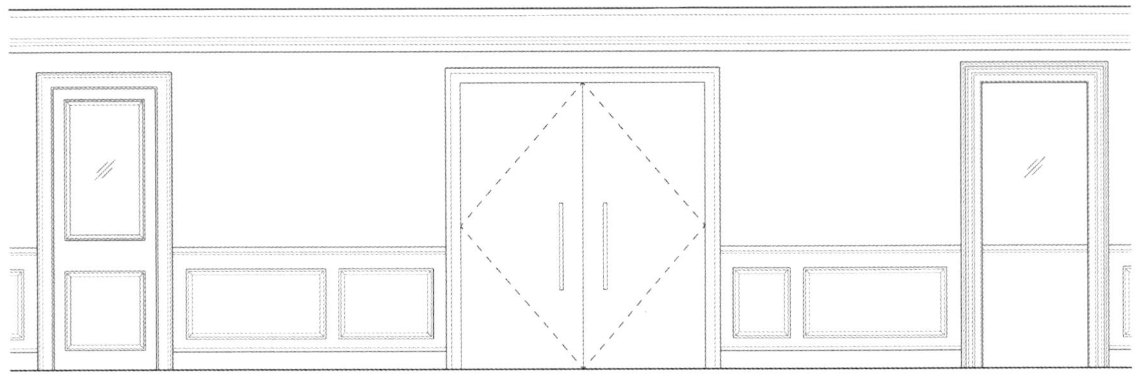

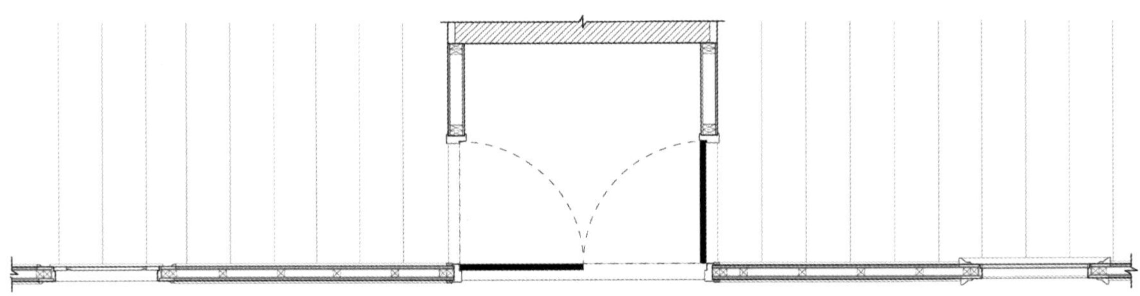

Typical threshold detail

     THE PARTICULAR AND THE PUBLIC

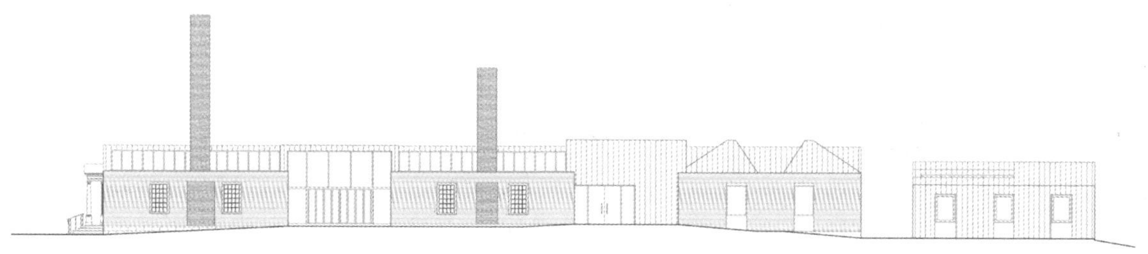

North elevation

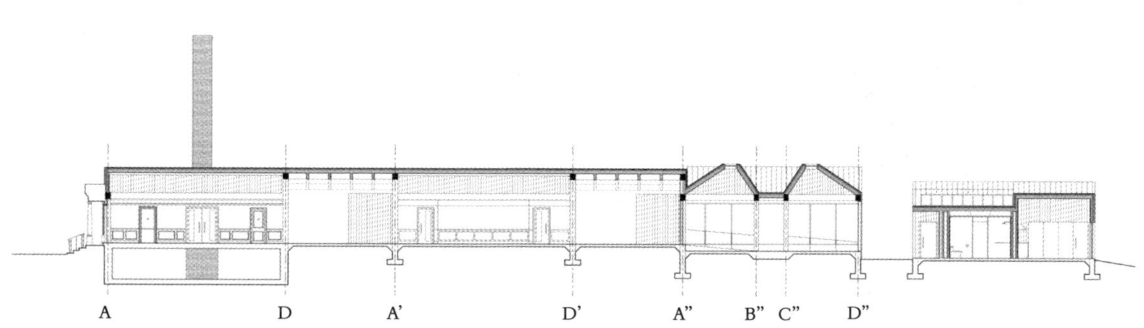

North-south section

ABBY REED

ALTERATION
4

THE PARTICULAR AND THE PUBLIC

The Joseph Webb House is not extraordinary except for the fact that it still stands after 270 years. Unlike contemporary buildings, it was not built with a 50-year lifespan. The attic was both systematic and ad hoc. Webb was a merchant who kept meticulous records of where materials came from. Timber was sourced locally and along the river for ease of transport. Today we see using local materials as ecological, but 270 years ago it was simply logical.

The framing echoes the house's particularities. The random beams and ad hoc nature of the building expose the craft and logic of how each piece of lumber was hewn and nailed into place. Joints varied based on material and the requirements of form. The redundancies of structure have led to small, enclosed spaces, limited openings, and a heaviness of enclosure.

The Webb House is a New England heavy-timber frame with diagonal bracing aligned to the studs for lateral supports. Since its construction, the logic of wood framing has become standardized as a two-by-four modular construction system. The introduction of engineering timber—glulam and cross-laminated timber (CLT)—has extended the span that wood construction can reach and allowed for more specific and particular conditions to be generated. The new framing reuses the original volume of timber through modern fabrication to produce a larger space. Our new methods and means of construction enable us to step away from the enclosed cellular spaces of the colonial house. We can achieve "bigness."

When bigness is reintroduced into this particular vernacular, a hyper-particular condition appears that realigns itself with the scale of the joint to reconcile the logic of these contrasting conditions. Bigness becomes relative in the acuteness of detail.

As the new skin adapts to the old, each joint must address the particularities of its host. The scale of bigness is broken down through its components, from the individual framing members and connections to the footprint of the house and pools. The adaptation loosens the house from its history and ties it to its contemporary social context.

With the introduction of bigness, the house can become much more than a house or an Athenaeum. Bigness opens the house up to its site, expanding to accommodate pools, gardens, and gathering spaces. It embraces the site, opening toward the canopy of trees. Bigness coexists with the vernacular. It embraces contemporary construction logics with the hope of making the ecological simply logical once again.

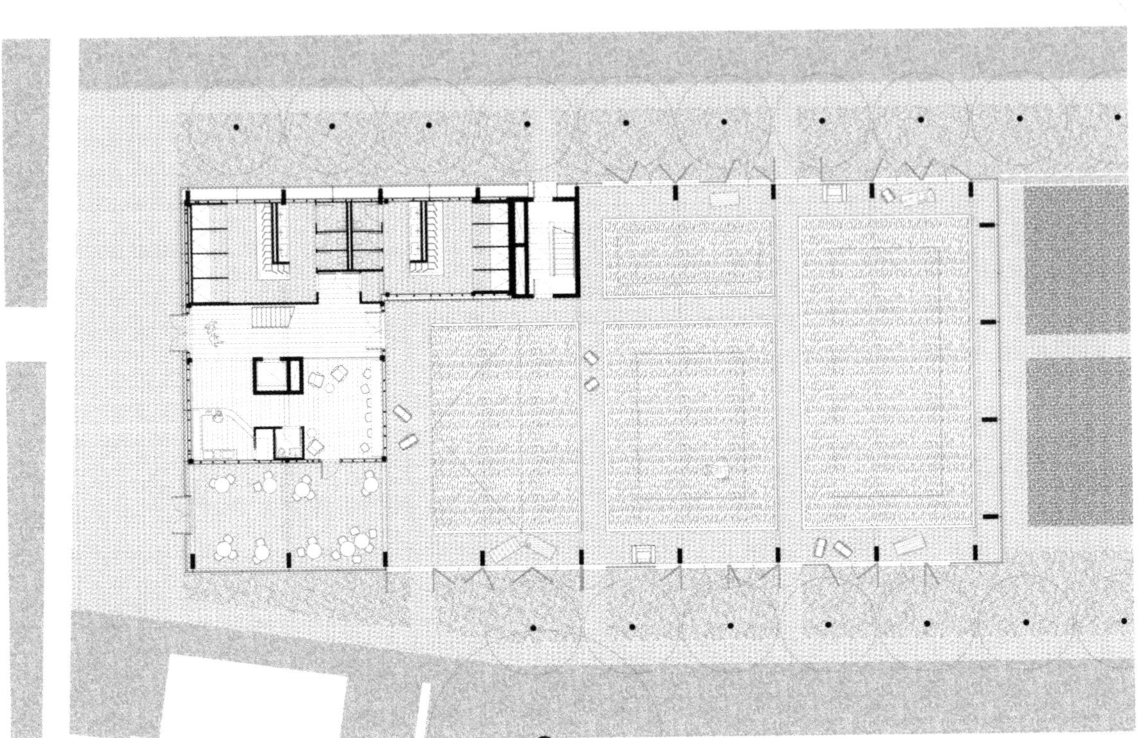

Ground-floor plan

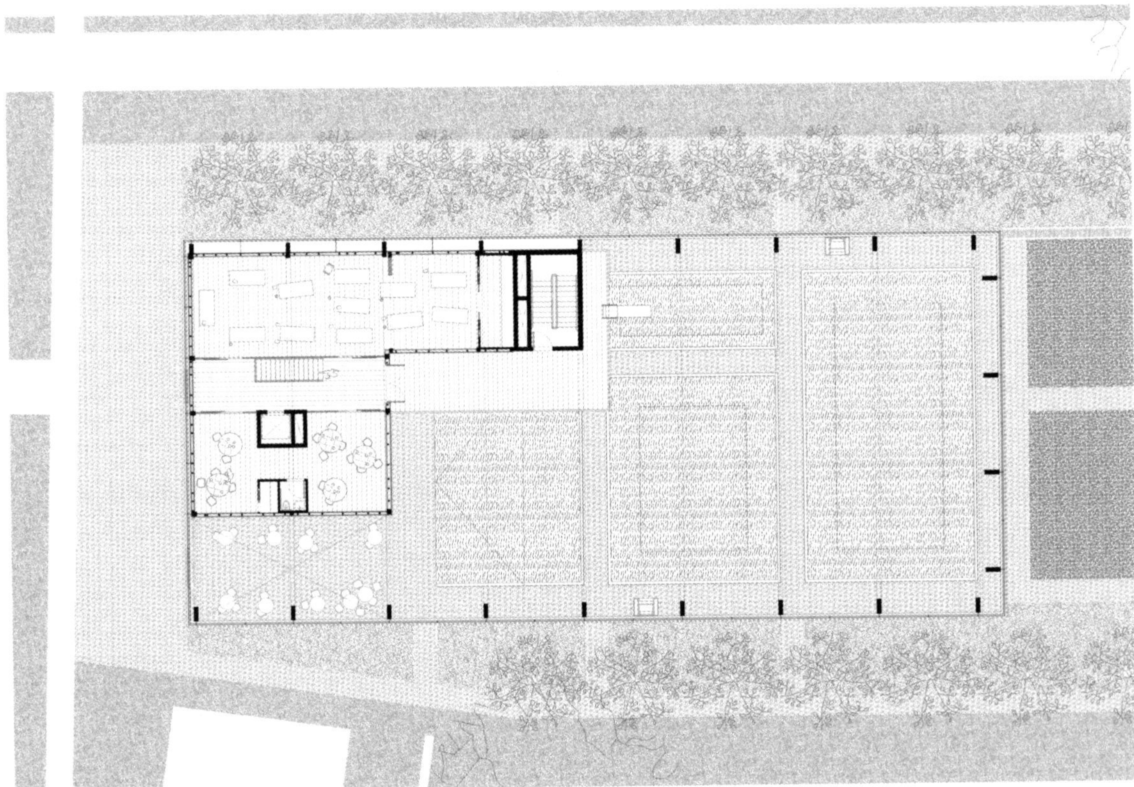

Second-floor plan

THE PARTICULAR AND THE PUBLIC

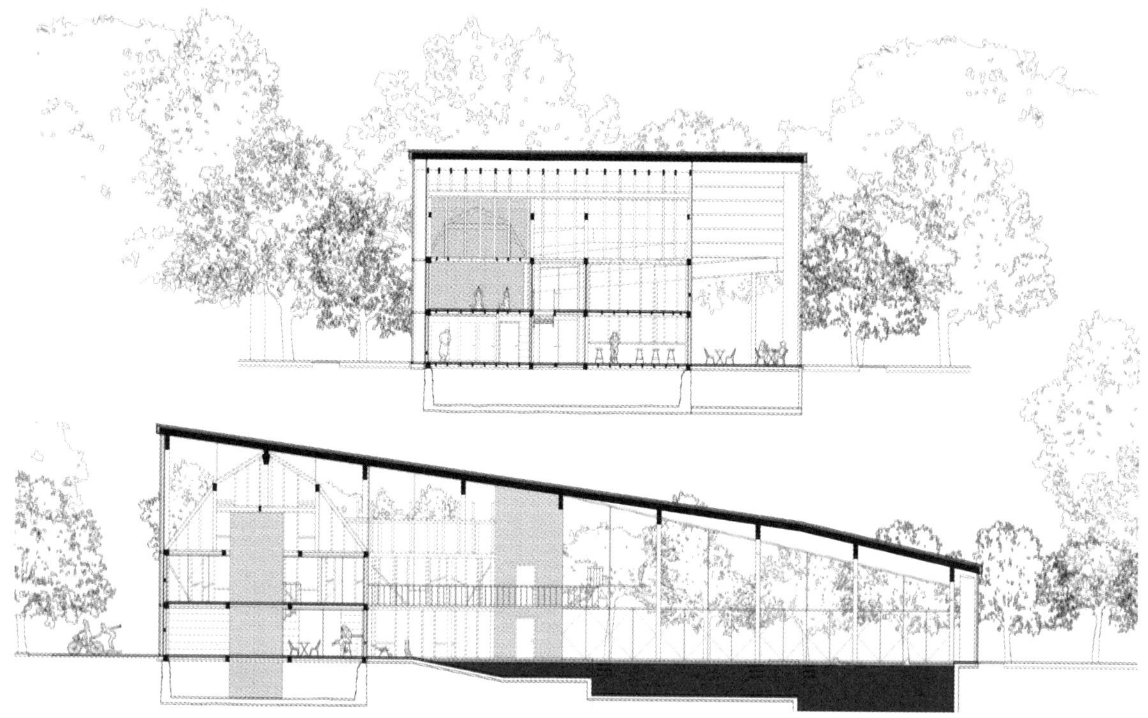

North–south section and east–west section

East elevation and north elevation

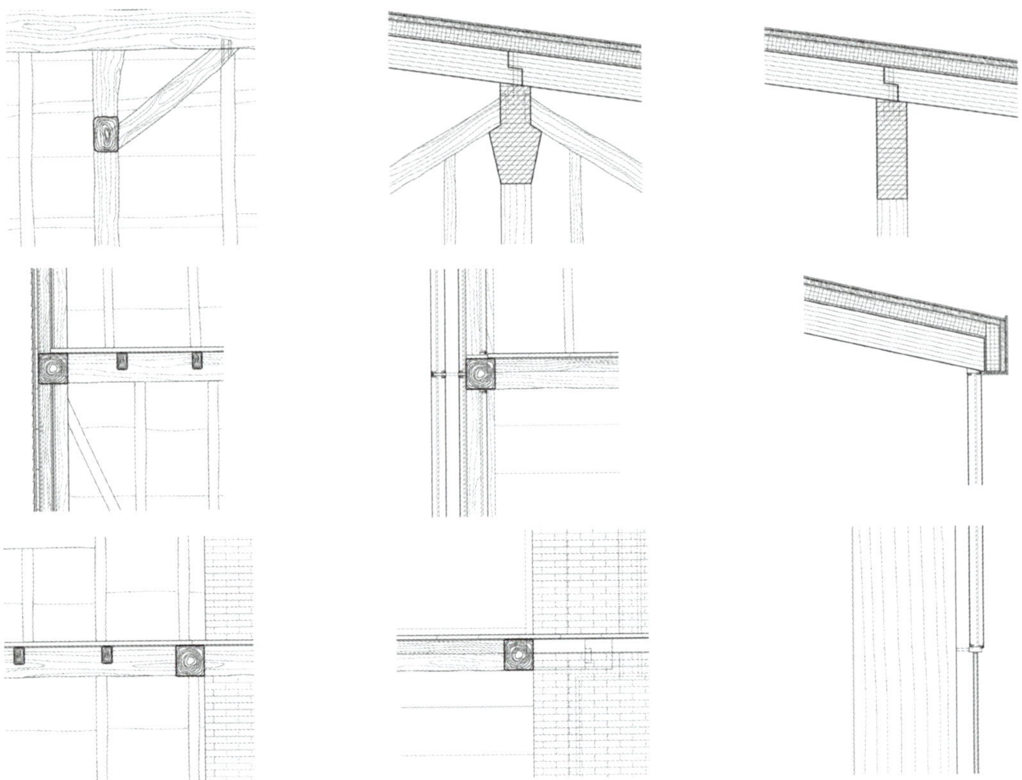

Typical details

Model, east elevation

Model, south elevation

Model, exterior corridor

Model detail

JERRY CHOW

ALTERATION
5

The Athenaeum project proposes to surface the latent, hidden, and forgotten histories and knowledge embodied in the Joseph Webb House with the aim of nurturing critical retellings and reinterpretations. It takes the form of spaces designed for sharing and studying in various ways.

Because the question of history is as important as futurity in this project, its scope is from roughly 271 years into the past—stretching back to the Joseph Webb House's initial construction—to 271 years into the future, for a total of 542 years. Additions have played a large role in the house's reconfiguration over the years. This project will pay special consideration to the barn (built ca. 1840, moved in 1921), the colonial garden (originally active in the 1920s, revived in 1999), and the ell addition (built in 1765). These appendages indicate changing perceptions, uses, and priorities over time, resulting in piecemeal interventions on the building and its landscape. They also suggest that a slower approach to conservation is possible and that the redirection of the house museum's trajectory can be intermittent, tentative, and contingent.

The gambrel roof and the attic are important elements of the house, given its historic role in the trade and storage of goods and slaves. Yet as an architectural construct, the house as a whole is largely unexceptional. Is the rest of the house simply connective tissue, a scaffolding for holding discrete, specific memories? Is it all fair game? Potential strategies for reframing the house are as follows:

Hem the building in so that its form matches its program and site.
Cut away that which is extraneous.
Repair the edges.

Soften our understanding of what is worth preserving; preserve that which is inherently soft, pliable, and fleeting. Think about the softness in the hard.

Make good in the sense of correcting, patching, and mending inconsistencies and imperfections—but also make interventions that further good.

Tell the story of the place; reveal the "as-found" that is not so easily found. Consider what it all means.

Starting anew does not erase history—it must be grappled with. I am in favor of humble, not necessarily concealed, work that wrestles with problems honestly, possesses a kind of conceptual earnestness, and respects its limits. This project does not promise to "do" anything except to identify and fill gaps in our knowledge through a recasting and revision of the Joseph Webb House and its history.

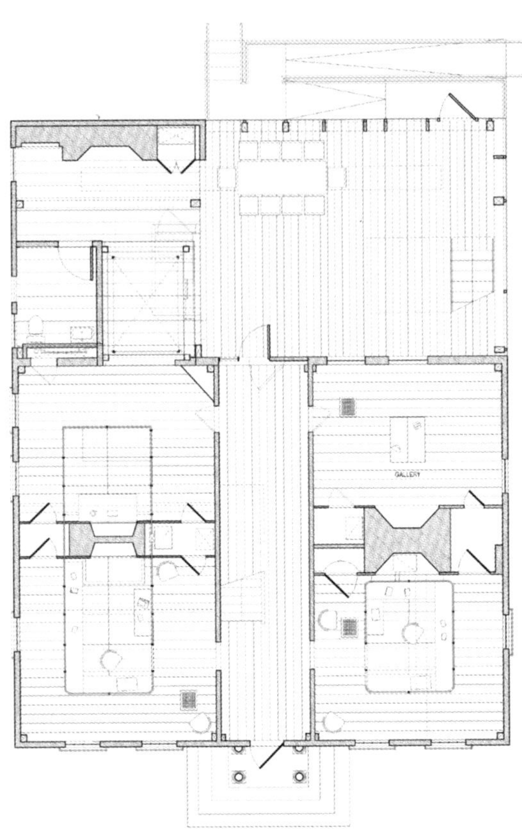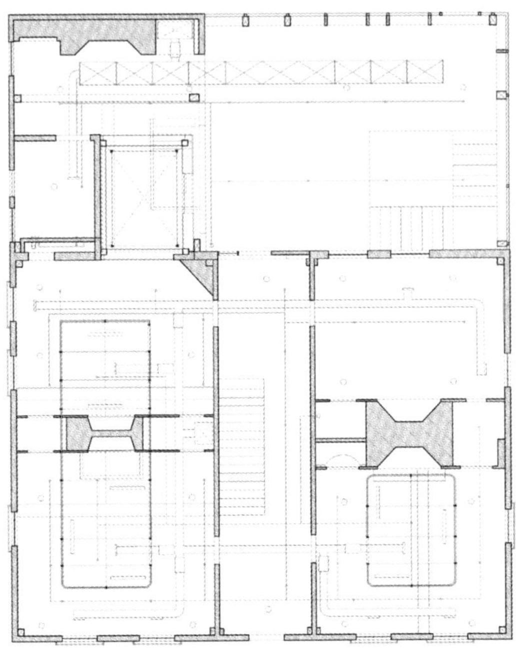

Ground-floor plan and reflected-ceiling plan

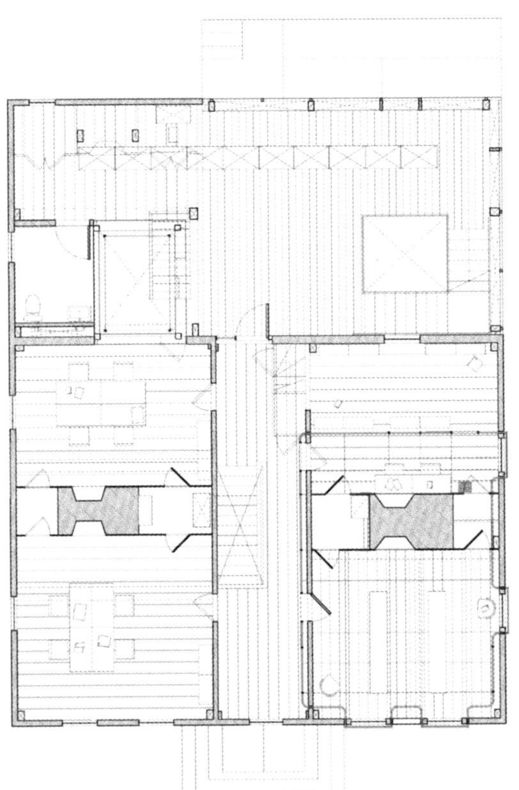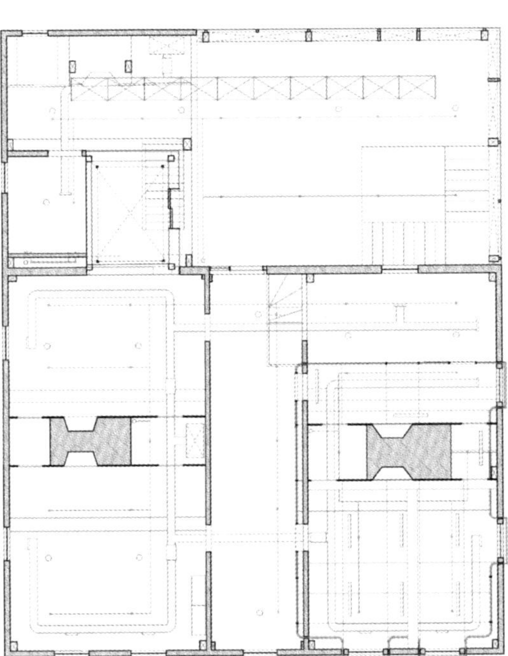

Second-floor plan and reflected-ceiling plan

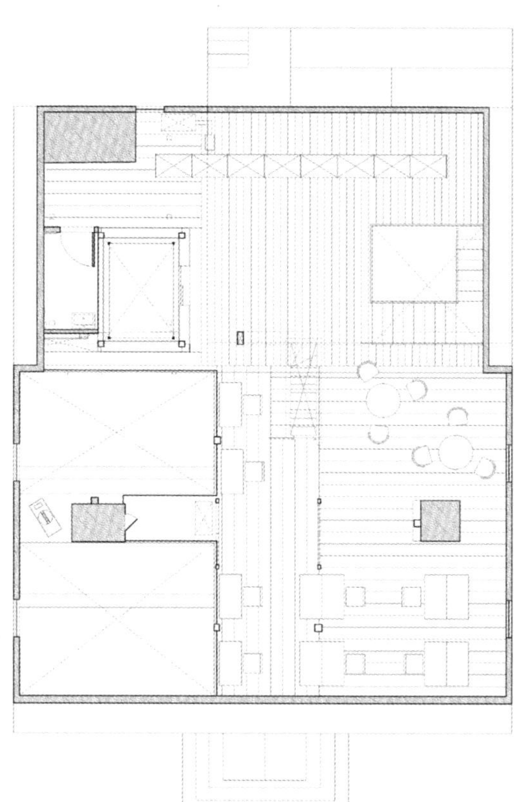

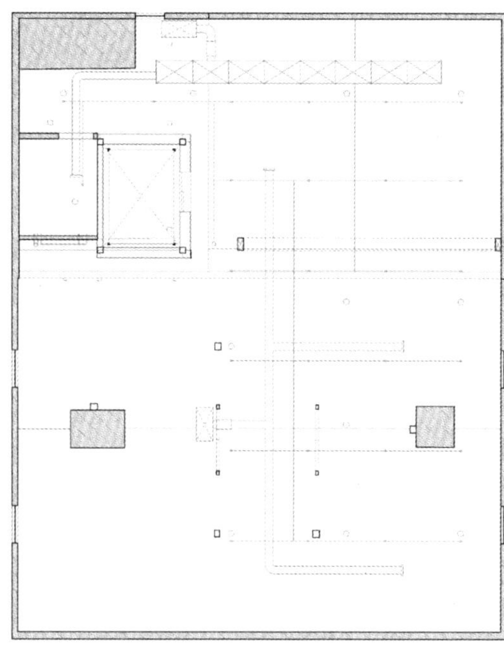

Attic floor plan and reflected ceiling plan

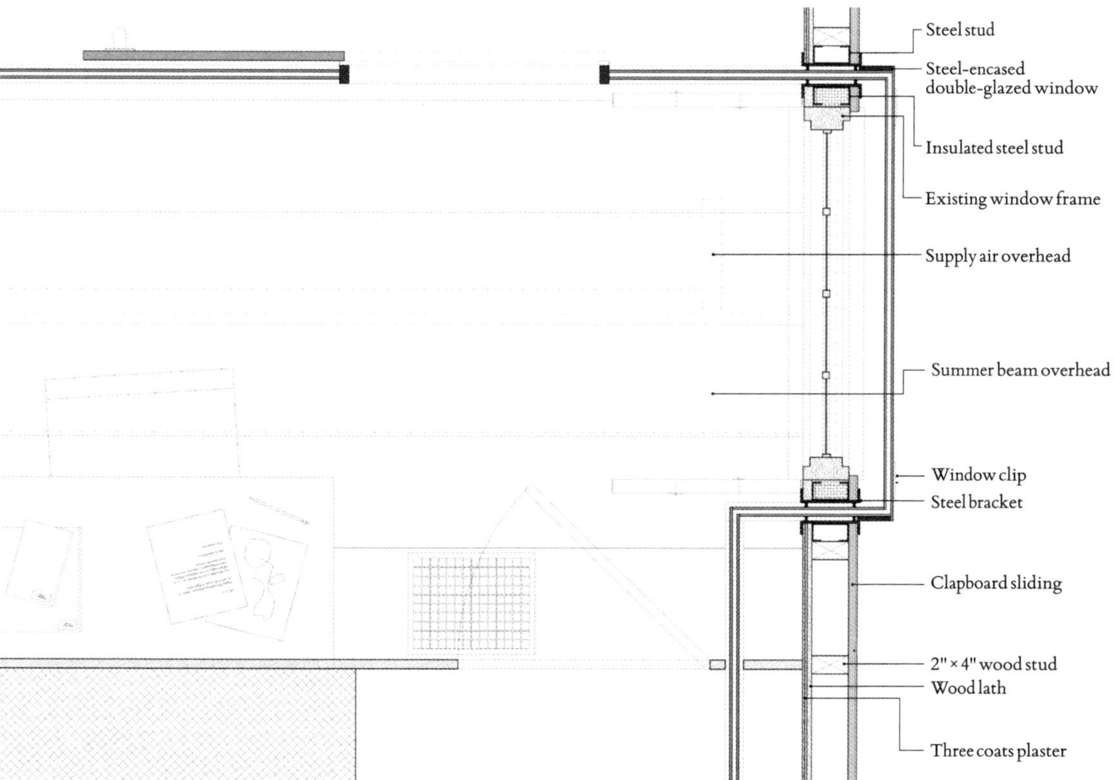

Typical window detail

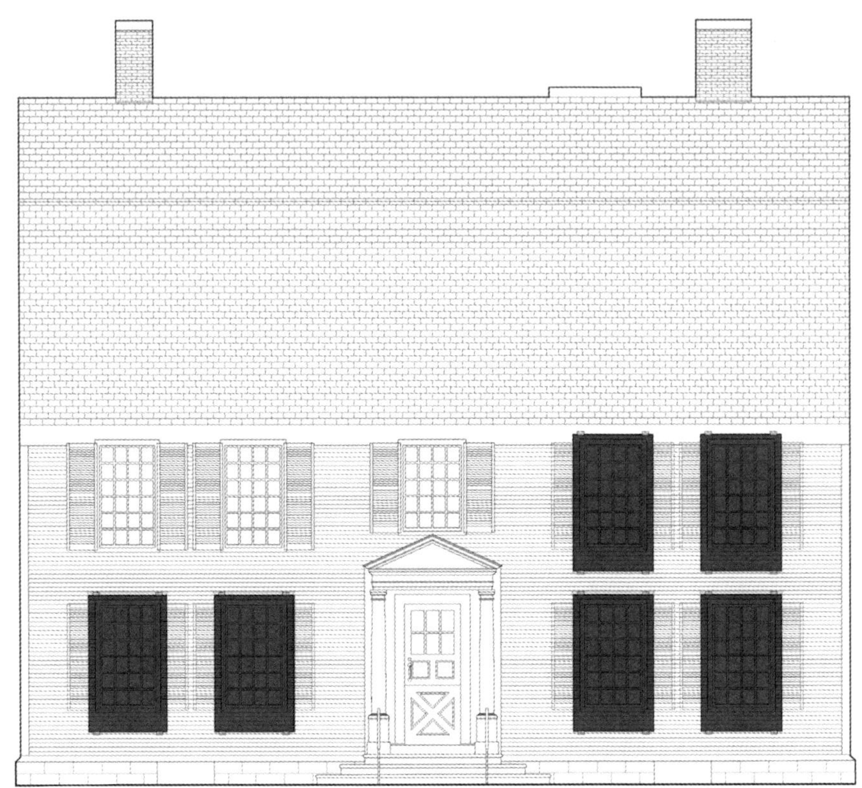

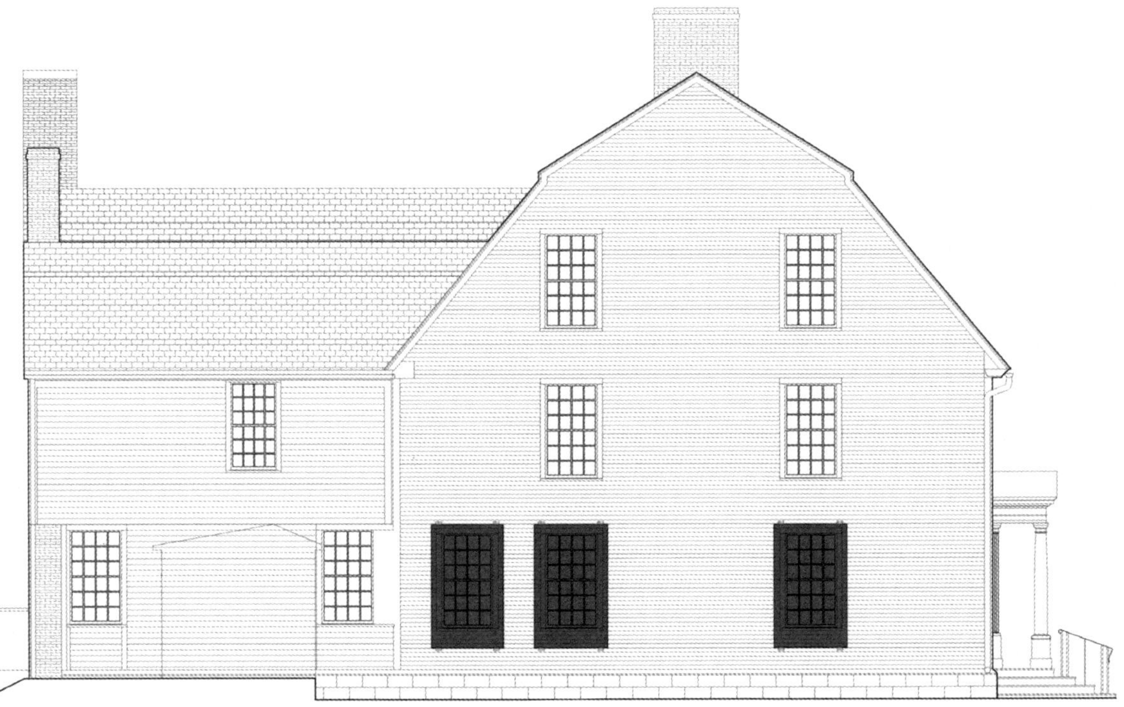

East elevation and south elevation

   THE PARTICULAR AND THE PUBLIC

Model, southeast

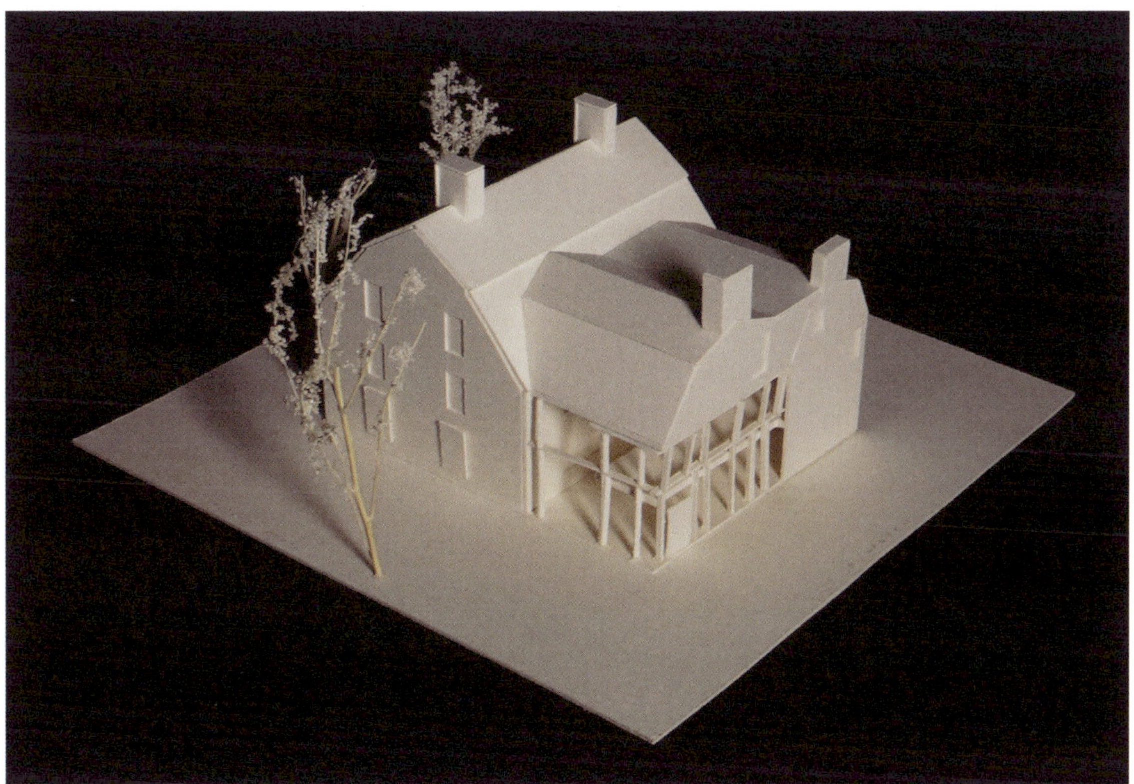

Model, northwest

IRIS YOU

ALTERATION

6

THE PARTICULAR AND THE PUBLIC

The Athenaeum will host a library or study space to encourage lingering and looking. Otherwise the program will remain unchanged: a cultural center with a museum addition and the activities of the Colonial Dames of America. The existing audience will be presented with a new experience.

Wood-paneled walls were instruments inserted into and readjusted within the cavity of the house, as was evident in the numerous alterations within the house's history. The alteration will continue to play on the precision and sharpness of one element or material against another. Employing variations on this history of dislocation, the existing rooms will be expanded by rotating the perimeter walls to a new boundary. The chimney and closet zone will be repurposed as a transitional space in an enfilade perpendicular to the original circulation. An updated facade on the north elevation will reorient the building to the visitors' first approach. The fireplace and its accompanying floor will be dropped to create a doorway linking the southern lower front room (existing exhibit space) with the upper back room.

Interesting comparisons are Tadao Ando's enclosure of the Clark Museum at the Williams College entrance as a courtyard, and Rafael Viñoly's courtyard enclosure at the front facade of the Cleveland Art Museum. The interior courtyards modulate the neoclassical entrances to convey approachability rather than the alienating sense of a yellowed Victorian picture postcard of a once grand edifice —a beached whale stranded in time. By limiting one's view of the whole from a distance, the new extensions break up the visual mass. Employing Modernist massing of a similar proportion to that of the original—without ornamentation— reintroduces the sense of elegance it once possessed without being overloaded symbolically. In that sense it closes the affective distance by creating a temporal wormhole where the marks of two eras are visible. I am interested in deploying the interior facades of the house in the same way, by turning a room inside out, just as those museum facades were turned outside in. The question is, what composition of those panelized wall portals could create an alternate "warm-up cool-down" transition space?

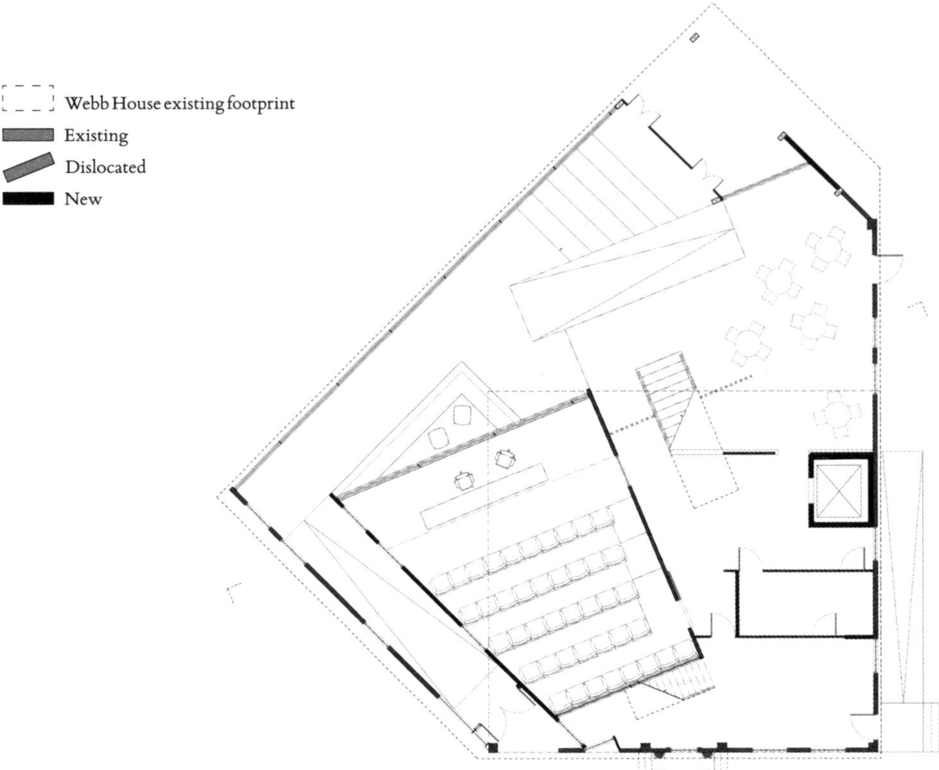

Ground-floor plan

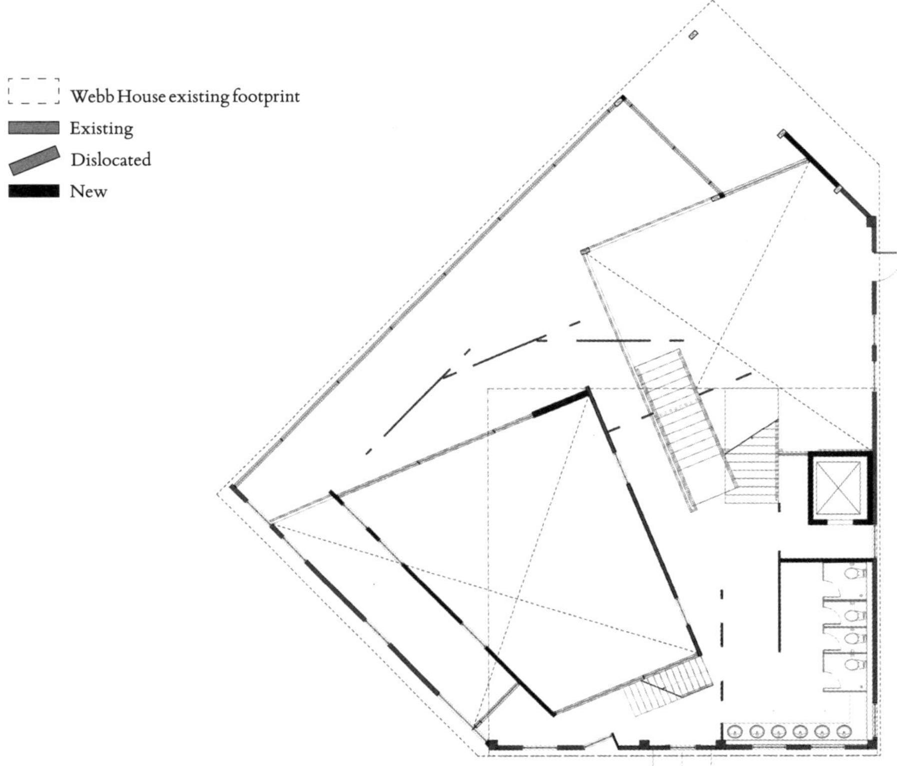

Second-floor plan

       THE PARTICULAR AND THE PUBLIC

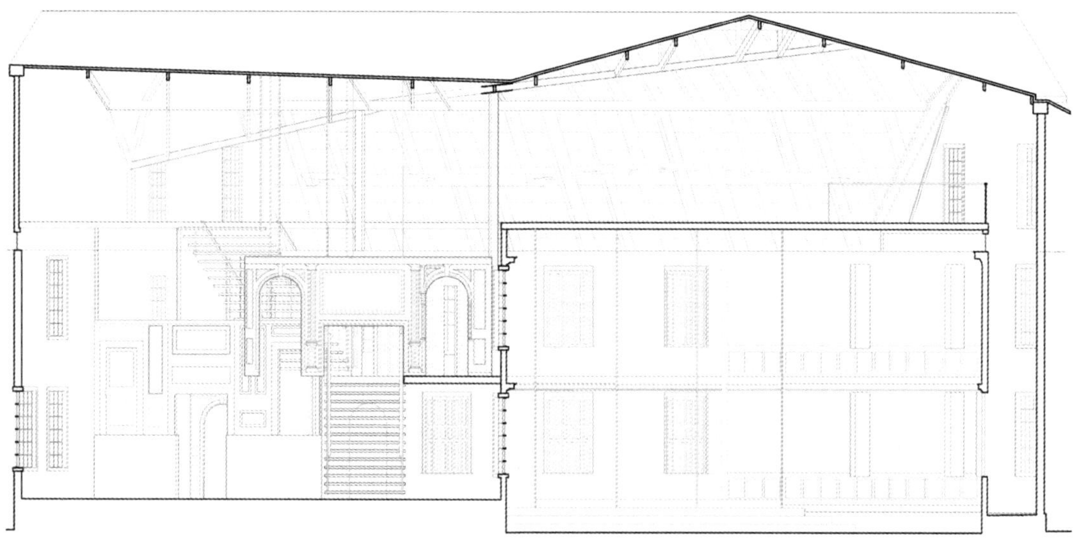

East-west elevation

North eleavtion

Site plan

 THE PARTICULAR AND THE PUBLIC

STUDENT WORK: IRIS YOU

JESSICA ZHOU

ALTERATION 7

The intervention for the Joseph Webb House should be conducted to preserve the original structure and, more importantly, all of its subsequent changes to express its multitude of identities. The operation should not try to narrate but to let the house speak. This is a proposal to amplify the Webb House as a place that celebrates the relationship between a building and changing times. Looking at the many identities the house has assumed—a family home, a wartime conference space, a public gallery, and a preservation museum, among them—what persisted was not a specific program but how it adapted forgivingly to human actions, both in the house and on the structure. The new design will focus on the ideas of gathering, pausing, looking, and examining; the possible programs include a public reading room, an open gallery space, and a café.

The intervention roots itself in the present; it does not try to unearth what has already been covered based on any understanding of what it "originally" was, and it does not restore what has already been removed. Reflecting on the drastically different approaches that Nutting and the Colonial Dames of America took toward preserving the house, the new proposal acknowledges all its past alterations. In a static sense, these are now part of the house; from a more active point of view, all manner of aging, sagging, and eccentricities will become integral parts of the house.

The design proposes modifications and additions in, around, and on the extended axis of the central hallway of the Webb House, including the interior finishes of the ground-level hall and the rear "piazza" and lot. The central axis provides an inherent antithesis to front (east end) versus back (west end), and the proposed design will operate mainly in the "back" portion of the structure.

The proposed design will transpose the building to highlight how the autonomous aging process acts in tension and conversation with generations of modifications, corrections, and additions; in other words, how the complexities of its past created a physical thickness to the building.

In the context of the house, there is value in seeing the building as an object rather than treating its entirety as the operating ground. Rendering the structure into another language that brings light back to the (loosely) axial plan provides a new lens through which to look at not what it should be, but what it could be.

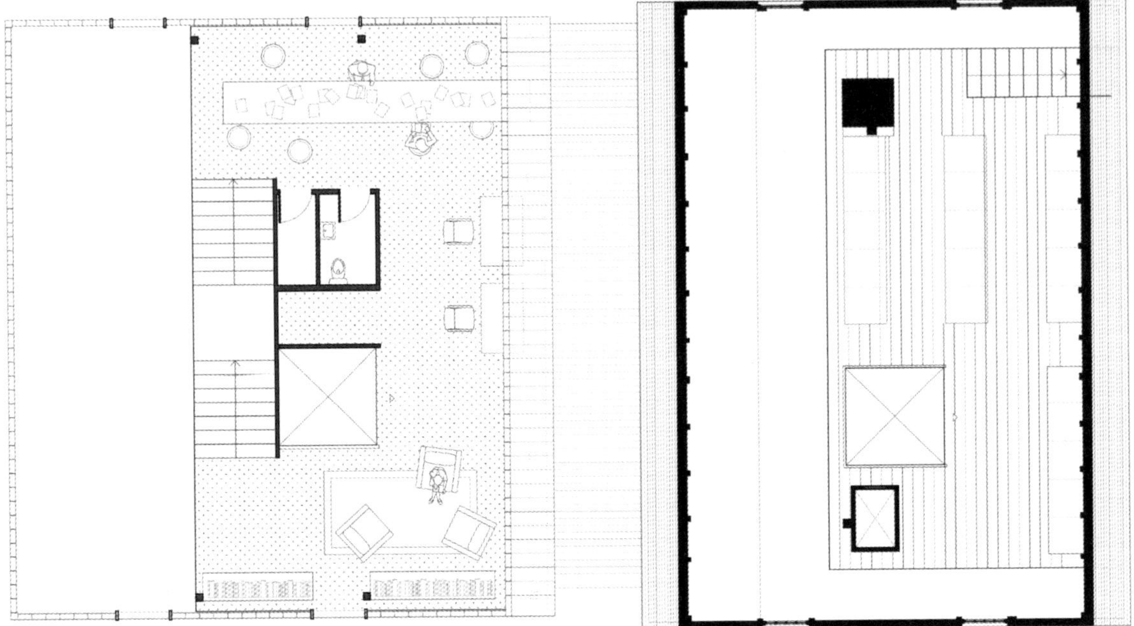

Ground-floor plan

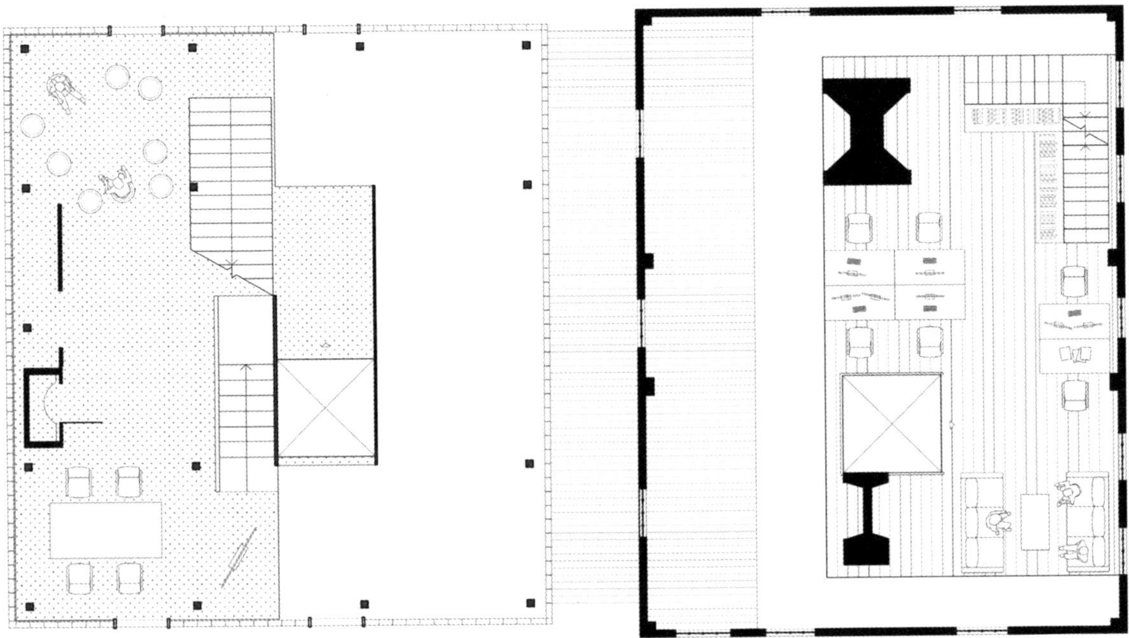

Second-floor plan

THE PARTICULAR AND THE PUBLIC

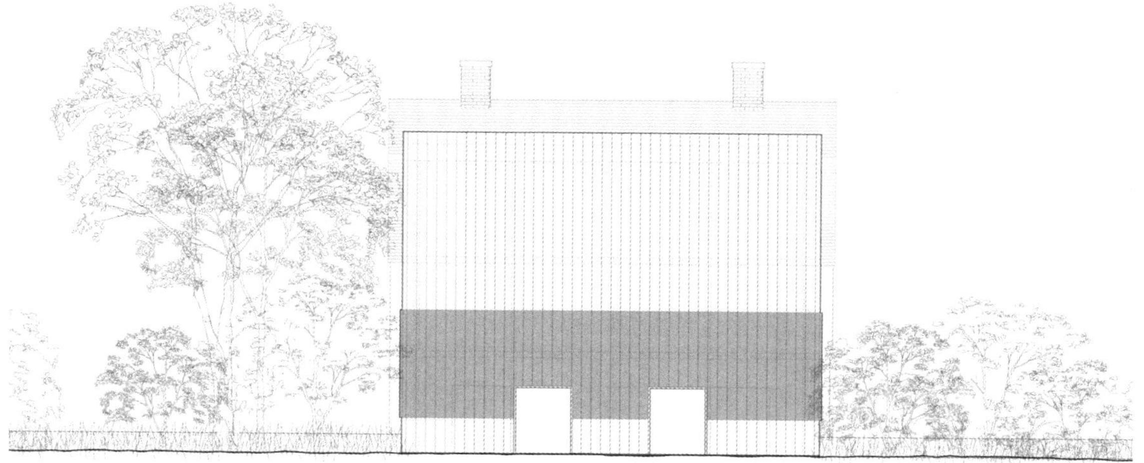

West elevation

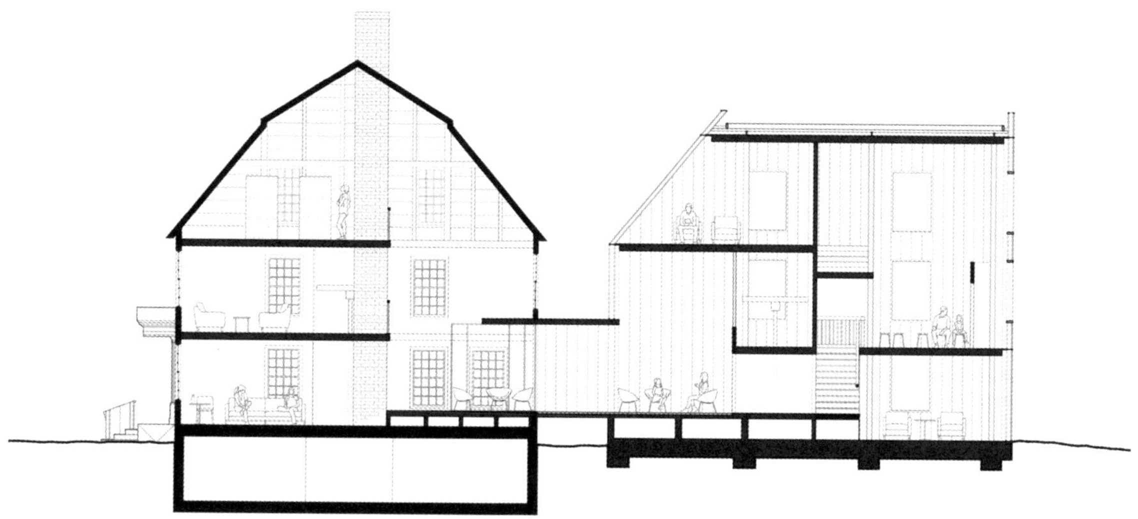

North-south section

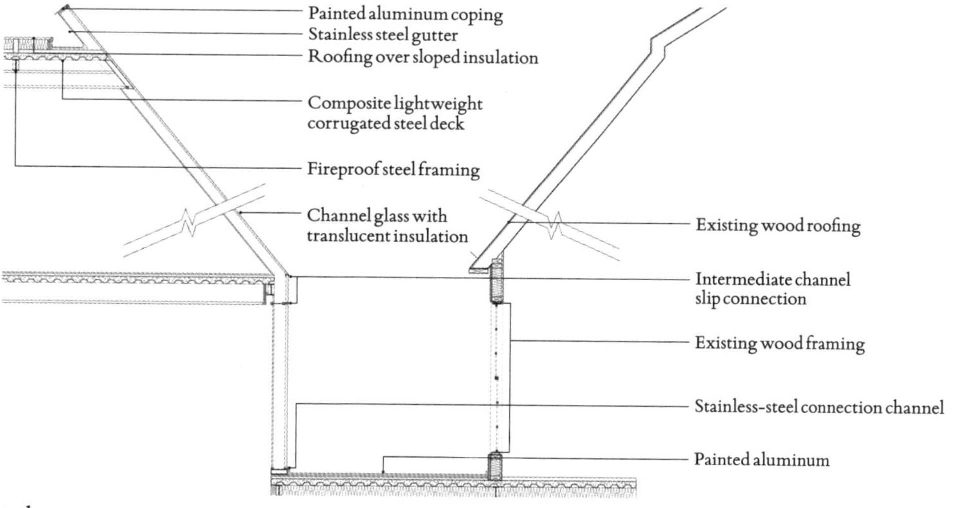

Typical wall details

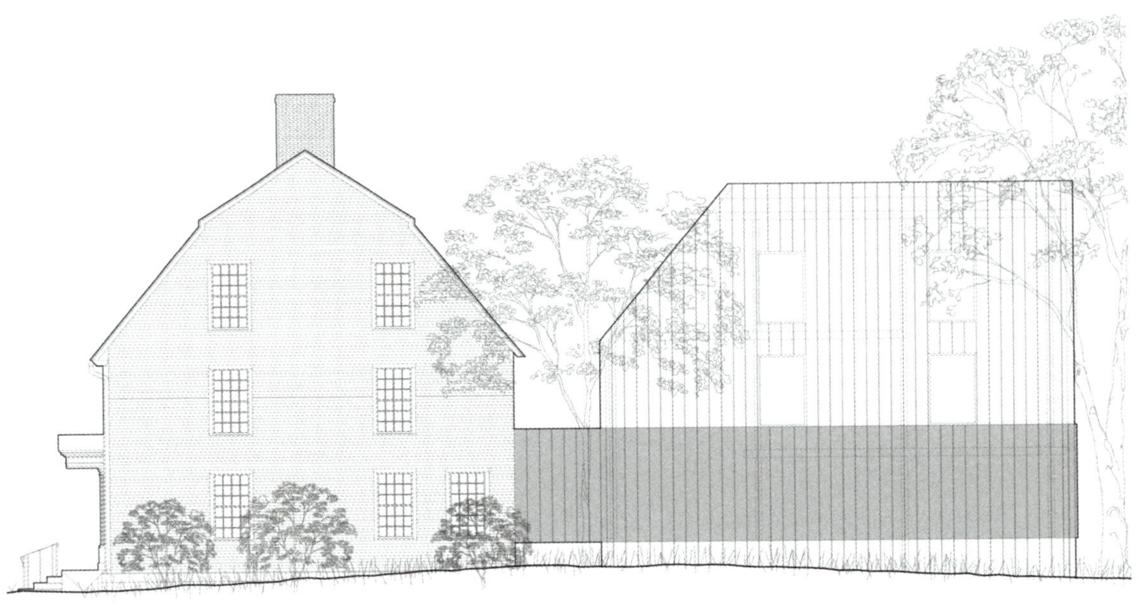

North elevation

Model details

 THE PARTICULAR AND THE PUBLIC

Model, north elevation

Model, west elevation

CALVIN LIANG

ALTERATION 8

The Webb House is lost in its identity, toggling between historical diorama and architectural artifact. Hidden among all the vestigial growths it has gained is a loose understanding of its archaeology: we must recover and clarify this aspect of the building. We must also respect its adjacencies—an Athenaeum serves the community and, in the future, might expand its interface beyond to greater New England.

The Athenaeum must consider the past, present, and future. It is envisioned as an archive of artifacts and curiosities aggregated from within the house, which is also part of the archive. Presently these objects are scattered and hidden throughout the building as part of dioramas or displays, or in storage. The archive presents all of these things at an equilibrium: the storehouse becomes the display. The objects are presented as archaeological evidence of the house's subtly rich histories rather than parts of a fictitious still life. To liken the house as an artifact, scaffolding will be deliberately designed and positioned to service restoration and renovation while allowing visitors to inspect, investigate, and interact with its unexplored features, such as the roof hatch.

The proposal is organized in a series of acts. First is the placement and insertion of the scaffolding, which indicates the location of the various surgeries to be exacted on the house. When renovations are complete, some scaffolding will be removed where new construction has taken place, and others will remain to preserve accessibility to the exterior.

The process will start where the museum lobby connects directly to the house via the ground-floor extension—this connection will be removed. Scaffolding will wrap around the west facade of the house to direct visitors toward the front door, restoring the flow of the interior. The scaffolding will extend around to the rear, where the Athenaeum is planned. Here an accessibility core is imagined, in addition to the archive. The scaffolding will climb over the house to provide access to the roof hatch. Once the construction work is completed, most of the scaffolding will be removed from the front facade, but some will remain at the back, emerging from the Athenaeum extension.

Three actions will be taken on the house. The first involves wrapping it in scaffolding, forming the foundation for the rest of the work. Second is the act of erasure by removing the attachment of the existing museum lobby to the house through demolition. The final act is one of elaboration of the Athenaeum addition. This development is not limited to the addition: since the house currently does not clearly express its role as either artifact or diorama, elaboration within it will help restore its identity as a historical artifact.

Although the house has played various roles throughout its history, most notably as a site of George Washington's campaign, its significance as a physical artifact of the colonial period has been lost. This notion is presently confused and will be embodied in the house as an outgrowth of the new museum lobby.

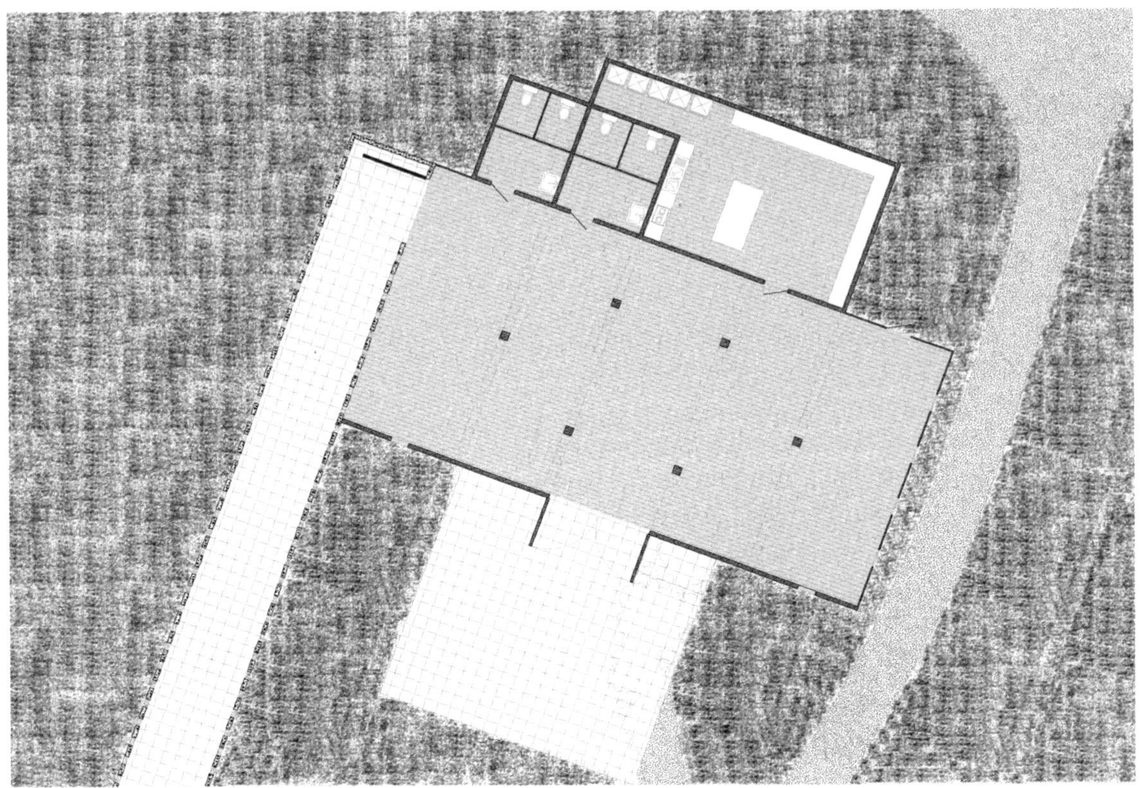

Ground-floor plan of barn

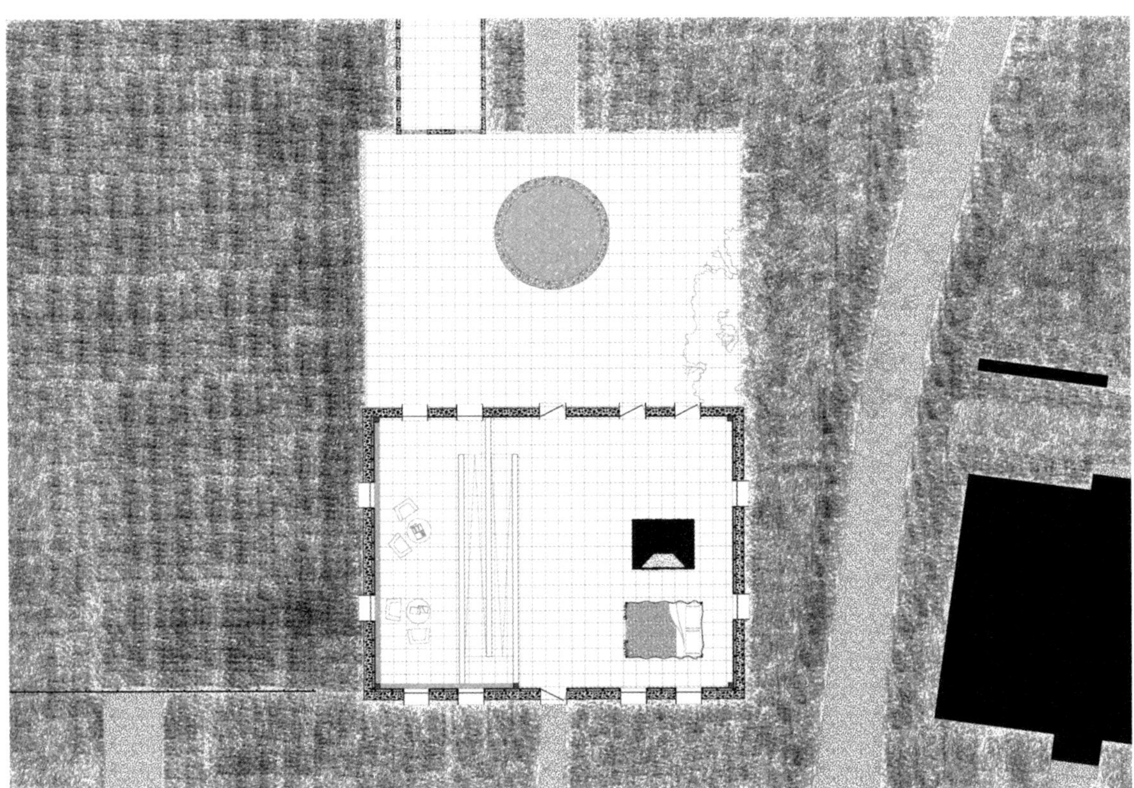

Ground-floor plan of house

     THE PARTICULAR AND THE PUBLIC

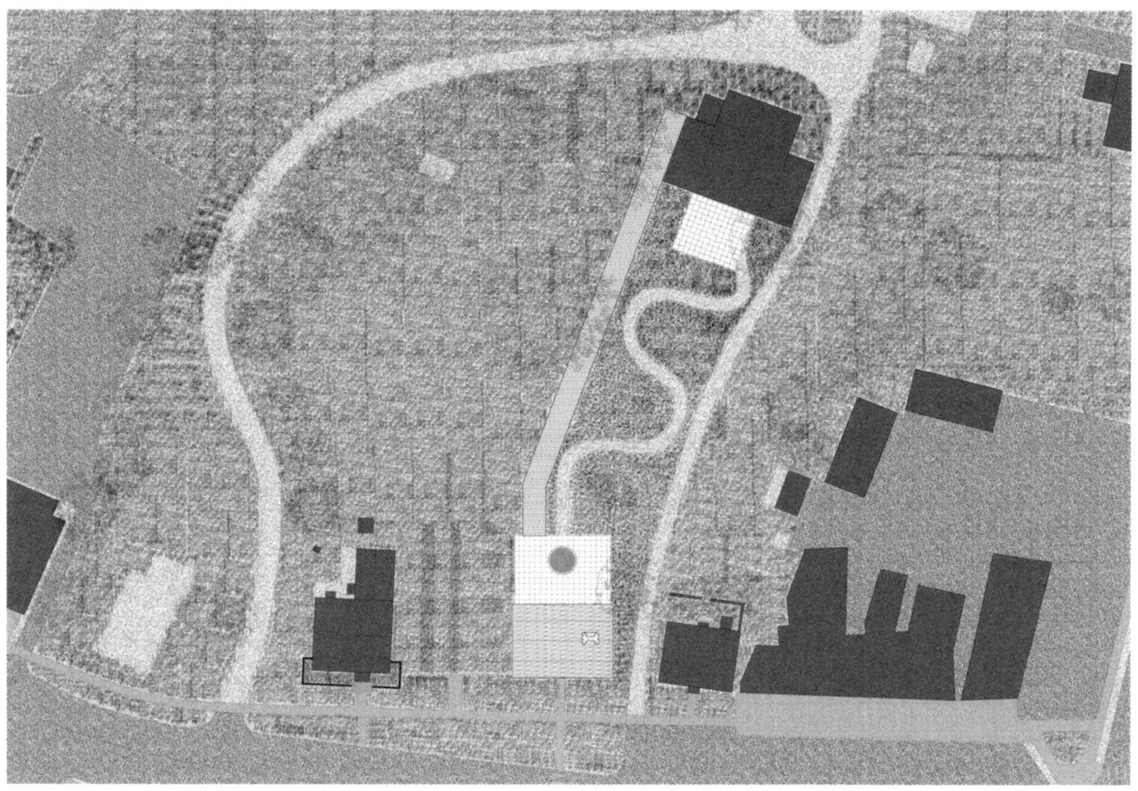

Site plan

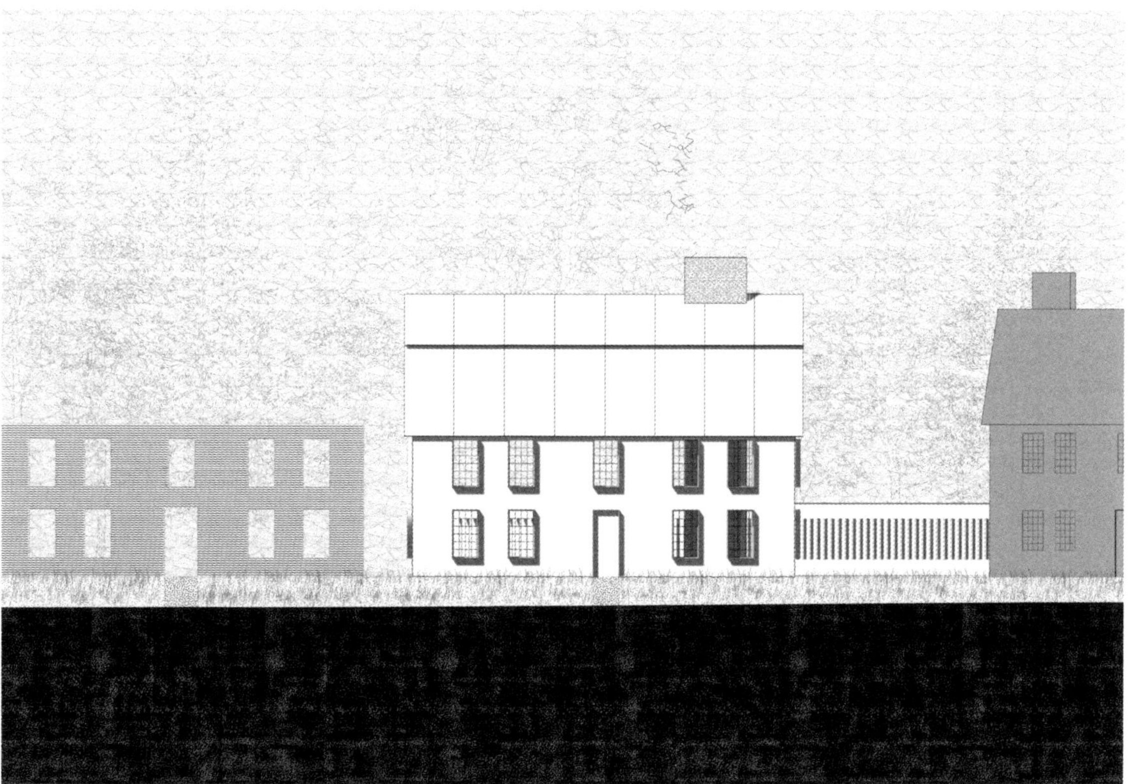

East elevation

North–south section

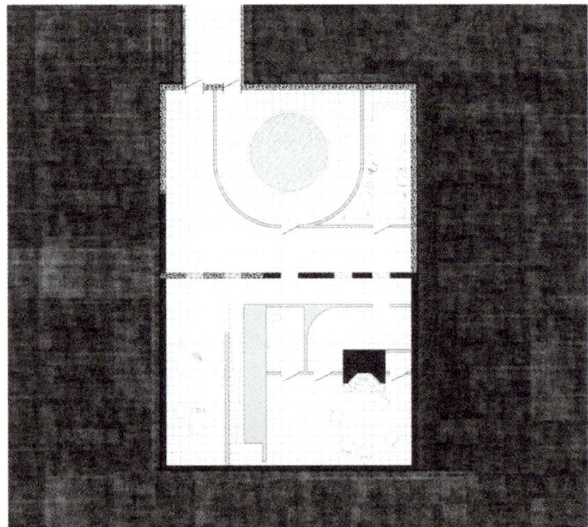

Section floor plan of house

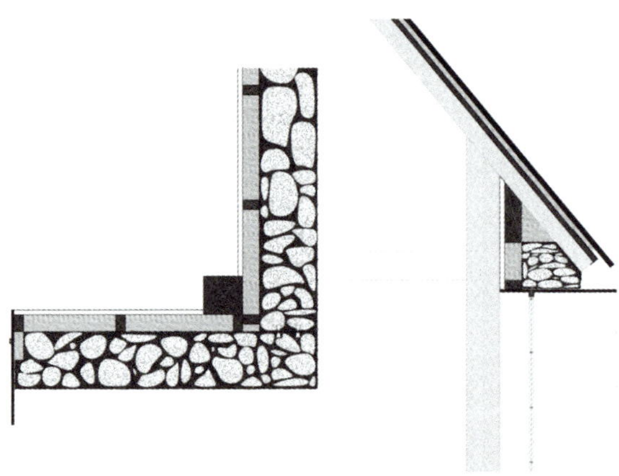

Typical details, plan and section

Model, east elevation

 THE PARTICULAR AND THE PUBLIC

Model, east elevation detail

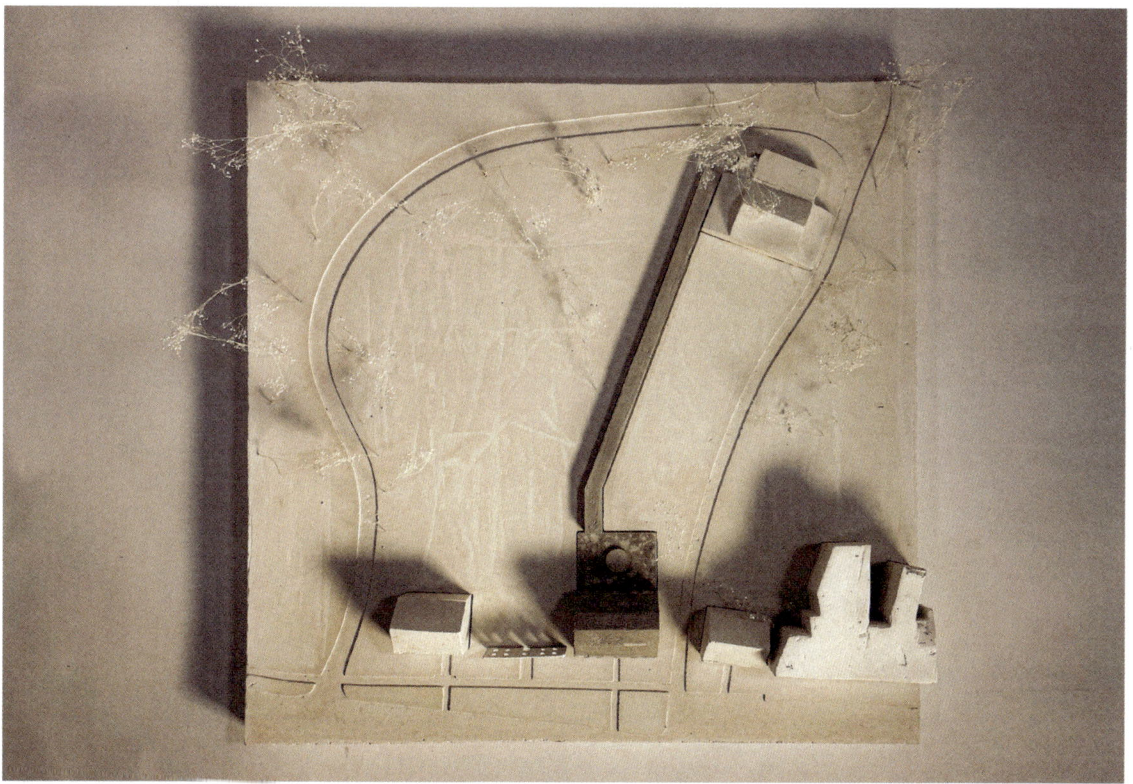

Model of site

INGRID PELLETIER

ALTERATION
9

Like the eighteenth-century design of the Webb House, this project caters to a variety of uses and conditions. Hyper-specificity can lead to a building's stagnation, so the Athenaeum should be considered a space hosting a wide range of uses for the general public. At first glance, the house might seem like every other home of its era in New England, but it has attained some unique qualities as it has been adapted to the environmental conditions and residents who have lived within its walls. This project will enhance the building's particularity, not merely as a site visited by historical figures but as a structure that has emerged from the Connecticut landscape.

The Wethersfield Athenaeum will allow visitors to study without the usual constraints of a museum. The house hosts an array of eighteenth-century furniture that tells many stories. The Athenaeum will allow for the study of the furniture and more. The library will be designed as a place for public gatherings and events, as well as respite from the outside world, as a sort of indoor park.

The reuse of the structure features surgical incisions to maintain the house, along with its well-crafted furniture, while making it adaptable for new functions such as a café. This may include multifunctional furniture extending out of the walls or floors that can recede when not in use; walls that open and close; skylights that appear with the pull of a ceiling board. What are the extents that a room can go to?

The building comprises layers of past lives. The goal of this renovation is to add an exterior layer and adapt the existing elements to make them more functional while maintaining the house's original character, as follows:

EXPAND AND CONTRACT

Maintain elements of the existing structure but alter the space with devices like movable walls and expanding molding to allow users to adapt it to their needs.

ILLUMINATE

Install lighting (artificial and natural) that highlights or alters the way one views or feels in the space.

UNCOVER

Allow visitors to explore and study their environment without the use of barriers such as ropes and glass.

The house is a staple of its environment, and nothing should be sacred: a living structure, it can be transformed just as it has been over its centuries-old existence.

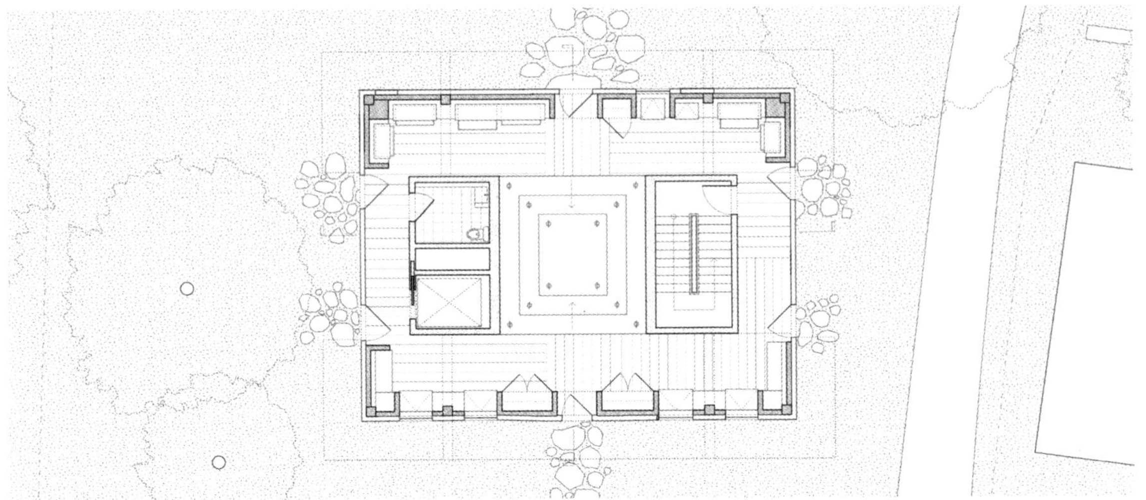

Ground-floor plan

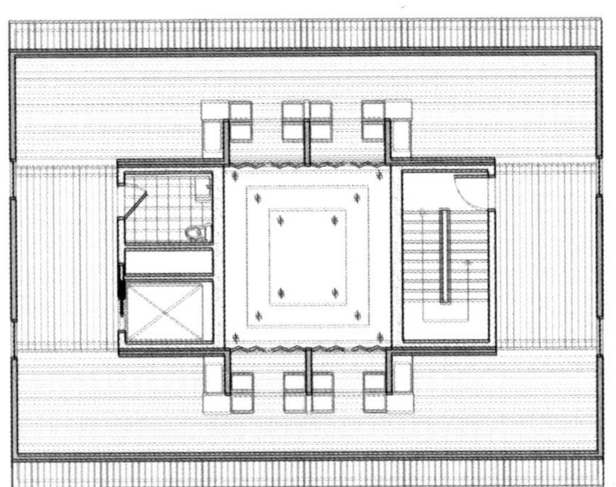

Attic and mechanical floor plan

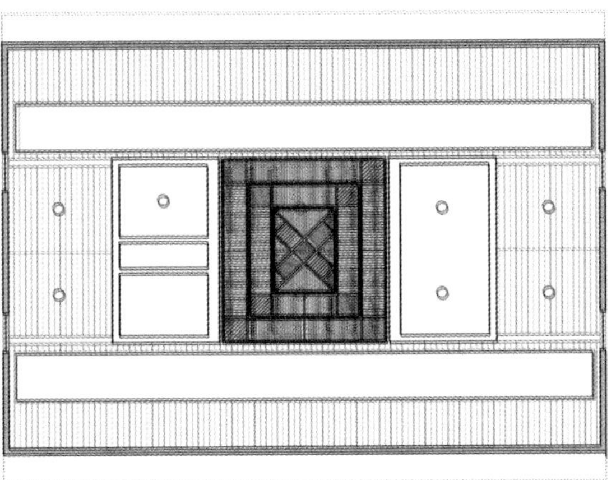

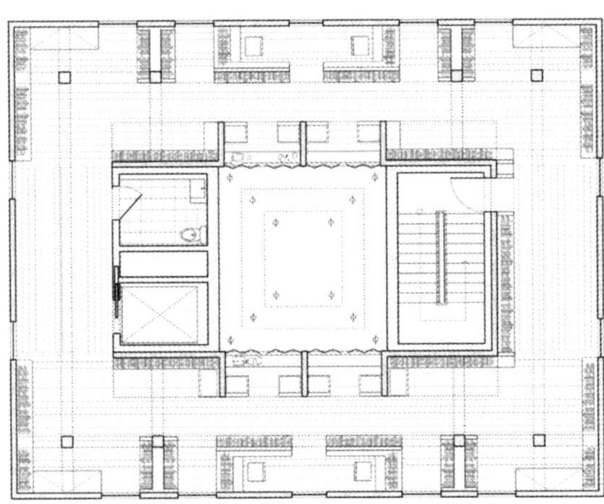

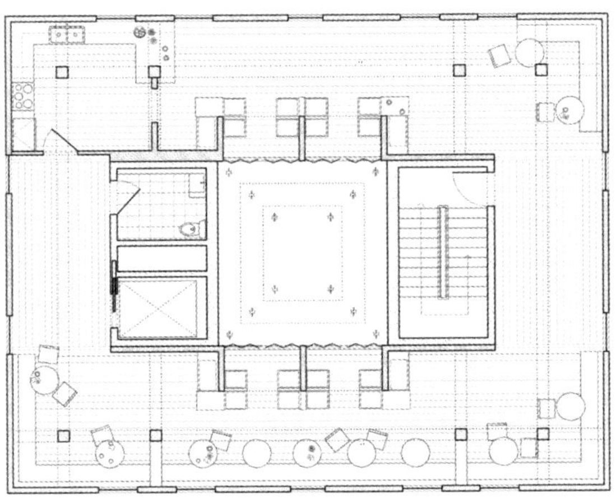

Fourth- and fifth-floor plans

THE PARTICULAR AND THE PUBLIC

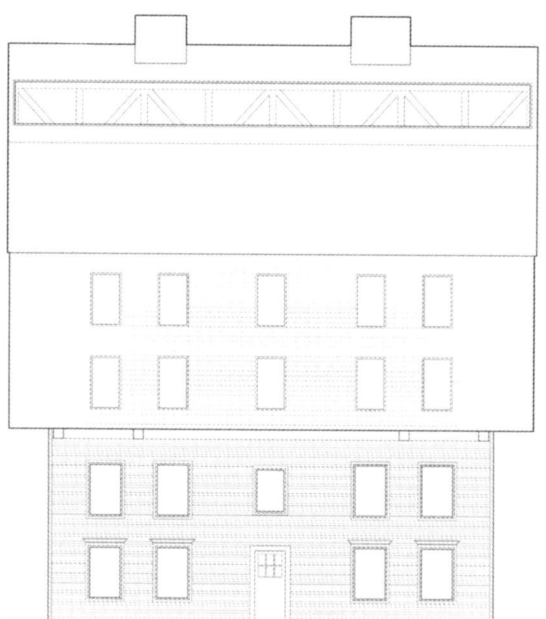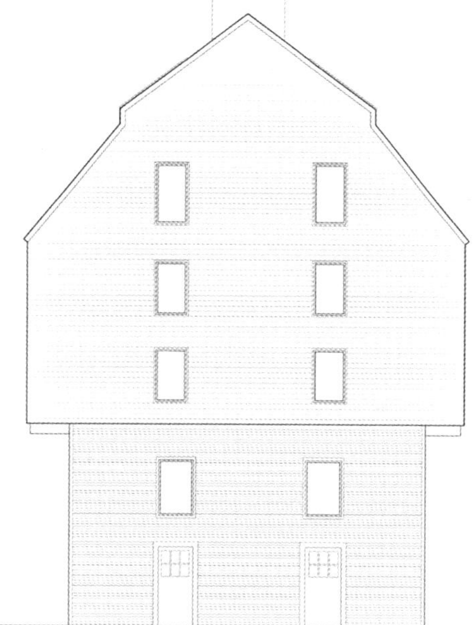

East elevation and north elevation

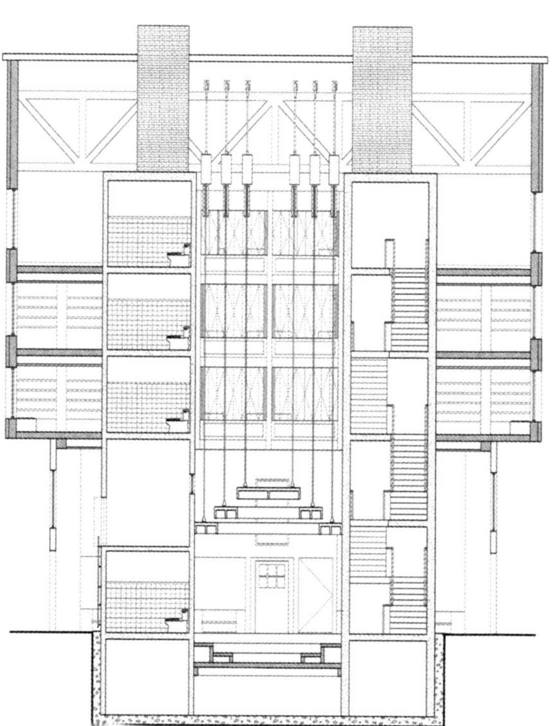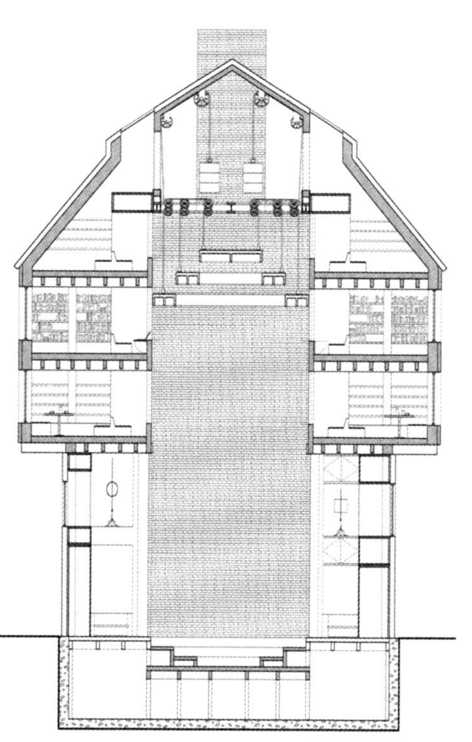

East-west and north-south sections

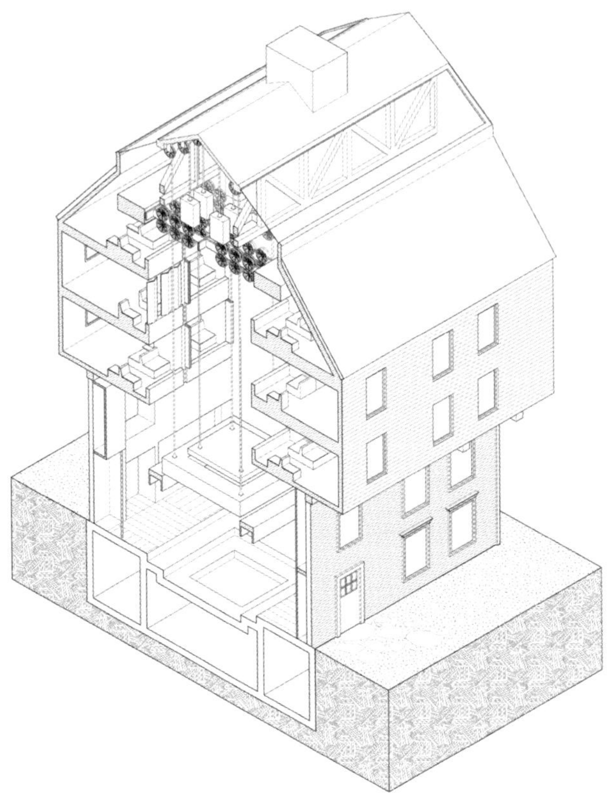

Section axonometric

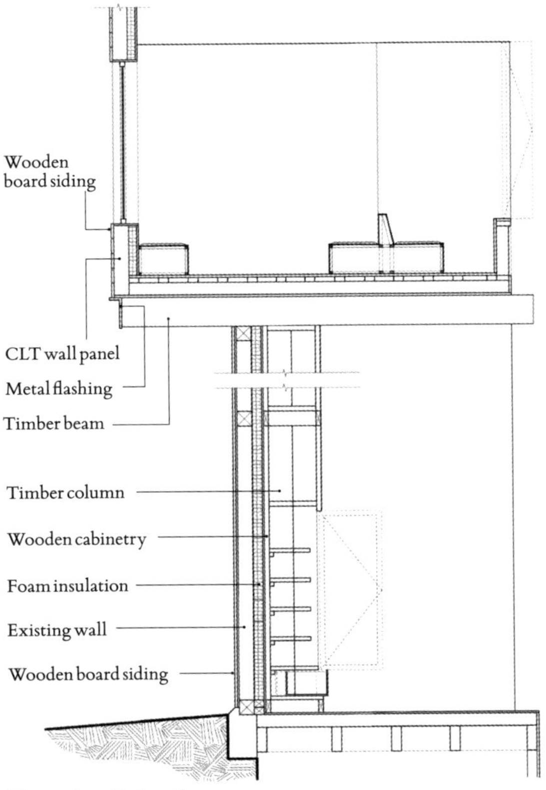

Wooden
board siding

CLT wall panel

Metal flashing

Timber beam

Timber column

Wooden cabinetry

Foam insulation

Existing wall

Wooden board siding

Typical wall detail

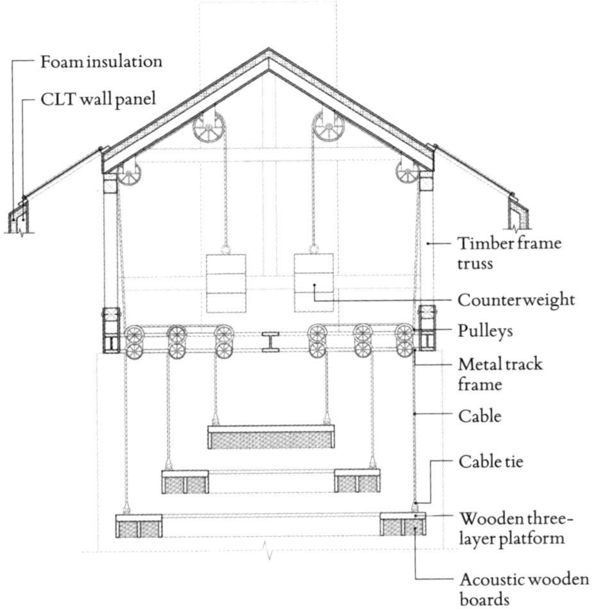

Foam insulation

CLT wall panel

Timber frame
truss

Counterweight

Pulleys

Metal track
frame

Cable

Cable tie

Wooden three-
layer platform

Acoustic wooden
boards

Pulley-system detail

     THE PARTICULAR AND THE PUBLIC

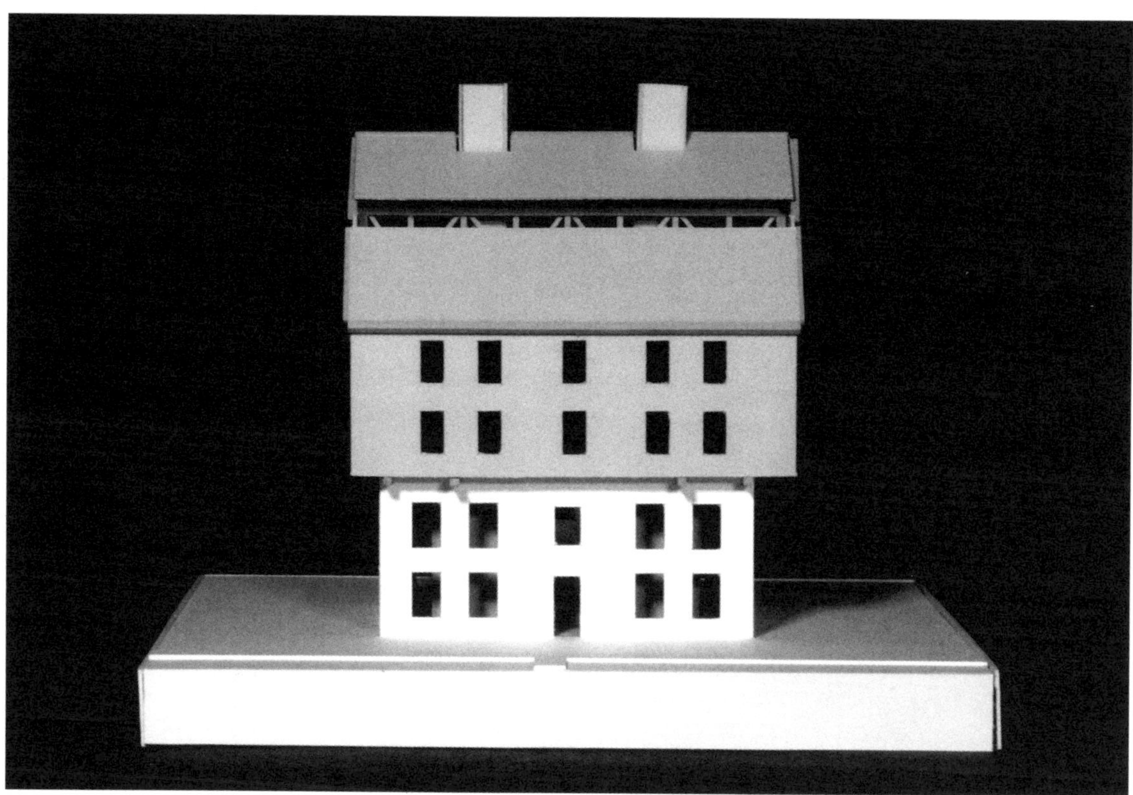

Model, east elevation

Model, north elevation

BOBBY CHUN

ALTERATION 10

THE PARTICULAR AND THE PUBLIC

In the middle of the seventeenth century, a series of witch trials took place in Connecticut. The victimization of the Wethersfield "witches" signaled the start of a mass hysteria that would see the unjust execution of many women throughout New England. Mary Johnson of Wethersfield was coerced into a confession and subsequently executed in 1648. She was convicted without any accusation or documentation of a fair trial. The residents eventually witnessed nine accusations and three executions between 1648 and 1668. Wethersfield was also not spared from the history of slavery. Historical records show entries of slave ownership by Joseph and Mehitable Webb, as well as their neighbor Silas Deane. Their enslaved servants would likely have been living in the attic, accessible only by a staircase inside the closet. The contrast between the ornate main staircase and the primitive attic stairway foreshadows a story of injustices and minority rights.

We cannot correct history. We can, however, recognize and learn from the past. To truly reconcile with the dark history of Wethersfield and the Webb House, we must educate ourselves beyond the glorified account of the colonial past. If the Athenaeum is a place to enlighten ourselves with knowledge, then it will help us understand and learn from history. It should be a common space where the minorities and majorities can coexist peacefully and voice their opinions respectfully. It will also be a legal archive and help center offering assistance to those facing the injustices and inequalities of our flawed legal system.

The Athenaeum is a project of the past, the present, and the future. It is about integrating the currently missing historical trauma into the narrative of the house.

The section of the main hallway will be the site of operation, as it contains the three distinctive stairs and the circulation axis of the house. The warping and subsequent correction made to the current structure will also be a site of alteration for the project.

History is not to be buried or painted over. Corrections should be made not to conceal the past but rather to highlight the mistakes we made as warnings to future generations. The same for the mistakes and distortions in the house: the warped stairs, balustrades, and joists are to be preserved. Reinforcements and braces needed for any structural correction will be made visible and beautiful to the untrained eye. These imperfections will be celebrated and given space to be seen and experienced rather than camouflaged. In its conversion from private to public, the main hallway will be opened both horizontally and vertically to accommodate its new purpose. The house's entry sequence will be redesigned, and the furniture will be rearranged to align with the new orientation.

To preserve a building is to honor its full history. The goal of opening this previously exclusive and discriminatory space to the public is to challenge the existing political narrative and develop a new, more balanced and accurate history. Alterations are integrated yet noticeable, calling attention to the complexity of history so that we recognize the changes we must make now and in the future.

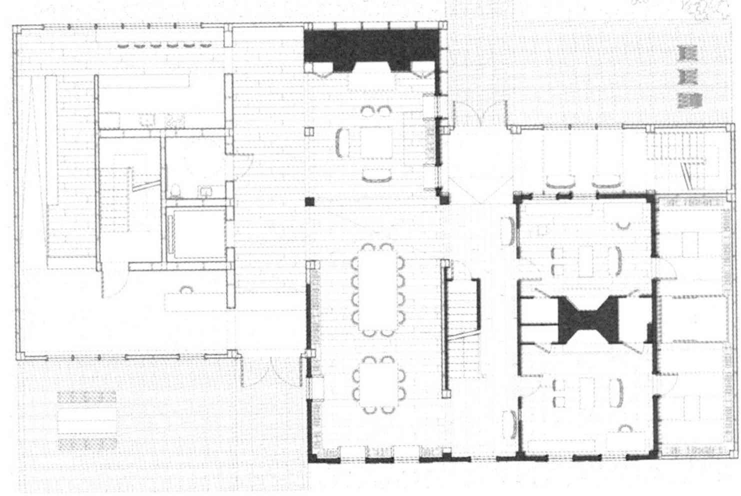

Ground-floor plan

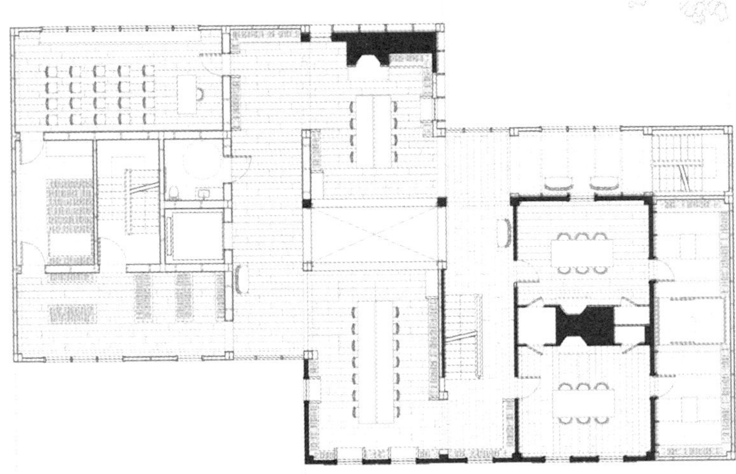

Second-floor plan

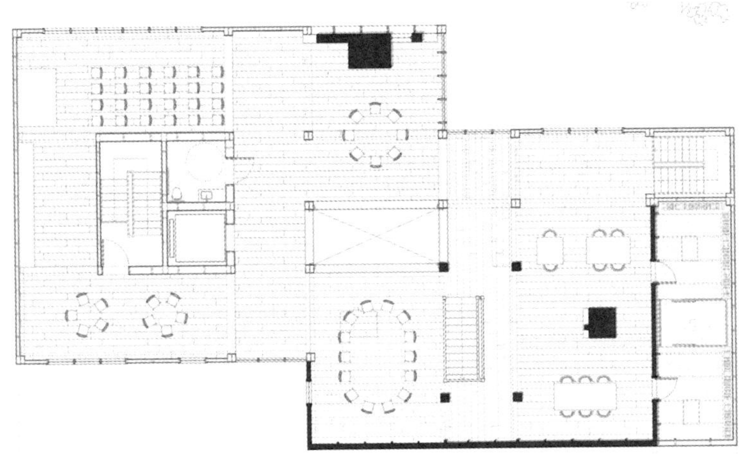

Third-floor plan

   THE PARTICULAR AND THE PUBLIC

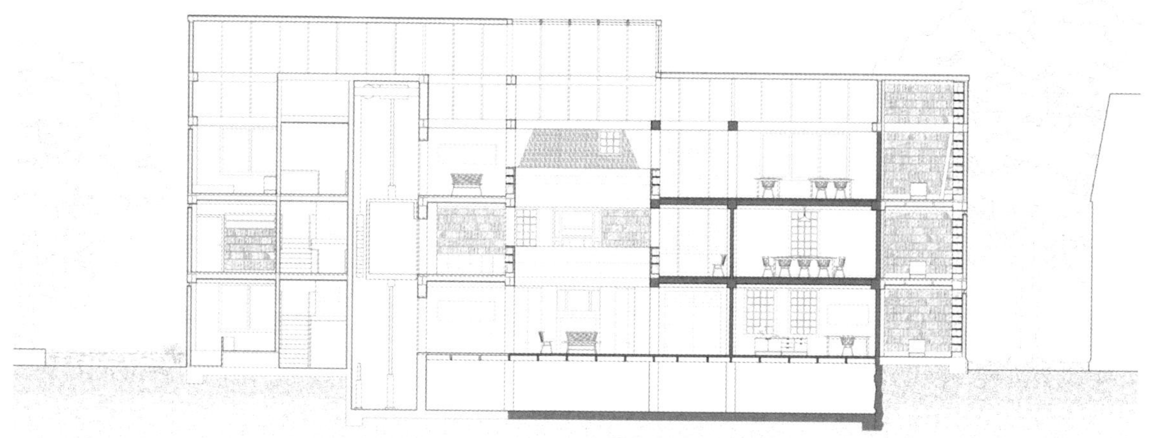

North-south section

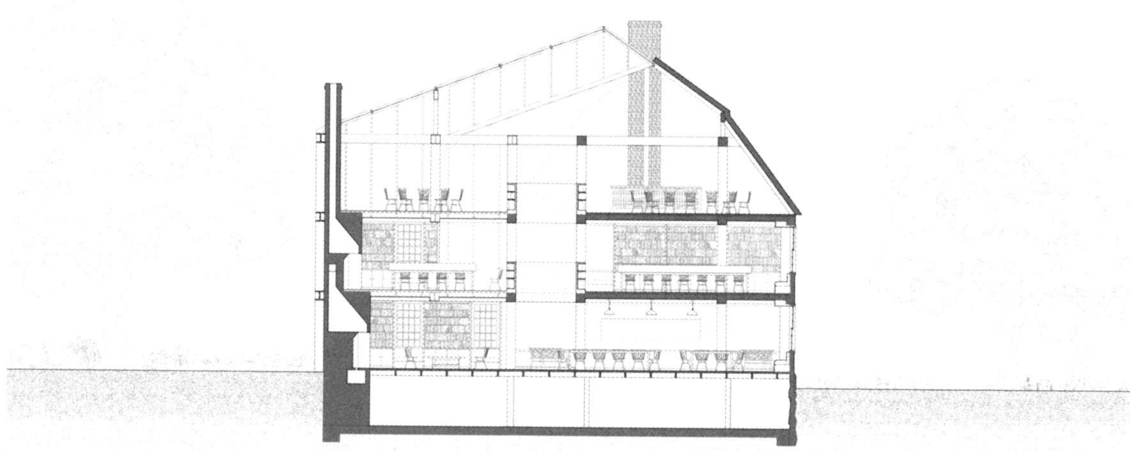

East-west section

Typical floor detail

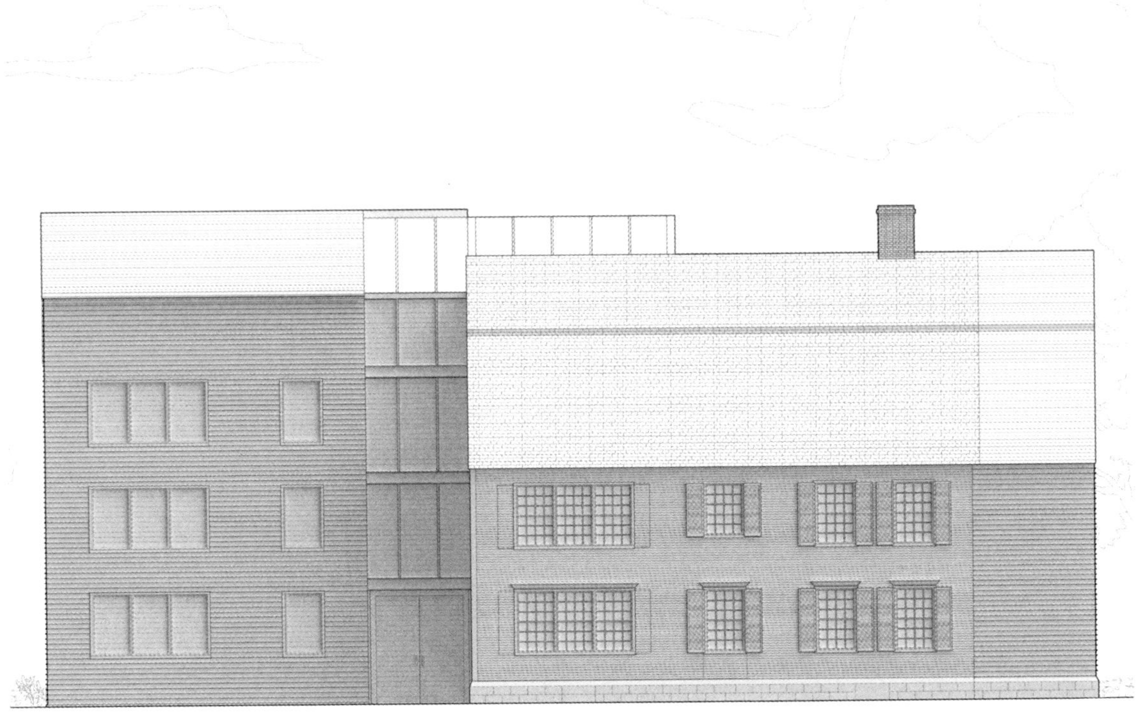

East elevation

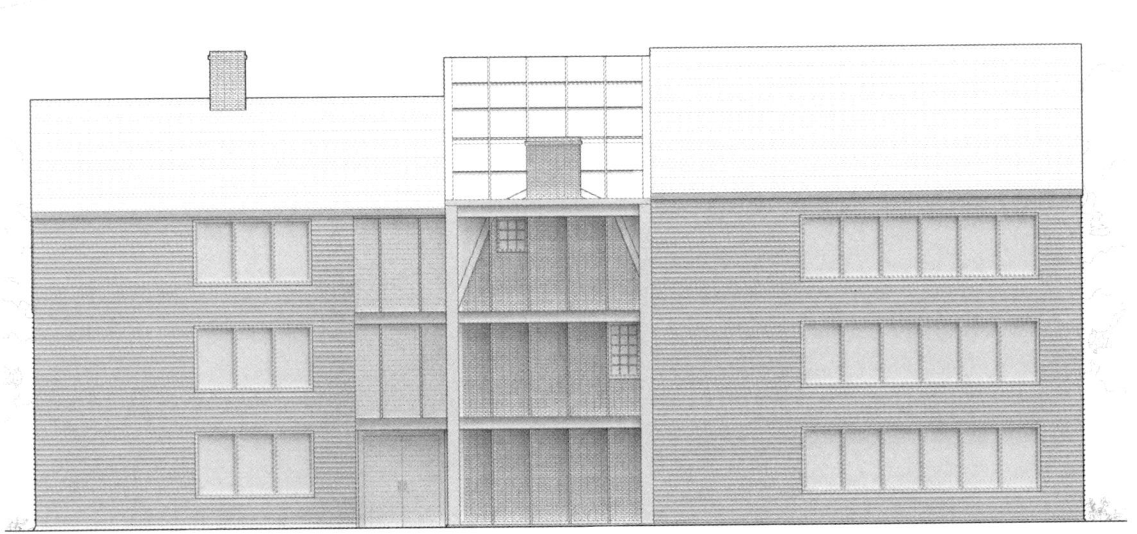

West elevation

     THE PARTICULAR AND THE PUBLIC

Model, east elevation

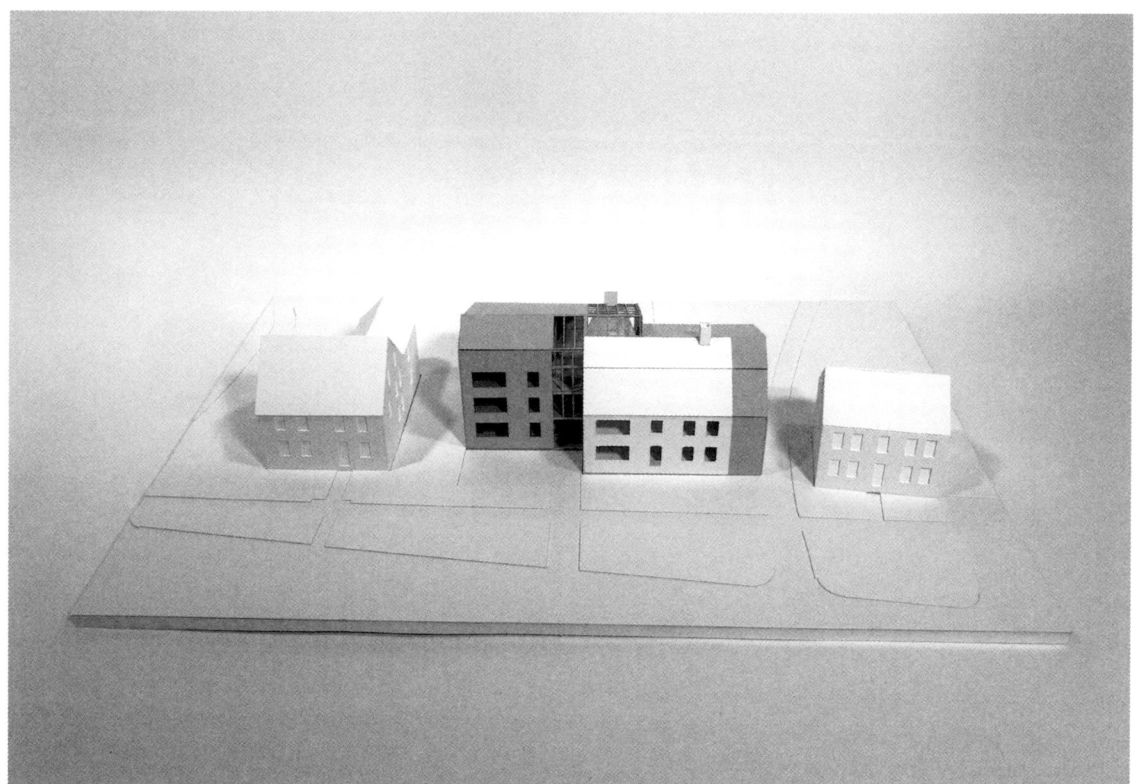

Model, aerial view

YE LOITE

CHAT TRAVIESO

The Boogie Down Booth (174th St.), 2015

Teenagers experience a distinct spatial predicament. They've outgrown playgrounds but are not yet old enough to go to college campuses or bars. They crave independence but lack spaces they can claim as their own. So they must, as Herb Childress puts it, "appropriate and occupy the places of others."[1] This sometimes takes the form of carving out spaces of autonomy in the public realm, where they are often rejected.

Whether gathering in parks, vacant lots, fast-food restaurants, streets, train stations, shopping malls, school grounds, or parking lots, teens routinely clash with security guards, business owners, school administrators, police officers, and other authority figures. Seen as nuisances or even threats, young people frequently find themselves subjected to legal, spatial, and social restrictions that limit their ability to find places to hang out and express themselves freely.

Take, for example, the rise of chaperone policies in retail spaces. If you have visited a Target store recently you may have noticed a sign stating, "All guests under the age of eighteen must be accompanied by an adult at this Target store." Atlantic Terminal Mall, in Brooklyn, New York, also restricts unaccompanied minors. Its code of conduct goes even further to limit groups of people (no larger than three), bench-sitting time (maximum of 15 minutes), noise levels (no "loud and boisterous behavior"), language (no "obscene or offensive language"), conduct (no "inappropriate behavior" or running), and even attire ("proper clothing is required at all times").

On New York City streets you are often met with a myriad of signs on residential buildings, schools, restaurants, and stores that read: "No Loitering," "No Sitting," "No Ball Playing," "No Skating," "No Biking," "No Loud Music,"

"No Hanging Out," "No Outside Food," and "No Trespassing." This is in addition to various hostile architectural elements such as concrete barriers and metal spikes, designed to deter sitting and skateboarding, an activity associated with young people.

Judging by these deterrents, it is clear that there is a general perception of youth as detrimental or offensive to the people and spaces around them. These negative stereotypes of teens as destructive and disorderly, coupled with racist tropes, create an intersectional condition that particularly impacts Black and Latine youth, who bear the brunt of zero-tolerance or "broken window" policing, along with the school-to-prison pipeline. These aggressive forms of enforcement can lead to dire consequences for youth, such as emotional distress, physical altercations with police, and cycles of incarceration.

The pandemic brought into sharp relief the mental-health crisis impacting teens today. While this issue predates COVID-19, the isolation and instability experienced during that time exacerbated the problem. Data shows that it particularly affected LGBTQIA+ youth, who are struggling in an increasingly hostile climate.[2]

WHAT IF DESIGNERS CENTERED THEIR WORK ON THE NEEDS OF TEENAGERS?

This advanced studio, focused on urban design, challenged the unjust rejection of teenagers in the built environment, asserting that young people have a right to the city. It prompted architecture students to propose ways to make the city more inclusive for teens and offer alternatives to adult spatial hegemony.

This studio was a continuation of "Yes Loitering,"
a collaboration with a team of seven South Bronx teenagers
between the ages of fifteen and eighteen to investigate the
ways young people in the city are ostracized and criminalized.
The project, carried out from 2017 to 2018, developed
preliminary design and policy ideas for creating
youth-powered spaces that are safe and welcoming.

The initial recommendations included the following:

1   Youth involvement: Engage teens in decision-making
    about the spaces affecting them to give them a voice
    from the start.

2   Social equity: Create inclusive, accessible spaces that
    are free from social or financial barriers and actively
    redress historical injustices, especially for youth from
    marginalized groups.

3   Safety: Focus on community safety and encourage
    conflict resolution without relying on police presence.

4   Location: Provide multiple decentralized spots for
    youth to gather near schools and public transit
    and reimagine the entire city, including sidewalks
    and streets, as a youth-centric environment.

5   Food: Offer affordable, culturally diverse food outlets
    with no customer-only rules or time limits, allowing
    teens to stay without pressure to purchase.

6   Seating: Design environments with varied and informal
    seating options that allow teens to rearrange the space
    to suit their activities.

7   Weather protection: Provide shaded outdoor areas and indoor public spaces for year-round use that don't require teens to spend money.

8   Technology: Offer free Wi-Fi and charging stations in parks and public plazas.

9   Sports: Support a variety of sports, including skateboarding, parkour, and other nontraditional activities—and decriminalize skateboarding in public spaces.

10   Activities and events: Create places to socialize, play games, or organize with regular programming and flexible spaces for events led by teens.

11   Art and culture: Provide creative spaces along with art materials, instruments, and technology that allow teens to experiment artistically.

12   Maintenance and amenities: Keep spaces clean with accessible trash and recycling receptacles, gender-inclusive bathrooms, and free water stations.[3]

Following up on this initial research project, the students rethought our social-spatial relationships and priorities to envision an environment characterized by conditions allowing young people to thrive and feel free, joyful, and secure in the city.

1
Herb Childress, "Teenagers, Territory, and the Appropriation of Space," *Childhood* 11, no. 2 (2004): 195.

2
The Trevor Project, *2023 U.S. National Survey on the Mental Health of LGBTQ Young People* (West Hollywood: Trevor Project, 2023), https://www.thetrevorproject.org/survey-2023/assets/static/05_TREVOR05_2023survey.pdf

3
Yes Loitering, "Yes Sitting, Yes Skating, Yes Music," *Urban Omnibus*, March 8, 2018.

This studio focused on the following questions: How might we deconstruct an adult supremacist mentality and begin to trust youth? How might we act in solidarity with young people and actively listen to what they have to say? What current infrastructures, systems, and beliefs are incompatible with a youth-justice approach to design? By focusing on the needs of young people, this studio sought to transform the city into a supportive and equitable environment for all.

Site and Program
The studio focused its efforts in the Bronx, the borough with the highest percentage of people under the age of 18. In particular, students considered the South Bronx neighborhood of Morrisania and its surroundings, home to the studio's community partners, DreamYard and the Women's Housing and Economic Development Corporation (WHEDco), which includes the Bronx Music Heritage Center (BMHC).

Morrisania has a rich history and was a hotbed of hip-hop, beginning more than fifty years ago, as well as other musical styles. It has experienced cycles of systematic neglect and disinvestment—and recently, fears of encroaching gentrification.

Building on the groundwork laid by the community partners, key findings gathered from direct observations of the site, and recurring engagements with community youth, students were tasked with developing a comprehensive set of citywide policy ideas, as well as site-specific urban design proposals aimed at making the area youth-affirming.

Students visiting a Bronx Land Trust community garden

Students visiting The Point CDC

 THE PARTICULAR AND THE PUBLIC

Student projects did not simply scatter more youth-centric amenities throughout the area; they proposed new social and spatial imaginaries and reconsidered how spaces were designed, managed, and operated. The programs, scales, and exact locations for students' projects were constructed through research and analysis, allowing for a wide range of themes to be tackled, including education, labor, transportation, physical and mental health, food, safety, housing, culture, and more.

Studio Methodology
Drawing inspiration from Black feminist thought, this studio adopted an anti-racist, feminist, and intersectional lens, recognizing that although all young people encounter oppression, their experiences may differ based on various intersecting identities and forms of marginalization. The studio uplifted underrepresented narratives of youth who were Black, Latine, LGBTQIA+, immigrants, disabled, neurodivergent, and from low-income backgrounds.

The community-centered design studio engaged in a sequence of exercises that provided experience in connecting with, learning from, and collaborating with stakeholders. Students combined participatory research and design approaches to understand user needs grounded in real-world insights and formulated impactful and radical design responses through an iterative process guided by active listening.

While considering stakeholder needs and concerns, the studio employed an assets-based approach. Instead of focusing solely on deficits, this framework emphasized the opportunities already present within the community. We sought to learn from and build upon these successes, the embedded knowledge, and the resources of the area to co-create visionary place-affirming responses.

Students worked closely with community partners WHEDco and DreamYard. WHEDco is a community development organization that serves more than one thousand young people in the Bronx through its youth development programs. DreamYard is an arts organization that fosters equity and social justice among Bronx youth through its visual and performing arts programming.

Students also collaborated with a group of six youth advisers, a dedicated team of teens from WHEDco and DreamYard, who consulted with students throughout the semester and participated in reviews. Recognizing that often young people's needs are ignored and their views not taken seriously, this studio stressed the importance of including them in the decision-making process—especially Black and Latine youth, a demographic commonly overlooked or excluded by architecture and urban design.

Students began the semester by remembering their experiences of traversing the built environment as teenagers, and visualizing, through collages, the places where they felt free. This exercise aimed to root their work in lived experiences, foster a sense of solidarity with the realities faced by today's youth, and develop a catalog of youth-centered spatial tactics they could draw from throughout the semester.

A key insight emphasized the significance of both spatial and temporal factors. Several students shared how their sense of freedom was influenced not only by their location but also by timing. They highlighted their commute from school as a rare moment of autonomy during which parents and other authority figures were unaware of their whereabouts or activities, leading them to want to prolong the journey. These reflections also underscored that the location of freedom isn't always a static place;

CHAT TRAVIESO

Students visiting Concrete Plant Park

rather, it can be a dynamic experience in which movement —whether walking, driving, or riding the subway—provides a fleeting sense of liberation.

Another important finding focused on the value of different kinds of stimulation for young people. While some students felt freest when there were no prescribed activities or schedules, others thrived in a structured after-school environment. Some found excitement and community in athletic settings or while shopping with friends, whereas others found comfort in solitude. Many students visualized nature, art, and music as significant contributors to self-discovery in their younger lives, and others emphasized the role of a rebellious spirit in shaping their sense of autonomy.

For the second exercise, students watched youth-themed films and examined the social-spatial elements within which young people found or created moments of independence, happiness, refuge, community, love, care, and power. These moments were often parallel to, outside of, or in opposition to a hostile world. Students made diagrams for a collective catalog that started in the first assignment. The films included *Skate Kitchen*, *Raising Victor Vargas*, *Paris Is Burning*, *Pariah*, *Style Wars*, *Class Divide*, *Moonlight*, *Fenced Out*, *Crip Camp*, and *Namens de kinderen van de Pijp*.

Fuad Khazam's diagram for the movie *Pariah* conveys the bedroom, club, and beach as spaces where the main character, Alike, who is exploring her identity as a lesbian, feels she can be her true self, away from the watchful eyes of her religious mother and the catcalls on the street. In *Raising Victor Vargas*, the main character hangs out on the rooftop, a place that significantly influenced Miranda Clark and Odette James's final project.

The students then collectively conducted secondary research and analysis of the site to uncover key context-specific issues and opportunities. They also designed and created community-engagement tools to connect with Bronx teens during the studio trip.

SITE VISIT

Students were fully immersed in the Bronx for the duration of travel week. They visited several youth-oriented and community-based organizations that are doing transformative work, including Bronx Land Trust, Bronx Documentary Center, The Point CDC, Rocking the Boat, the Bronx River Alliance, DreamYard, WHEDco, the office of City Council Member Althea Stevens, Bronx Music Heritage Center, Caldwell Enrichment Program, and the NYC Department of Youth and Community Development.

The studio focused on building long-term relationships and maintaining multiple touchpoints throughout the semester with community partners and youth advisors. Students facilitated three engagement sessions with the youth advisors during the studio trip, one of which included over twenty-five Bronx teens. For these sessions the students designed playful activities that encouraged young people to share their experiences, dreams, and concerns. Activities included crafting a graphic novel to represent their typical day, modeling their ideal spaces, and a mapping exercise where they identified favorite hangout spots, areas needing improvement, and community assets. A poster-making station allowed the teens to articulate issues they care about. Common themes that emerged from these sessions were safety, pollution, and affordability.

The youth participants were encouraged to share their memories of and thoughts about the neighborhood on a felt map.

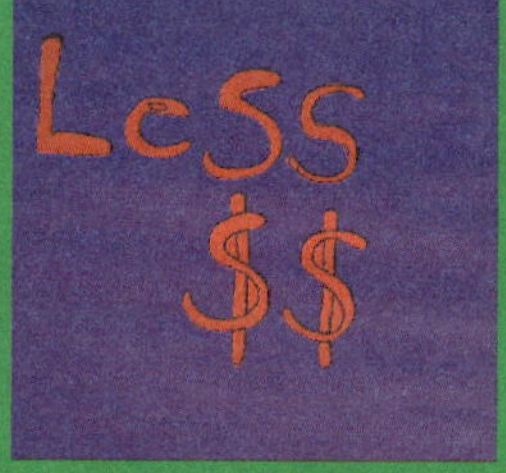

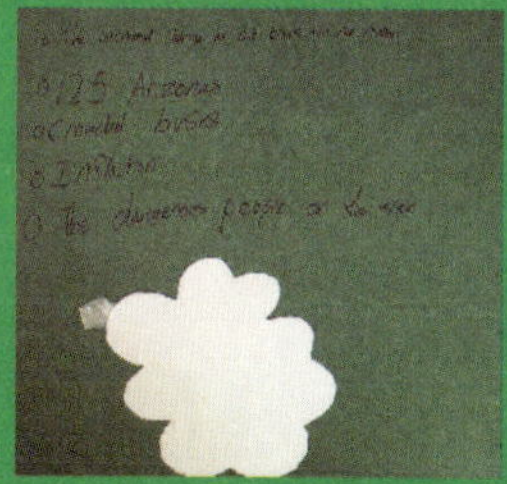

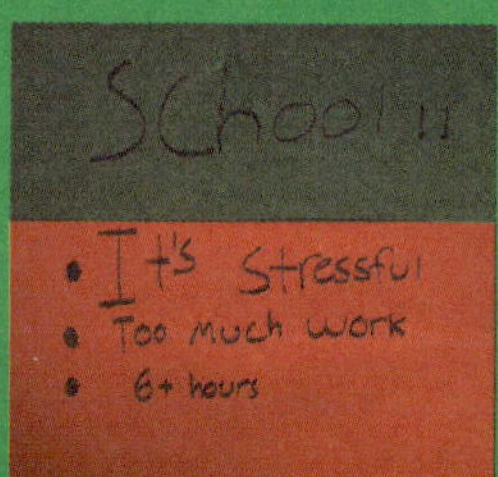

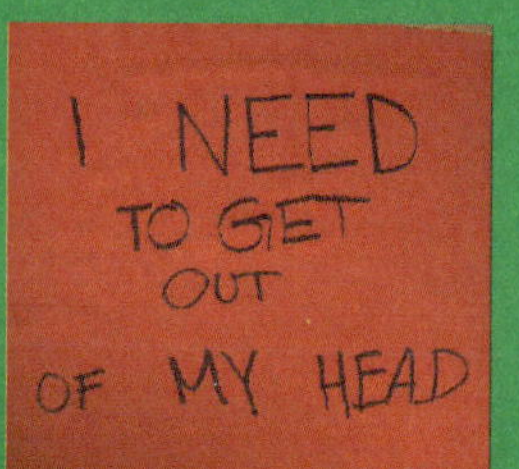

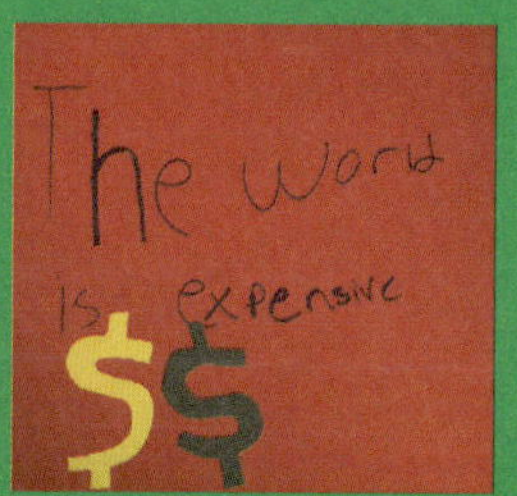

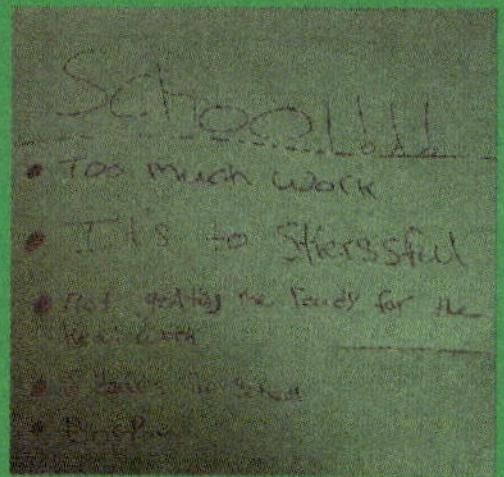

Protest posters created by Bronx teens at the workshop

ACKNOWLEDGMENTS

This community-engaged studio would not have been possible without so many collaborators. In particular, I would like to thank the youth advisors who provided invaluable feedback and ideas throughout the semester: Andy Duarte, Aneudy Carmona Castro, Skyla Santiago, Skyler Maisonet, Steven Vidal, and Wilber Perez.

I would also like to thank community partners DreamYard and WHEDco, who helped recruit the youth advisors and shared their wisdom with the students. I am especially thankful to Austin Greene, director of Art Center Programs at DreamYard; Chelsea John, associate director of Art Center Programs at DreamYard; Gloria Viveros, Middle and High School Programs Manager at DreamYard; Katie Aylwin, senior director of Education and Youth Development at WHEDco; and Kevin Contreras, program aide at WHEDco.

I am also grateful to all the people we met with during studio travel week: Ramon Andino, Bronx Land Trust; Michael Kamber, Bronx Documentary Center; Dariella Rodriguez, The Point CDC; Hatuey Ramos-Fermín, The Point CDC; Rob Buchanan, Rocking the Boat; Nathan Hunter, Bronx River Alliance; Journei Bimwala, Bronx River Alliance; Arianna Gil, Brujas; Jahtah Brown, Office of City Council Member Stevens; Elena Martinez, Bronx Music Heritage Center; Yolanda Hardy, Caldwell Enrichment Program Inc.; Reginald K. Gibson, NYC Department of Youth and Community Development; Cat Betances, Urban Design Forum; and the 2023 Forefront Fellows.

And thank you to all of the people who joined us for guest talks, pin-ups, the midreview, and the final:

Jim Lammers, Street Lab; James Mituzas, NYC Parks; Kerry McLean, WHEDco; Mariana Mogilevich, Urban Omnibus; architect and doula Kim Holden; Yeju Choi, Yeju & Chat; Writer Alexandra Lange; Jae Shin, HECTOR; Quardean Lewis-Allen, Youth Design Center; Tya Winn, Community Design Collaborative; Keller Easterling, YSoA; and Nina Rappaport, Vertical Urban Factory.

Chat Travieso, *Yes Loitering Sign*, 2016

STUDIO BRIEF

After the trip the students began their design projects, working in pairs. Each team tackled a different location within the site area, as well as different issues and themes. The goal was for each project to produce a case study of what is possible. To ensure a comprehensive set of design and policy ideas, students engaged in collective knowledge production.

The studio employed a design framework comprised of three stages: pop-up, permanent, and policy. This approach was intended to encourage students to envision ways their ideas might be implemented rapidly, over a prolonged period, or through systemic change. For the midterm the students considered pop-up designs to respond to a chosen site and issue. These consisted of spatial, programmatic, and operational strategies that were low-cost, high-impact, relatively easy and quick to construct, and temporary. Typically pop-up projects are meant to test ideas and gather additional input, activate a space quickly and respond to immediate needs, and/or function as advocacy and community-organizing tools.

After midterm the students received valuable feedback from the youth advisors and conducted a virtual visioning session with them. Some of the takeaways were the need for regular programming and the desire for affordable food options in spaces where teens like to gather. Students then developed longer-term proposals for their sites that, in some cases, included policy ideas. The scopes of the projects ranged in scale, from expansions on the pop-up and architectural solutions to urban design and/or planning visions.

Students were asked to produce the following for their final deliverables:

- Title and project description (150 words max);

- Site-analysis diagrams that build their thesis argument through relevant contextual information and interpretive analysis of key issues, opportunities, and community assets;

- Community-engagement drawings, visualizations, and/or diagrams that illustrate insights gained from the encounters;

- Comic book illustrating the experience of the project from a teen's perspective;

- Concept diagrams that clarify project intent and social-spatial-programmatic strategies;

- Physical model that describes the project at an appropriate scale;

- Construction/material diagram illustrating materials and the construction and/or installation system;

- Orthographic or axonometric site plan showing the project within the site context at an appropriate scale;

- Sections and/or elevations at a project-appropriate scale;

- Plans at a project-appropriate scale;

- Perspectives of at least four views.

The youth advisors participated as jury critics during the final review. Instead of following the traditional front-facing chair arrangement, this session was conducted around a large table, where youth advisors were positioned at the same level as distinguished scholars, promoting inclusivity and open dialogue. The format allowed the teens to be recognized as experts in their lived experiences and offer some of the most insightful and critical feedback. This setting also added an element of levity and fun to what is usually a serious occasion; it's unlikely that any Yale architecture final review has ever had such an engaging discussion on the importance of Doritos.

ADDITIONAL CONTEXT

This studio took place at a critical time, coinciding with significant community organizing efforts to develop a long-term economic program, the Bronxwide Plan, grounded in economic democracy and racial justice. There was also interest from the city at the time, through the Urban Design Forum's 2023–24 Forefront Fellowship, to consider youth in the design of the built environment.

Guided by a participatory planning process, the Bronxwide Plan constructs a shared vision for the borough that empowered residents and workers to take control of the economy. The plan was led by a coalition of twelve community, faith, and labor organizations from across the borough, including WHEDco. Among their values and principles was the commitment to "apply an intergenerational lens," recognizing that all voices are important, including those of youth (https://bcdi.nyc/bronxwideplan).

Additionally, the Department of Health and Mental Hygiene and New York City Public Schools partnered with the Urban Design Forum on the 2023–24 Forefront Fellowship, titled Free to Grow. Over two phases, the cohort of fellows aimed to imagine "a New York City where youth are free to grow and learn" (urbandesignforum.org/initiative/free-to-grow). Phase I focused on developing a "playbook for outdoor learning environments for public school students," and Phase II involved proposing youth-affirming public spaces.

This studio maintained contact with representatives from both initiatives, hoping that the students' work would help inform ongoing efforts, and vice versa.

CONVERSATION

This is an excerpt of a discussion with Chat Travieso published in *Constructs.*

CONSTRUCTS

You look at ways in which infrastructure and the built environment—or *active form*, to use Keller Easterling's term—affect people and spaces. You also published the article "A Nation of Walls," in *Places Journal*, about segregation walls and infrastructures of division. Your own interventions, such as amenities for seating and playing music, have had positive effects on the environment. How do you make sure that the effects you're trying to produce as a designer are positive?

CHAT TRAVIESO

I see urban interventions as both direct responses to everyday needs and poetic gestures. The work I do as an independent artist and designer, as well as with Yeju Choi for Yeju & Chat, is very much invested in working with what's already happening on the ground. It's meant to uplift existing efforts, not start from scratch. People are already adapting their built environments to everyday needs. There are already social bonds and relations, and the work is designed to reinforce those and learn from them at the same time. I also see the work as a catalyst for larger actions. The temporary nature of this approach can be disappointing, however: it activates the space and people are excited, and then it goes away. So what is the afterlife of the intervention? Can it spur changes in policy? Can it exist at another site? In my research work I try to investigate the histories and policies that have shaped the built environment in order to start thinking more expansively about alternative futures and systems.

‹

One thing you do so well is to build theory from specific examples. What is your research methodology? And what new projects will you be taking on?

CT

My research process tends to be circuitous and multipronged, guided by conversations, connections, and relationships that blossom and multiply over time. "A Nation of Walls," my project exploring the history of segregation walls, is a good example of this. I'm originally from Miami, and in 2016 I read N. D. B. Connolly's book *A World More Concrete,* about the history of real estate and Jim Crow in South Florida. Connolly describes several race walls in Miami, including the one in the Liberty City neighborhood that was a model for others built throughout the country. There's a footnote that discusses a wall in Detroit. In my creative practice, I've always had an interest in subverting objects of exclusion in the built environment, namely walls and fences, and turning them into spaces of community and action. Naturally the subject of segregation barriers

Chat Travieso, *The Boogie Down Booth (Freeman St.)*, 2014

Chat Travieso, *The Boogie Down Booth (174th St.)*, 2015

deeply intrigued me. I emailed Connolly to ask, "Is there more information about these walls?" He replied that all the books he's read mention segregation walls only in passing, and there's no comprehensive study. So that triggered the research project. Concurrently I was talking with Tarell Alvin McCraney, author of the play that the movie *Moonlight* is based on, who started a youth program in Liberty City oriented toward theater. He's from there too — we both attended the New World School of Arts — and he wanted to bring in a more social justice community-based design aspect. He mentioned how when they were filming *Moonlight* he told the young actors about the wall, and they were shocked to learn not only that there was a wall built to separate Black and White neighborhoods but that there are still remnants of it today. That led to the "Wall (In)" project, a summer arts program in which local youth investigate the history of the Liberty City wall, talk to community members, and come up with ideas for interventions. I worked with Arts for Learning Miami and architect Germane Barnes to develop and facilitate the program from 2017 to '19. So "Wall (In)" informed "A Nation of Walls," and vice versa. In the *Places Journal* article you cited, I quote from interviews conducted by the youth with Melba Rose, Hattie Walker, and Phillip Walker, who were instrumental in this project. One thing led to another, and I heard about more segregation barriers. People I met in Miami were like, "Oh yeah, there was another wall over here." "Oh, I remember those." I wrote some things about this history online and started getting emails from people across the country telling me about walls in their hometowns. I also dove into the archives. So far I have uncovered evidence for more than thirty race barriers either still standing, removed, or planned in eighteen states. I try to ground this ongoing research in oral histories and community engagement.

❮

What will you be teaching at Yale?

❮T

I'm debating between going deeper with the wall research and exploring issues of borders and boundaries. Another side of my research is an interest in young people and creating a more open, inclusive city for them. Teens are not only seen as nuisances; they're actively criminalized in public spaces, especially Black and Latinx youth. They are also completely forgotten in the design process. We think somewhat about young children. They have playgrounds, although we can think more expansively about this too. And obviously we consider adults in the process because those are the people who are typically doing the design. But where can teens go to feel safe and autonomous?

Another idea for a studio is to interrogate spaces of privilege and Whiteness as sites that necessitate action. What if we work on those communities and institutions that have been hoarding resources and imagine ways to redistribute those resources more equitably? There are remnants of a race wall in the Coconut Grove neighborhood of Miami. Unlike spaces such as the Liberty City wall, where both sides are now predominantly Black due to White flight, the Coconut

Chat Travieso, *The Boogie Down Booth (Melrose),* 2016

Chat Travieso, *The Boogie Down (Youth) Booth,* 2019

Grove wall still holds that color line. You see the redlining maps, and then you see the Google aerial view. You can see how the tree canopy is different—it absolutely aligns with the redlining map, which also aligns with where the wall is to this day. To address the disparity between the two sides of the wall—the difference in the tree canopy being just a symptom of deeper systemic injustices—and enact a reparative praxis, we must focus our attention on dismantling the structures that perpetuate advantages for wealthy White neighborhoods to the detriment of communities of color.

What are you planning in terms of pedagogy for the year ahead? What are the things you're hoping to invite students to think about at this moment in time? What excites you about teaching now?

CT

Architects might not perceive how the law and policy have spatial consequences. I want to bring into the classroom an understanding of how policymaking can be a design tool that shapes our material geographies, as well as how architecture is a form of regulation. I also want to introduce students to participatory methodologies in which they would engage with community stakeholders, including young people, in the design process. Youth might not buy into some of the social, economic, and political assumptions that we make, so they are able to imagine alternatives that might allow us to see other worlds. That's the really exciting part of teaching a studio. The best kind of studio is not just a thought experiment but a potential tool for capacity building and imagining a world into existence.

Chat Travieso, *Imagine That!*, 2024

STUDENT WORK

THE PARTICULAR AND THE PUBLIC

CHLOE ZHANG
KAIWEN ZHAO
PRECIOUS NDUKUBA
KEVIN YAN
FUAD KHAZAM
BEN ACHEAMPONG
MARIEL LINDSEY
BARBARA NASILA
MIRANDA CLARK
ODETTE JAMES

CHLOE ZHANG KAIWEN ZHAO

ART, FRIENDS, STREETS: WELCOME TO OUR ARTISTIC HUB

Through our preliminary research we discovered that the Bronx has a strong artistic culture and is the birthplace of numerous art forms, including street art, visual art, and music. After connecting with various art organizations and youth advisors in the Bronx, we learned that many young people are engaged in a diverse range of artistic endeavors within the local community. Recognizing the pivotal role of expressive activities in well-being, we understood the importance of providing a space dedicated to personal growth, relaxation, and creative exploration. Our mission is to establish an outlet for self-expression that also functions as an after-school artistic hub. This dual-purpose space will empower teenagers to express themselves freely in an environment that fosters personal development.

The project unfolds in two phases. The first focuses on creating a dynamic artistic hub around the Morrisania Library equipped with amenities such as woodshops and computers. We envision Beatty Plaza transformed into an outdoor art space with a café to foster community interaction and engagement. A proposed youth art center, located across the street, connects to the art plaza via an underground art gallery to exhibit artworks by the teens.

In phase two we envision a pop-up installation system designed to amplify youth voices throughout the Bronx. We carefully selected sites of varying scales, from streetlights and existing scaffolding to empty parking lots, to be transformed into dynamic street exhibits. A modular framework will allow easy assembly, disassembly, and reconfiguration. Inflatable air packages serve as visually captivating skins and interactive furniture elements. Our goal is to make art accessible to foster cultural self-confidence among young people. The installations also become conversation starters that encourage social engagement.

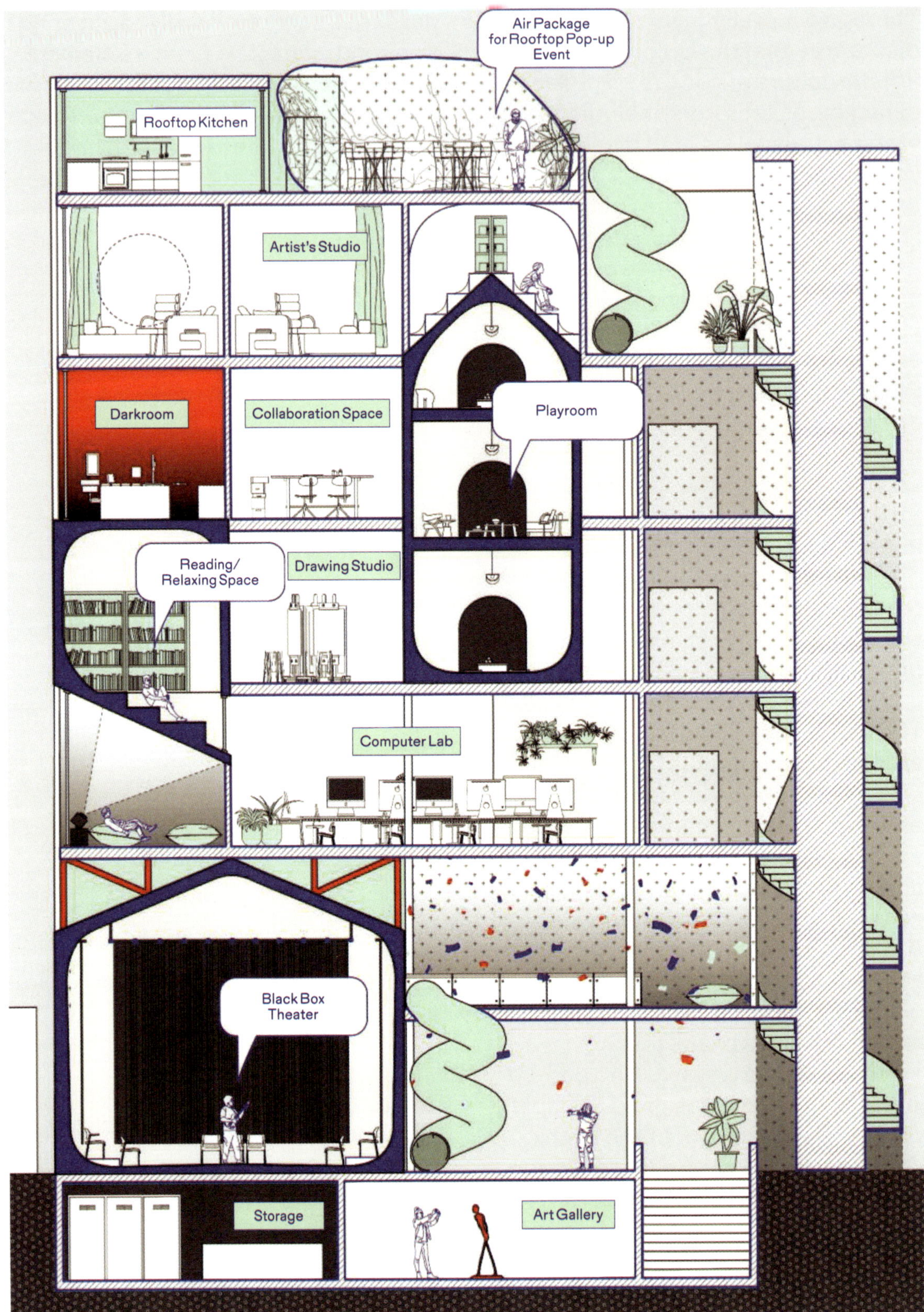

Cross section of the Youth Art Center

THE PARTICULAR AND THE PUBLIC

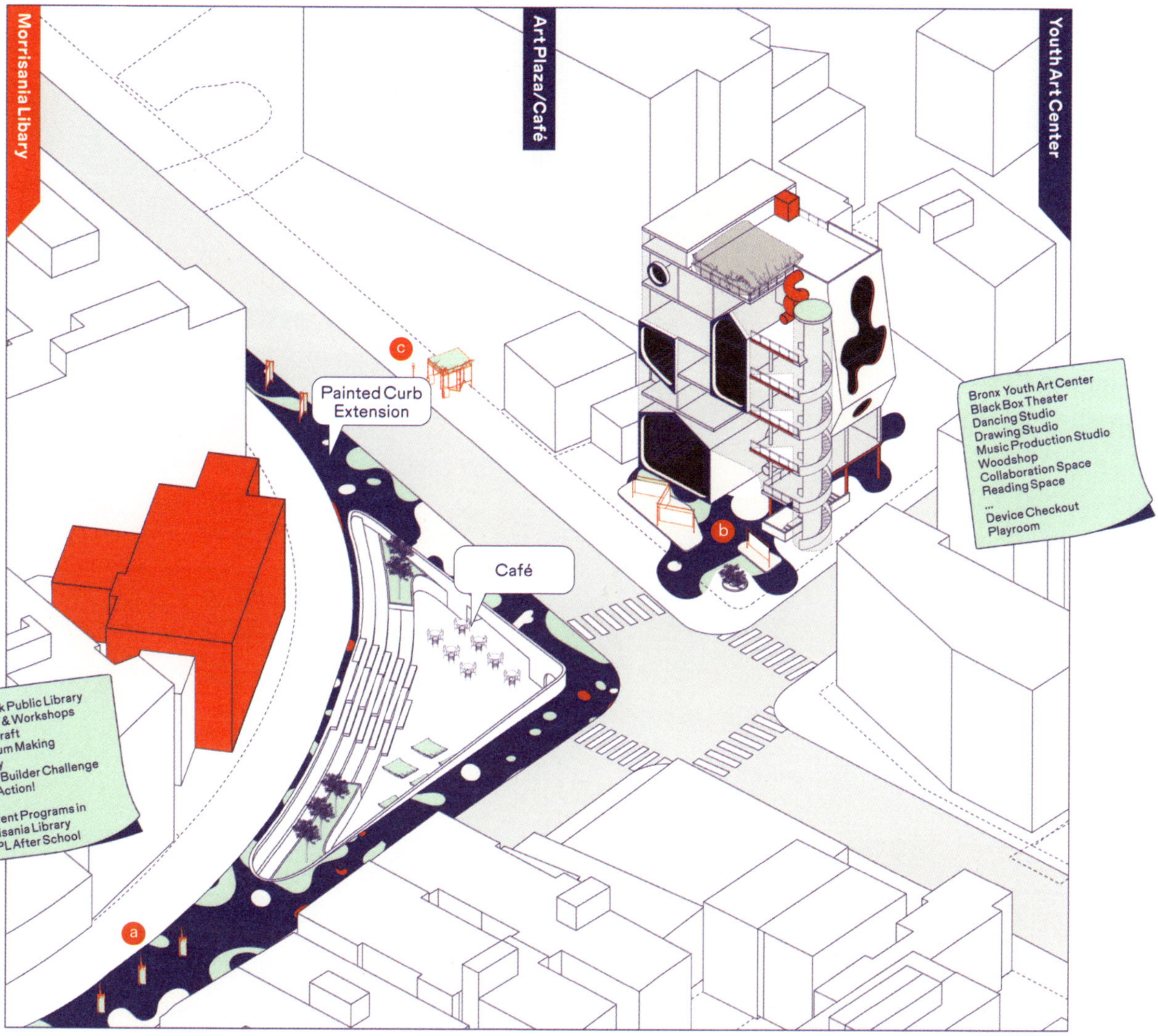

Axonometric site plan showing existing Morrisania Public Library and proposed Art Plaza/Café and Youth Art Center

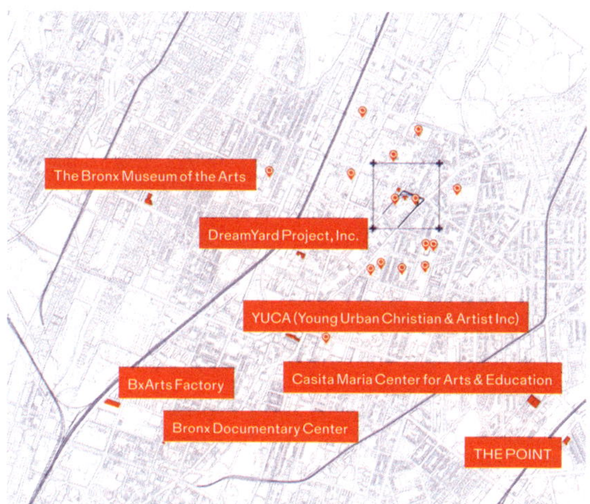

Concept diagram showing the locations of existing youth arts organizations and nearby schools

Section model showing the Art Plaza, café, underground exhibition space, and Youth Art Center building

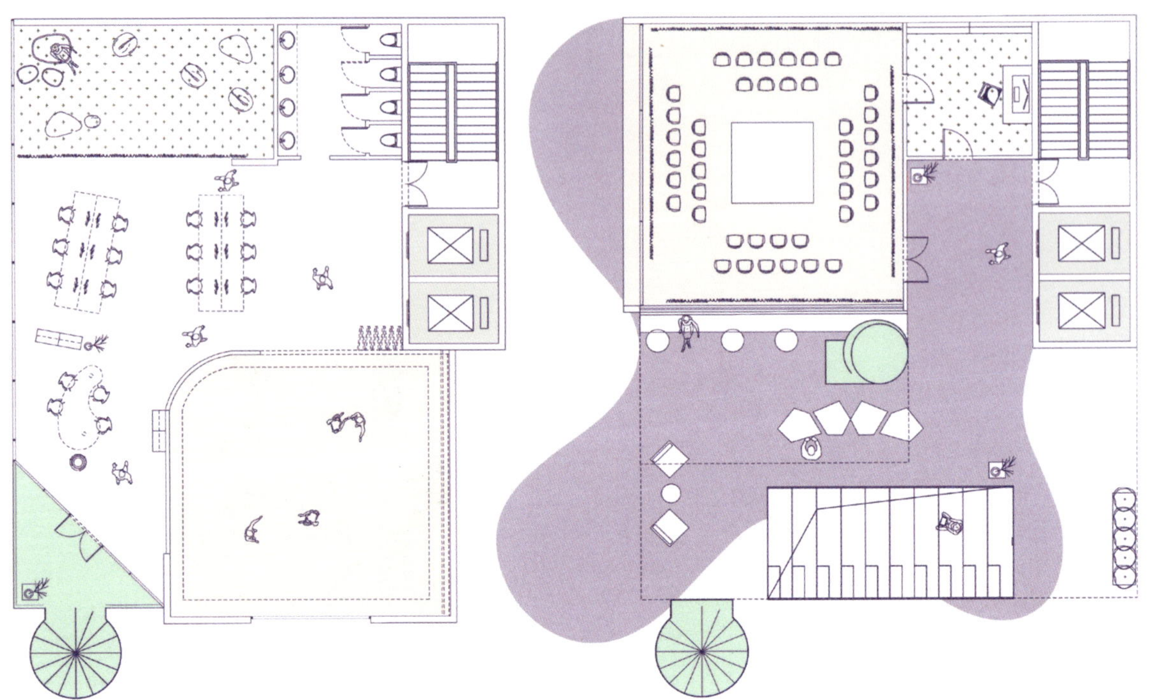

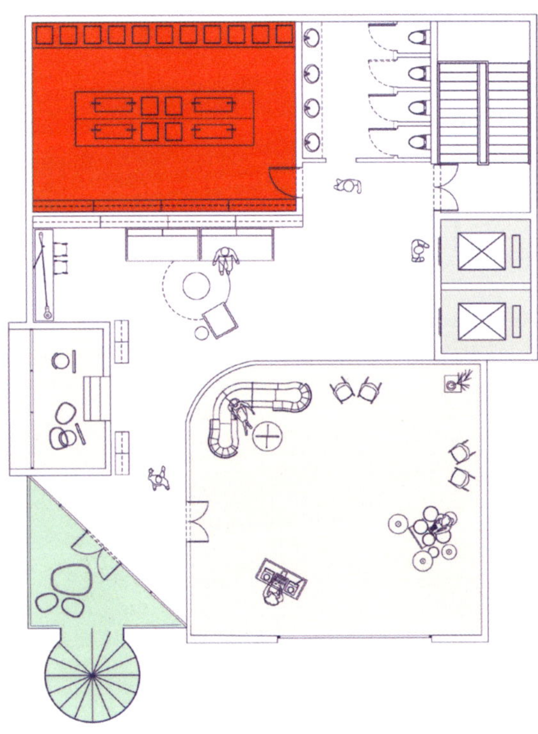

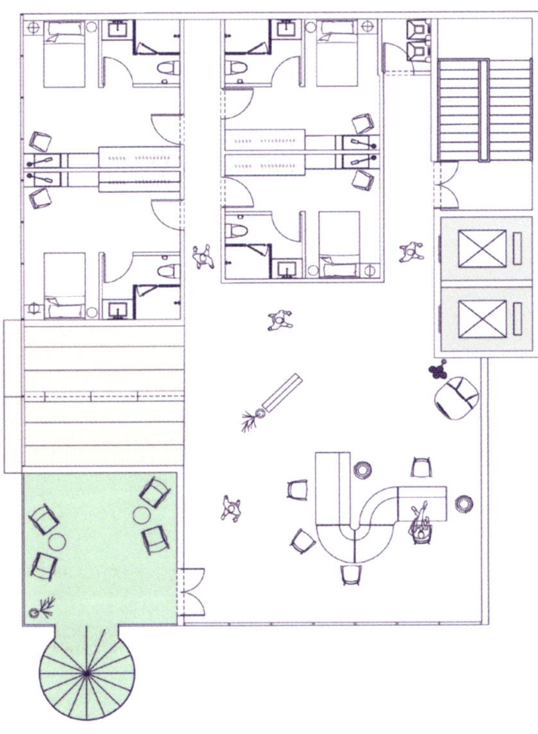

Selected floor plans of the Youth Art Center

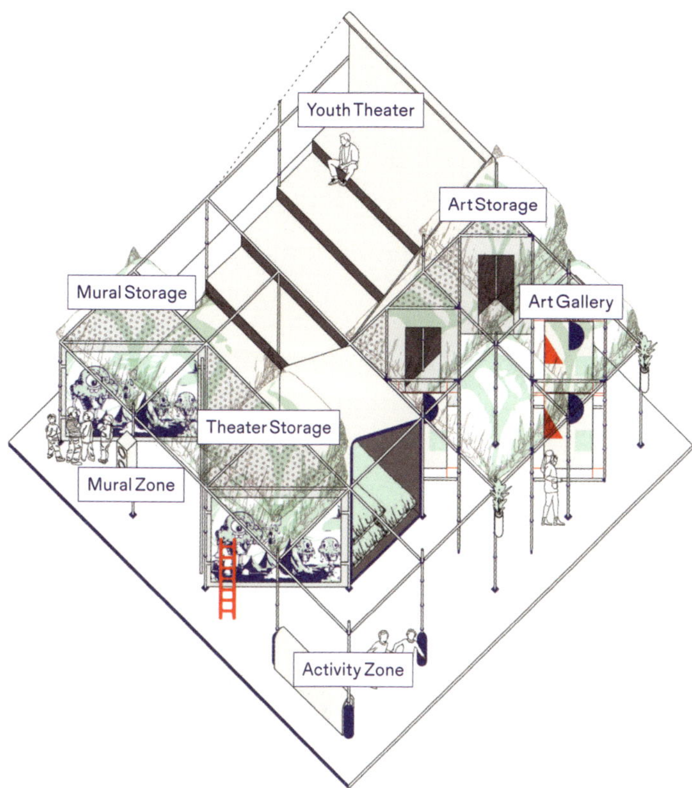

Large-scale pop-up installation for one-day event

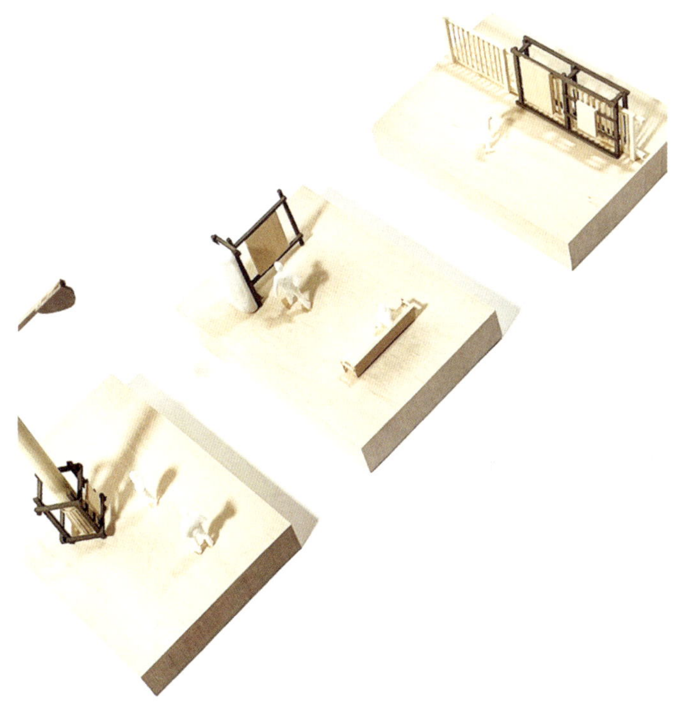

Physical model for small-scale pop-up installations

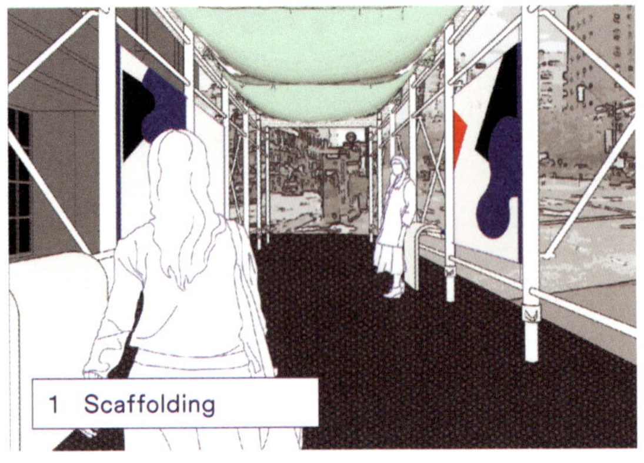

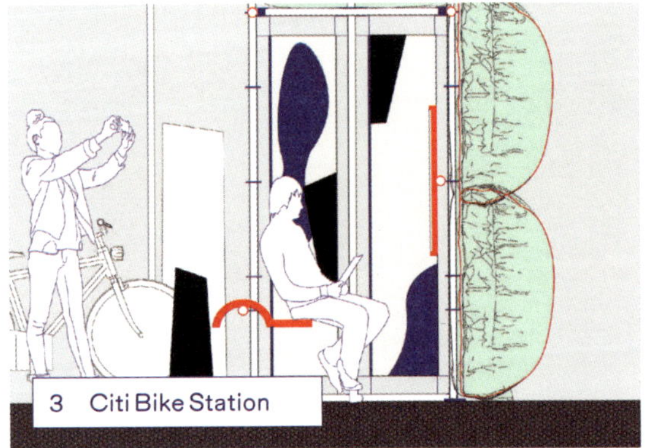

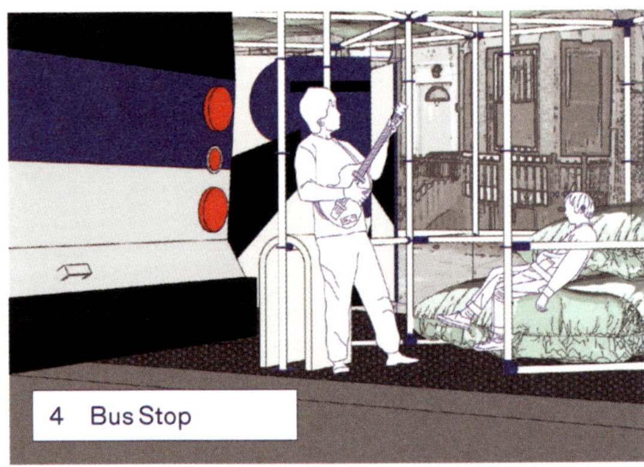

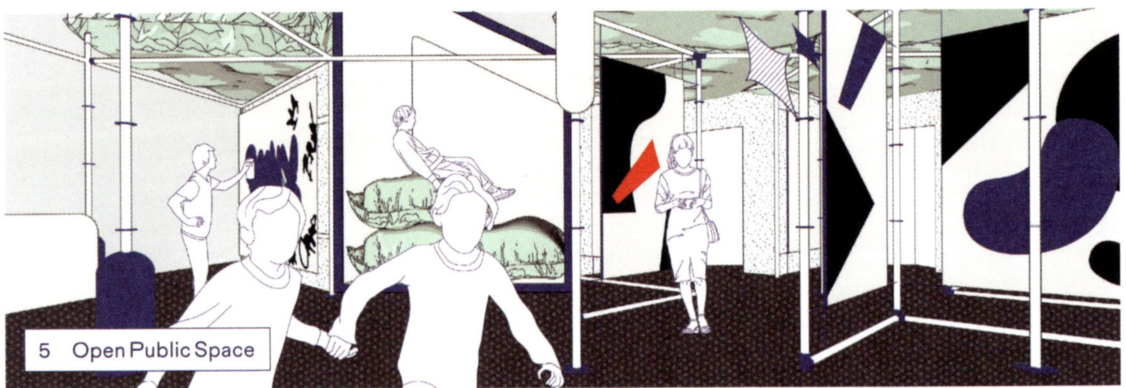

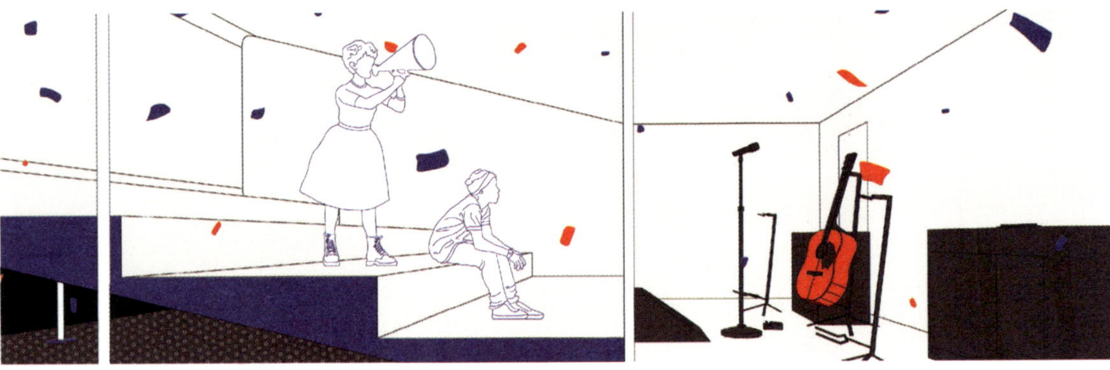

Decentralizing art across the Bronx

"My Easel, My Street" comic drawing

Rendering of the art studio

PRECIOUS NDUKUBA
KEVIN YAN

GENDER, TRANSIT, AND A BIT OF FUN

The Bronx is home to a wealth of community leaders and organizations that provide creative programs and spaces for local youth. However, these organizations face a consistent drop in enrollment after daylight saving time begins. As daytime hours grow shorter, parents pull their children out of the programs because they perceive a lack of safety after dark in the Bronx. This project proposes to boost the impact of these rich community resources through a series of interventions that improve nighttime safety for youth and make the act of transit just a bit more fun.

Spaces for youth in the Bronx are scarce and overly scrutinized. During our workshops with local teens we found that safe spaces for young women are the hardest to come by. With girls and gender minorities in mind, we designed interventions that reclaimed space—not by contesting youth spaces like baseball fields or basketball courts but by activating underutilized areas near places where youth already gather. These interventions were informed by interviews with local teens and the understanding that youth spaces are not created simply by designation. We hope that these spaces will provide agency for teens to claim and remake them on their terms.

Our first intervention is a collection of swings on the medians just outside the Yankee Stadium subway station. As a transit hub, it is a place where people often sit on the under-illuminated sidewalk while waiting to transfer to a bus or train. We installed swings of different sizes and configurations so that teens—perhaps after picking up a snack from the bodega or McDonald's —can sit, eat, hang out with friends, or wait safely for the next train or bus. We envision expanding the public space with an "open street" between the medians, which would host pop-ups and other activities.

Continuing down the street toward DreamYard, we will transform the long and claustrophobic Lou Gehrig underpass into a community garden, a multimodal skate park, a social services center, and a covered market. The adjacent residential segment will be upgraded with various lighting methods determined by community workshops, and the street will be expanded to accommodate a two-way bike lane and bus loading zones.

A little further beyond, at the Bronx Music Hall, a public performance space and open street will be set up for youth to sing, dance, and shop at the nearby pop-up market stalls and food trucks. Lastly, on the final stretch to DreamYard, neon signs signaling the presence and services of automobile and trade shops will illuminate the street, creating multicolored shadows that infuse the sidewalk with life.

Diagram connecting community assets

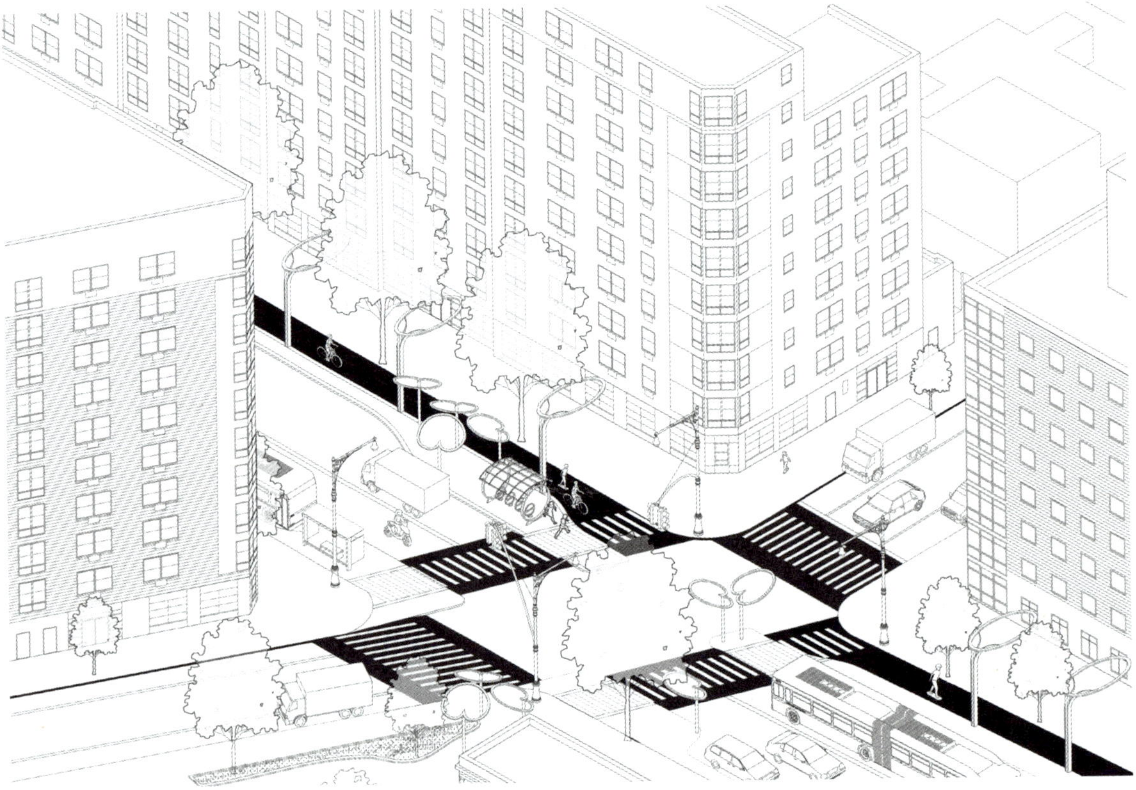

Street proposal

Event posters

Bathroom proposals

Comic spread

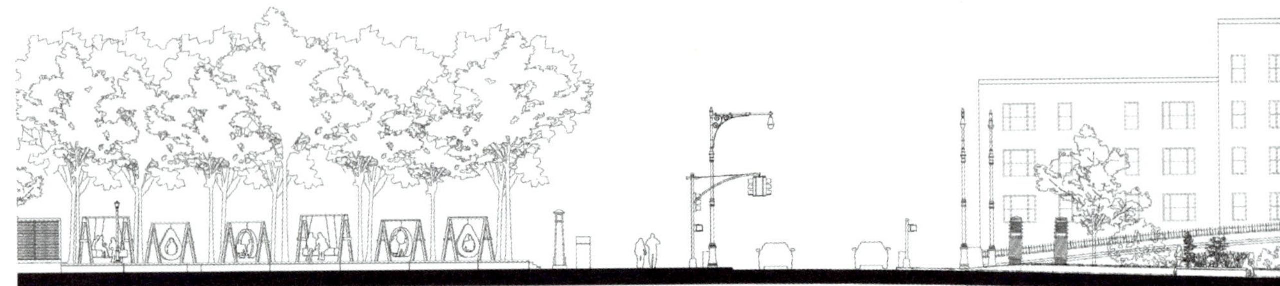

Project section

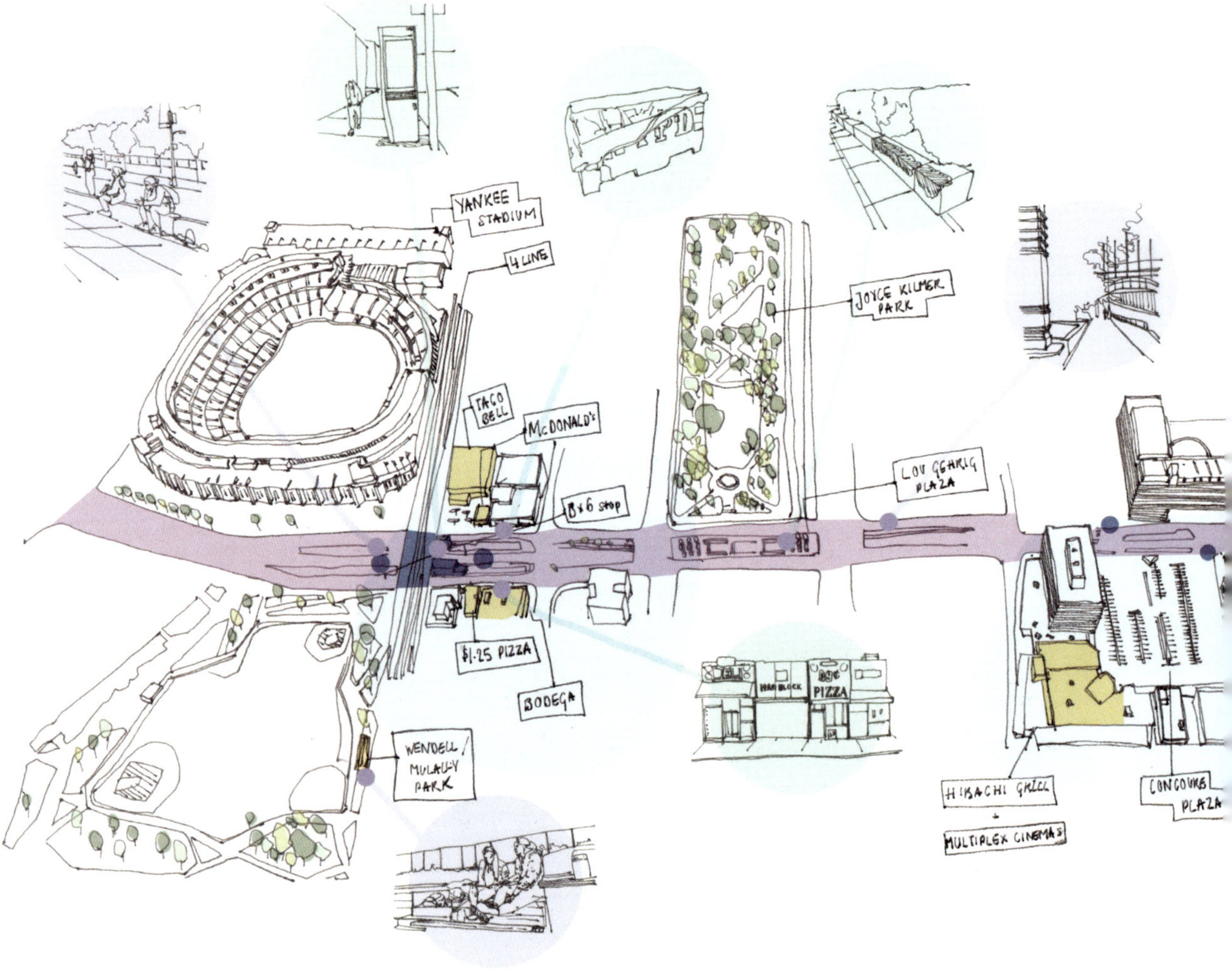

Site diagram showing 161st Street and the existing opportunities and observations along the route

THE PARTICULAR AND THE PUBLIC

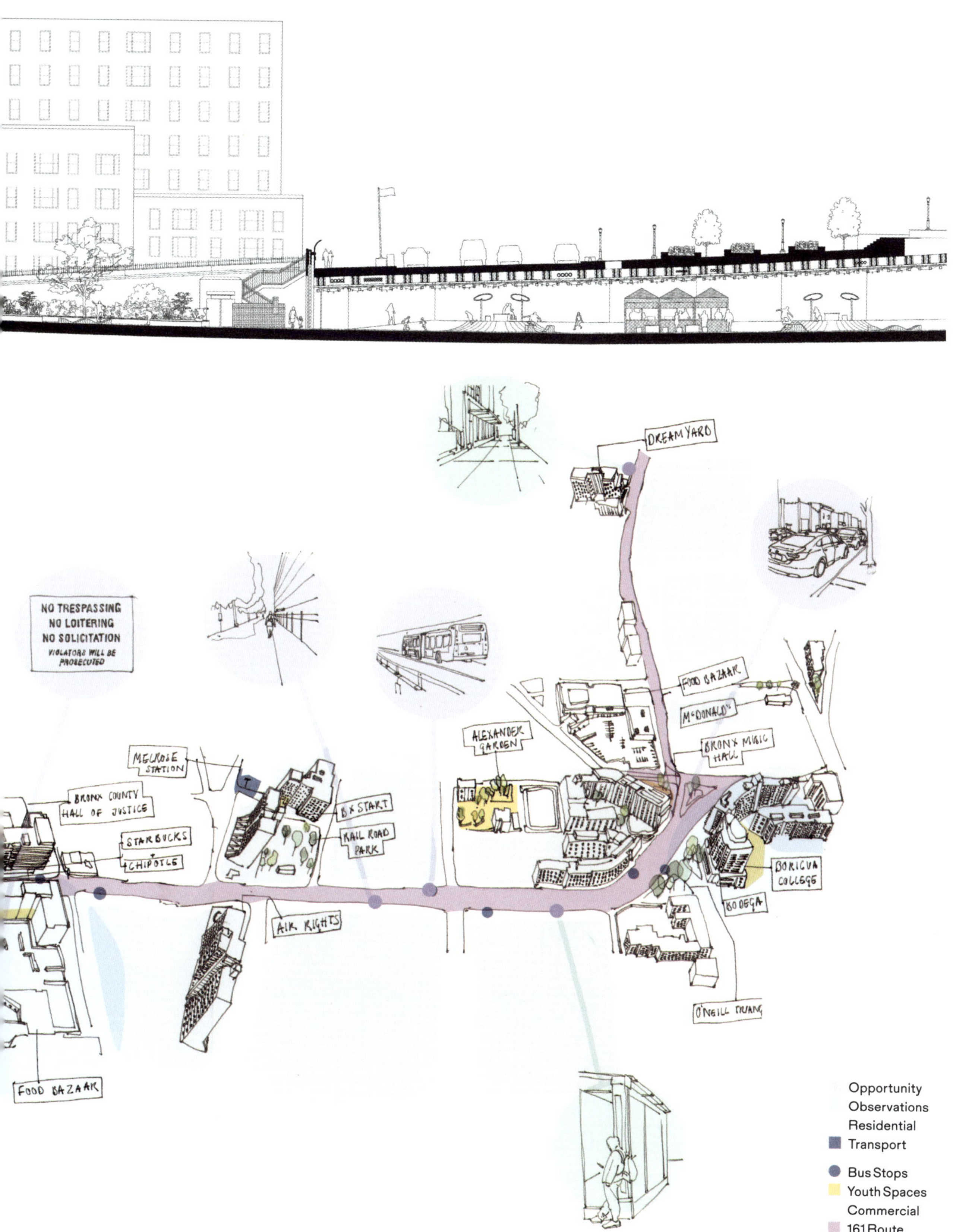

NO TRESPASSING
NO LOITERING
NO SOLICITATION
VIOLATORS WILL BE PROSECUTED
DREAMYARD
FOOD BAZAAR
McDONALD'S
BRONX MUSIC HALL
ALEXANDER GARDEN
MELROSE STATION
BRONX COUNTY HALL OF JUSTICE
BX START
RAIL ROAD PARK
STARBUCKS
CHIPOTLE
BORICUA COLLEGE
BODEGA
AIR RIGHTS
O'NEILL PLAZA
FOOD BAZAAR
Opportunity
Observations
Residential
Transport
Bus Stops
Youth Spaces
Commercial
161 Route

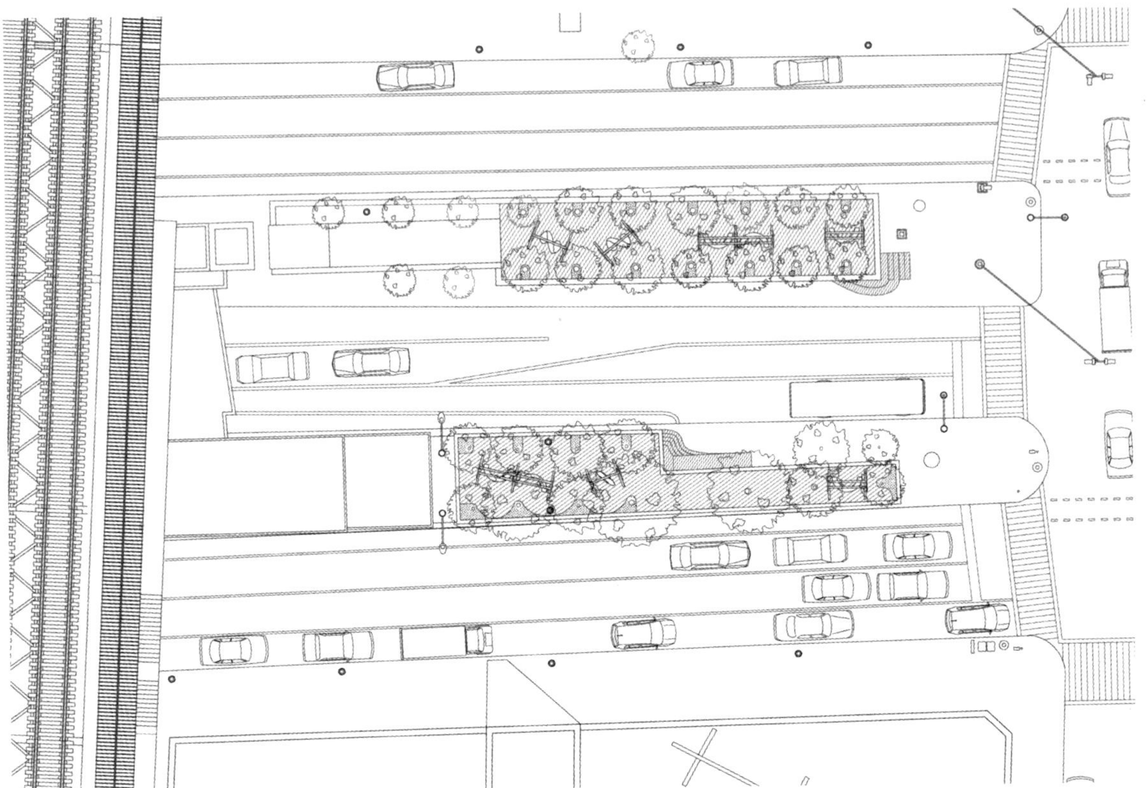

Yankee swings proposal

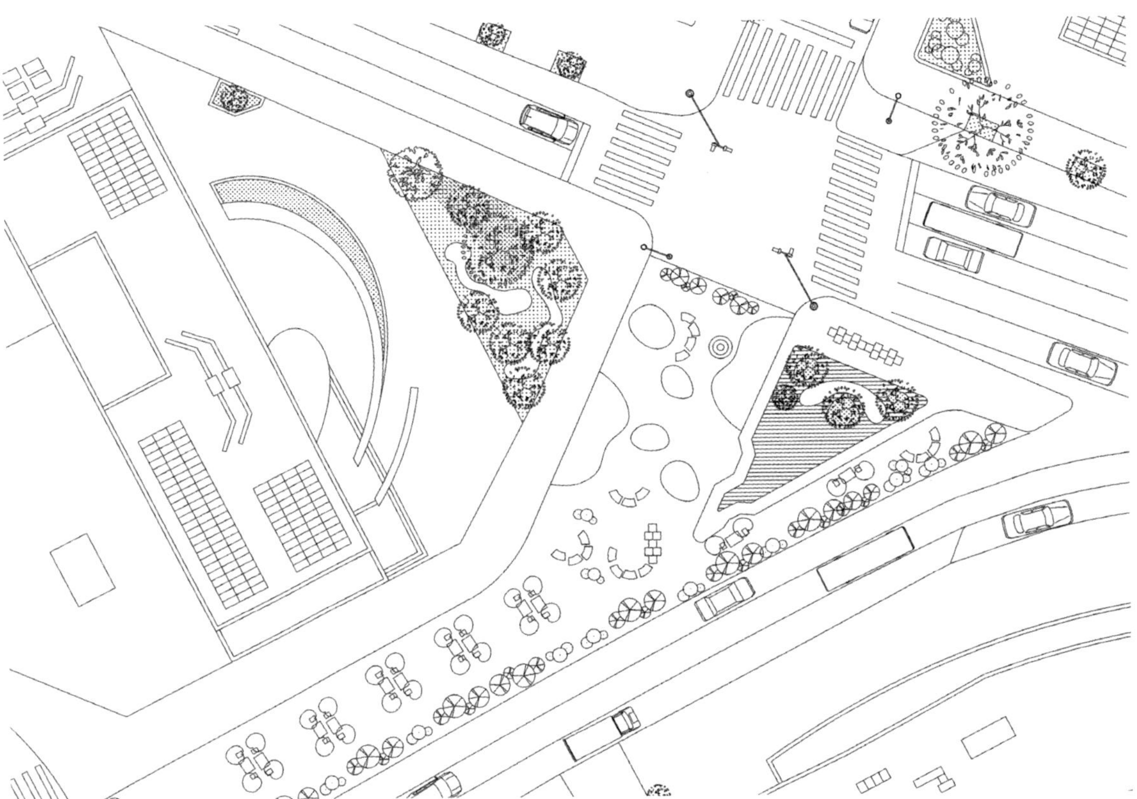

Music hall site proposal

THE PARTICULAR AND THE PUBLIC

Comic book spread

FUAD KHAZAM

WITH BEN ACHEAMPONG

BRONX GREENWAYS

The Bronx has an urban vehicle service
industry that provides a local source
of income but is harmful to residents'
health. Health and safety issues have
been exacerbated by top-down city
planning, which isolated deep-rooted
Bronx communities through highways
and industrial hubs. One proposal is
the Bronx Greenway—a borough-wide
urban intervention that remediates the
toxic air quality. This project addresses
the heavy infrastructure of the car-repair
area by installing permeable surfaces
and greenery on heat-reflecting
elements. Car parts are recycled from
surrounding junkyards and repair shops,
repurposing the corpse of former car
cultures into a new youth environment.
As a result, the project brings the
community together in an engaging and
youth-supportive network of green
spaces offering refuge, social activities,
and urban farming.

Concept collage

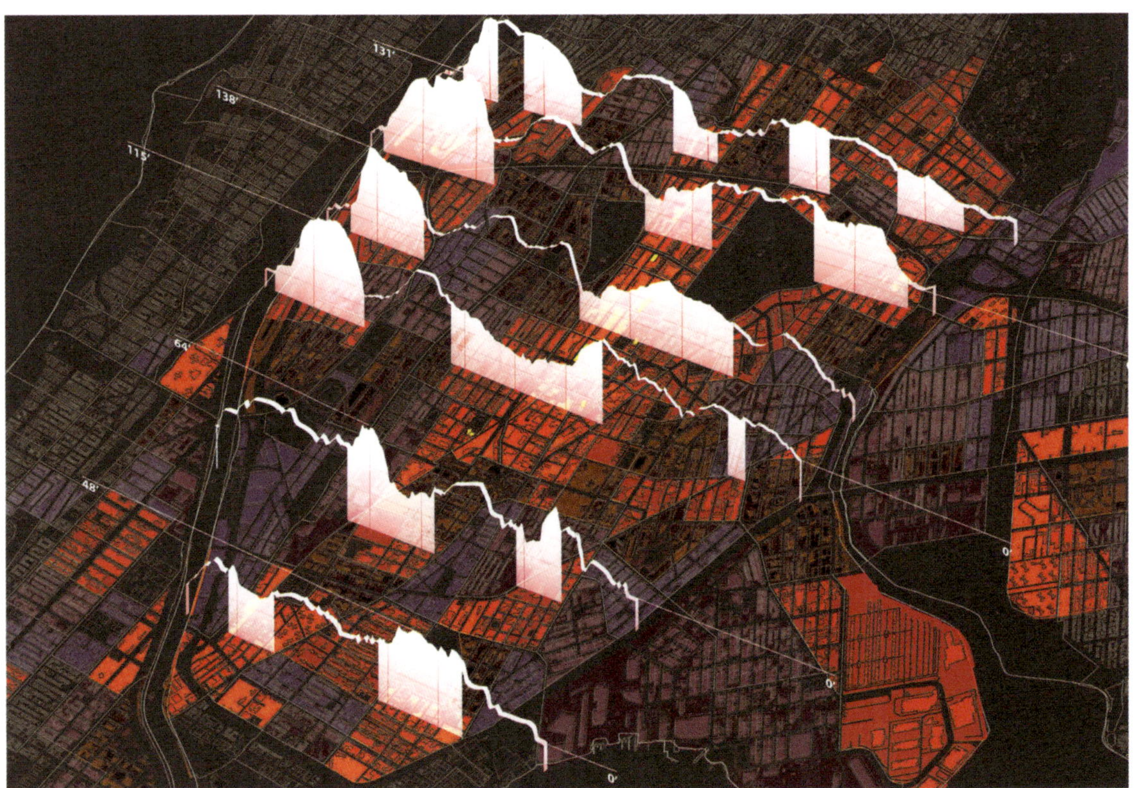

Diagram correlating section cuts of the Bronx with asthma rates

Diagram illustrating how salvaged car parts could be used to create different spatial and programmatic configurations

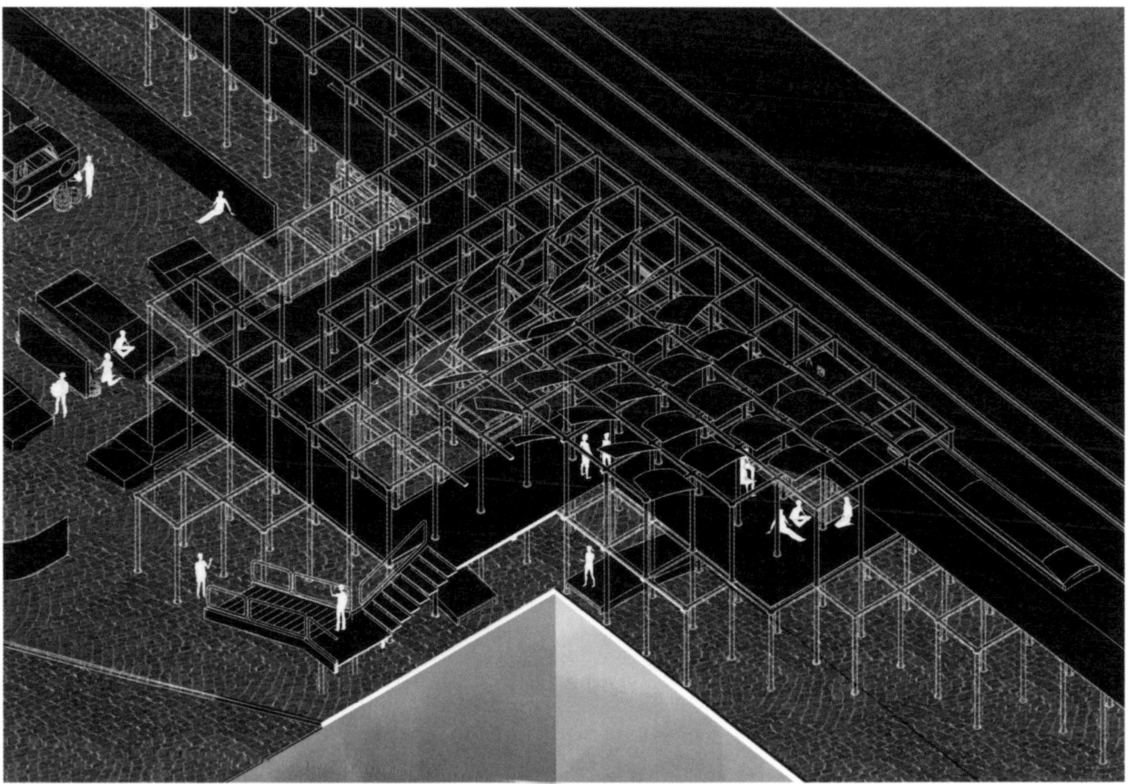

Project site axonometric

Project site plan

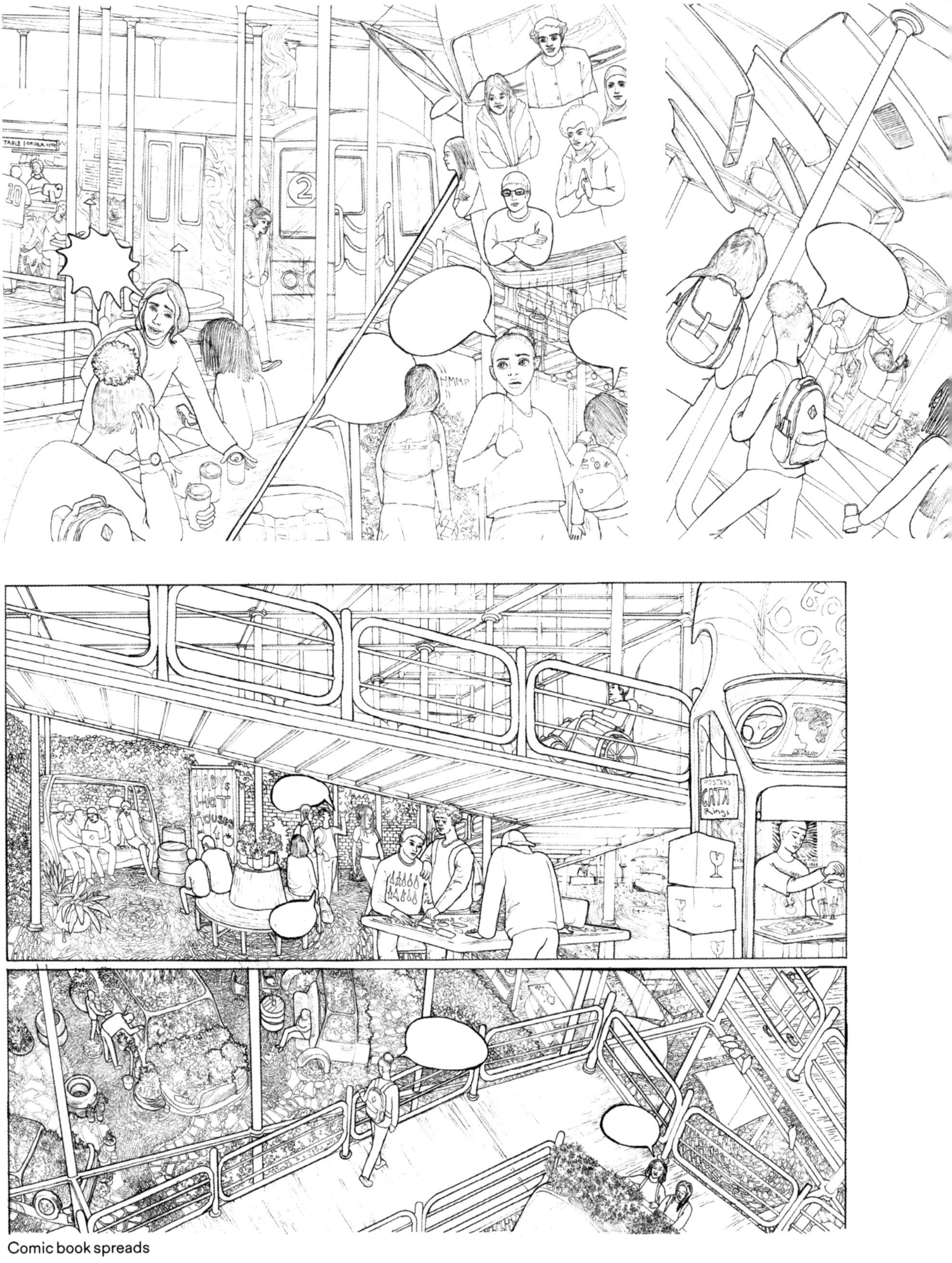

Comic book spreads

lets
GO
ARTS & CRFTS
FAIR
of 2023

MARIEL LINDSEY

BARBARA NASILA

THIS LAND IS OUR LAND: MORRISANIA COMMUNITY LAND TRUST

This project addresses the historical use of landownership as a tool of dispossession and violence against communities of color. We propose a Morrisania Community Land Trust (CLT) to reclaim power for residents through a community-controlled model of landownership. This initiative challenges traditional landownership structures and fosters conversations about what it means to put land in the hands of the public. The goal is to move beyond conventional CLTs and encourage a reimagining of landownership that prioritizes community control of public and private land. The project creates safe and equitable public spaces that empower young people to participate actively in governance.

The Morrisania Community Land Trust initiates pop-up installations designed to engage all community voices, especially teens, in methods for land reclamation. The first mode focuses on small sites where community organizations help residents reclaim government-owned land throughout the borough by physically marking it with colorful stakes. This staking process serves as a temporary monument symbolizing the start of land reclamation and creating visual markers for community members to engage with and to recognize that the land is in their hands.

The second mode targets larger sites to reactivate spaces for community organizations. This involves semi-permanent installations using the visual language of staking to support gatherings and mobilization efforts. These installations could take the form of theatrical stages or digital bulletin boards to promote ongoing community initiatives. Through these actions the Morrisania CLT envisions a future where landownership is centered around the community, fostering collaboration and ensuring that land remains a resource for the people.

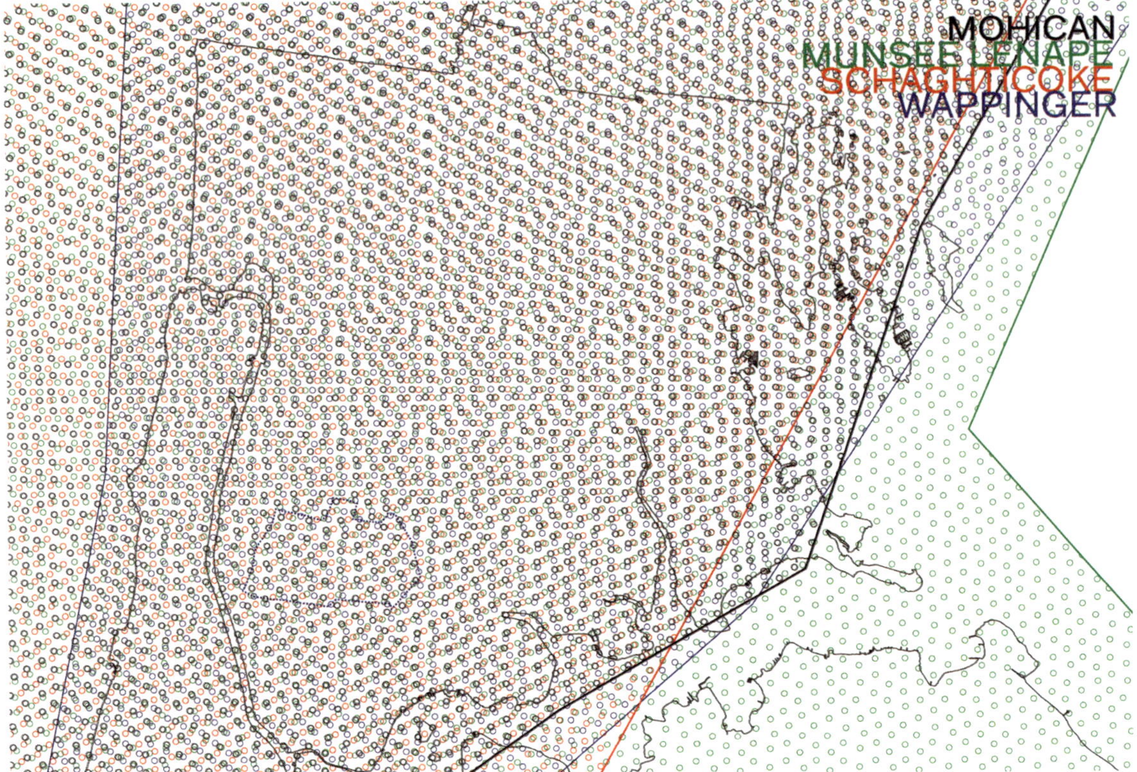

Diagram documenting the Indigenous stewards of the land that is now known as the Bronx

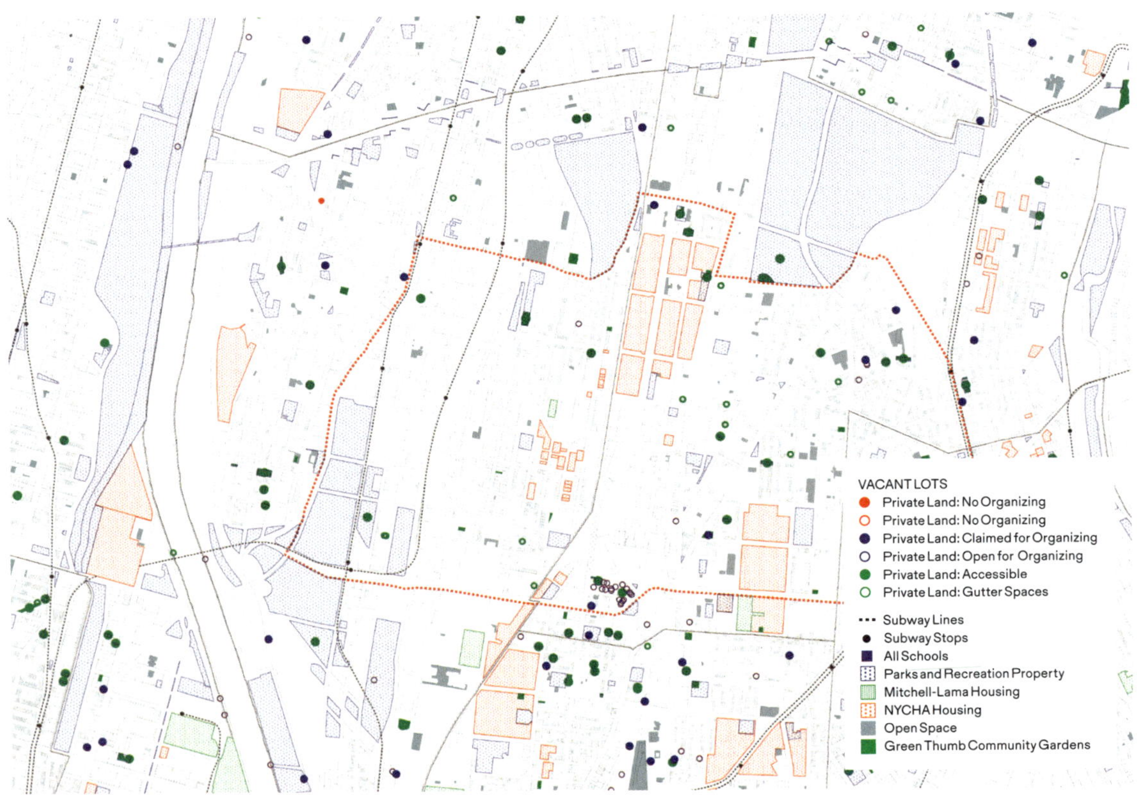

Land-reclamation opportunities map

People have been fighting over land since the creation of our country. The framers of the Constitution treated private property as the cornerstone of free society and as a capitalist society our government values the rights of wealthy individuals over the needs of the whole.

Community Land Trusts fight against this and work to put the power in the hands of the people and promote community-controlled land over individual ownership.

As a CLT, a community can reclaim land in its neighborhood by petitioning the government to relinquish its rights to unused or ill-used public land.

"Take back your land" comic strip

Longitudinal section showing phase two of a small pop-up

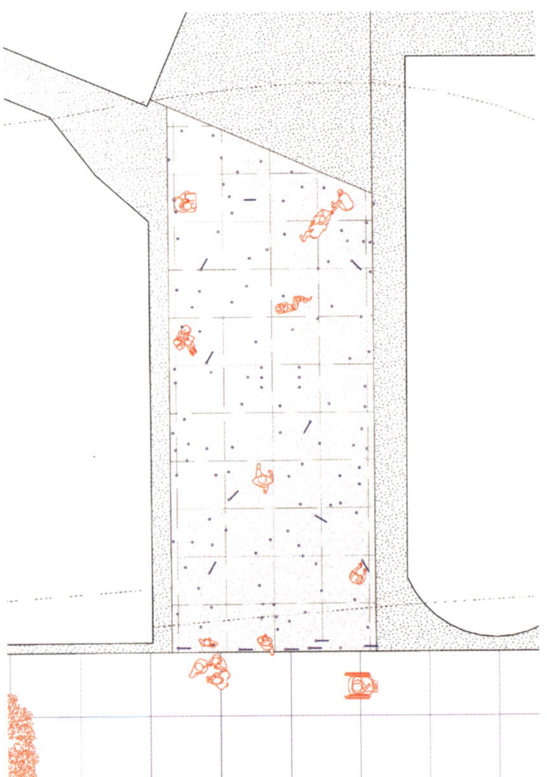

Plan showing phase one of a small pop-up

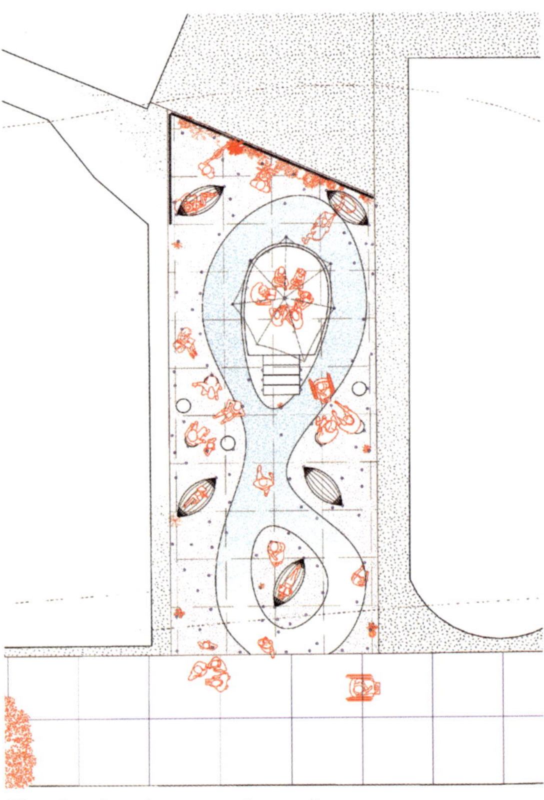

Plan showing phase two of a small pop-up

THE PARTICULAR AND THE PUBLIC

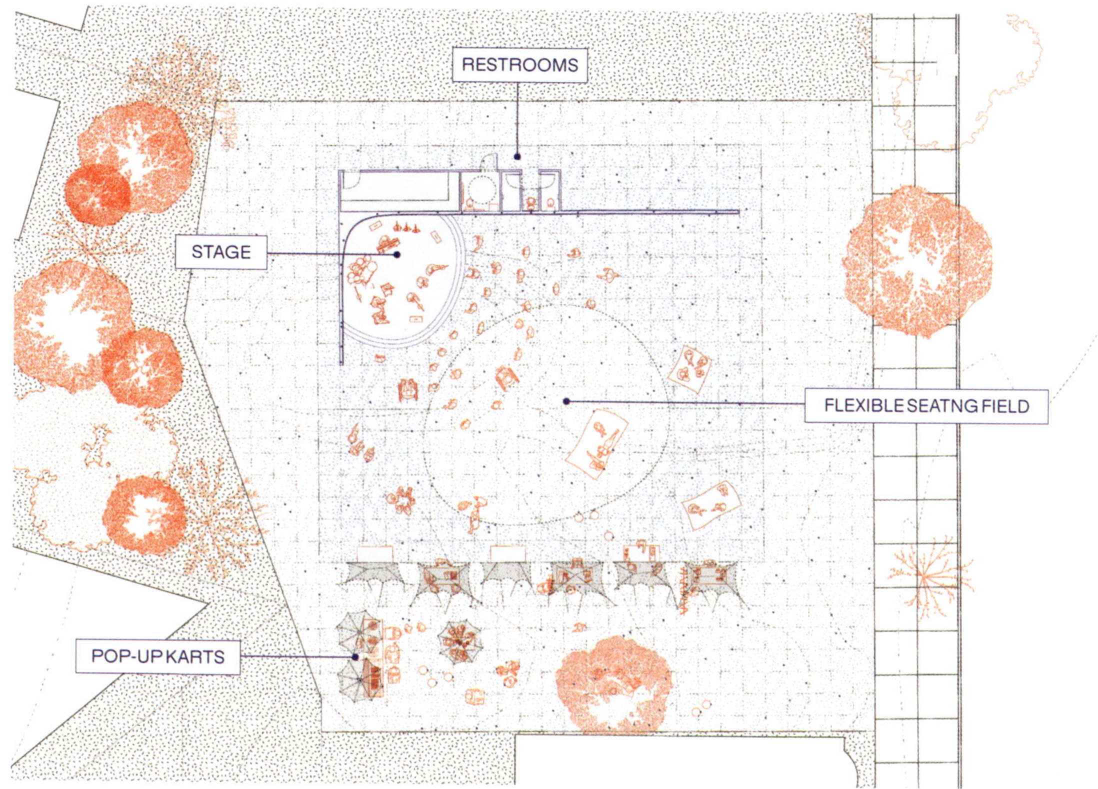

Plan showing phase one of a large pop-up

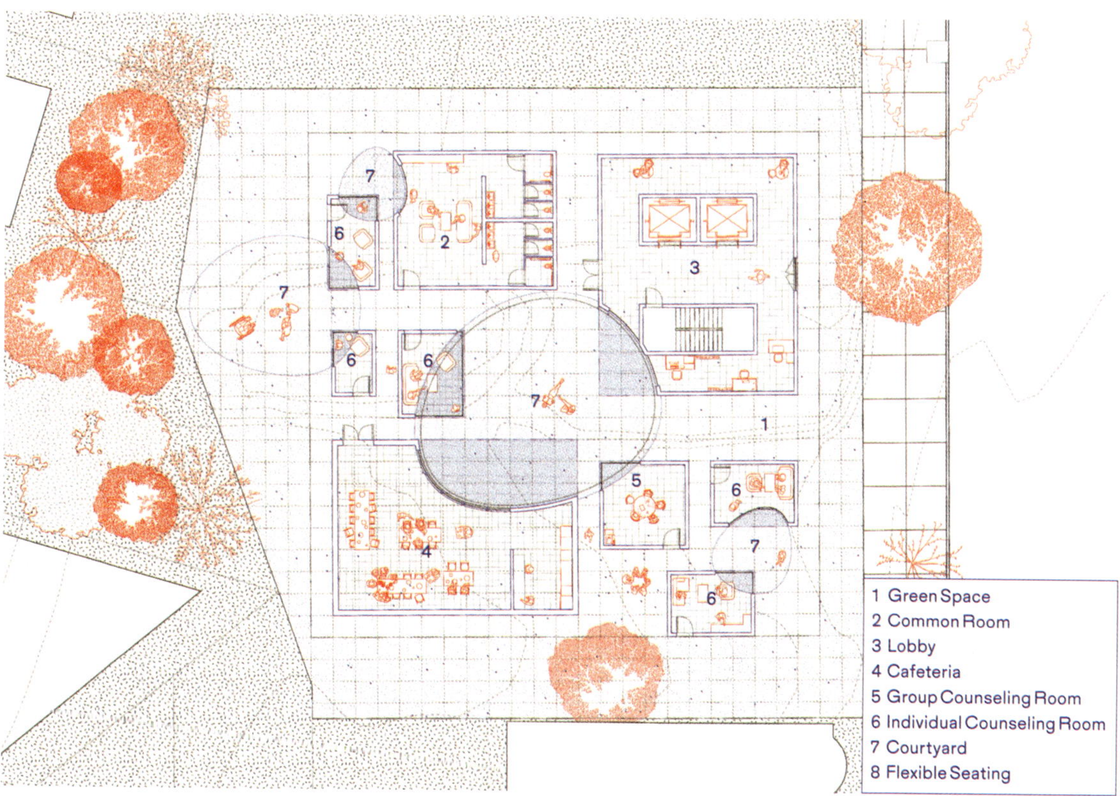

Plan showing phase two of a large pop-up

Perspective views showing different phases and scales of the Morrisania CLT pop-ups

THE PARTICULAR AND THE PUBLIC

CLT

MIRANDA CLARK

ODETTE JAMES

RAISE THE YOUTH

This project proposes a nonprofit organization called Raise the Youth, which would create spaces for youth in the Bronx by developing and adapting rooftops in the blocks of Morrisania with the highest population of young people. The studio adopted an asset-focused mentality, taking inspiration from the work currently done in the Bronx to support the needs of young people. Issues of safety, independence, affordability, and belonging are critical to the youth experience. In the Morrisania neighborhood, the youth movement is constrained by both time and space. The spaces occupied by young people during the fleeting moments of freedom and independence when they move between school, after-school programs, and their homes are lost to street infrastructure and controlled by conditions of surveillance. The spaces of the "open streets" break these constraints but are limited to the times they are open and do not serve commuters.

In our search for places beyond the streets and sidewalks, we identified the largely unused rooftop as a "third space" for youth. Rooftops are often residential terraces with chairs and tables, planters, solar panels, small playgrounds, and greenhouses. Our project proposes that Raise the Youth works to negotiate spaces for youth via the development and adaptation of rooftops in Morrisania. Youth members, employees, and building owners can take advantage of new incentives that we have designed based on existing New York zoning ordinances and programs. The resulting spaces, used and largely managed by youth members, provide places of refuge for recreation, community events, extracurricular programs, and social gatherings.

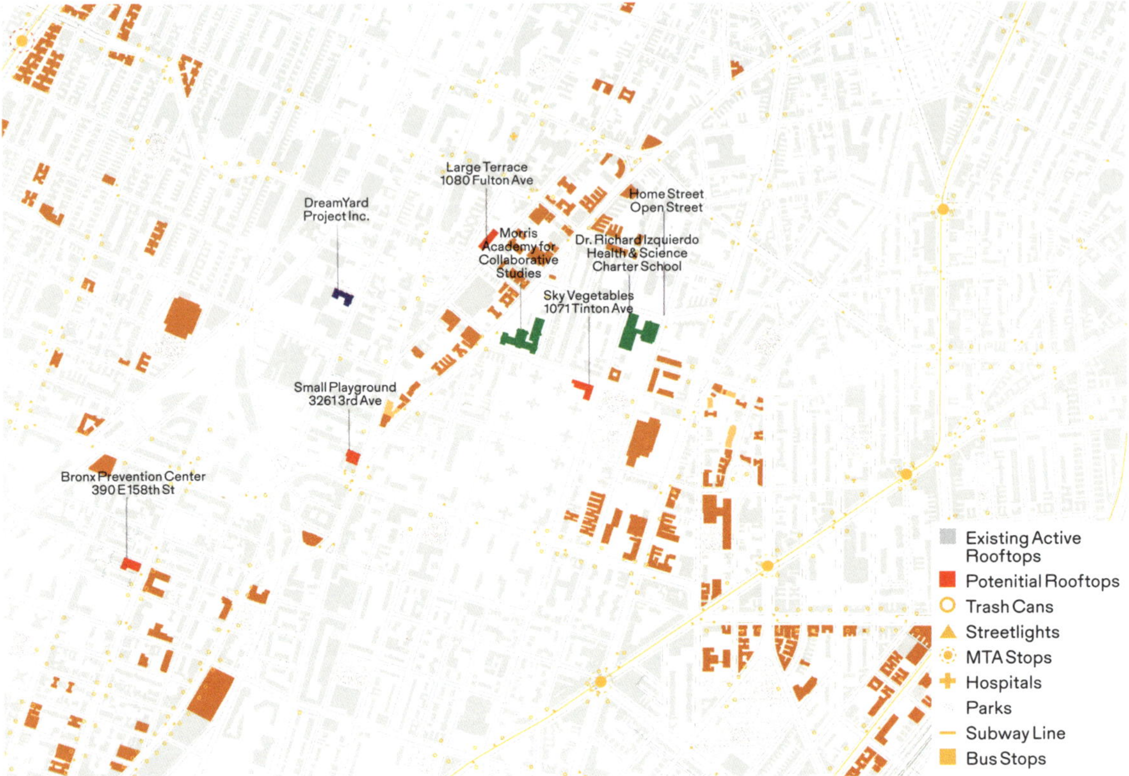

Morrisania rooftop analysis map

Future Imaginings rooftop water park

Future Imaginings basketball city

Section of one of the proposed rooftop interventions on an existing building

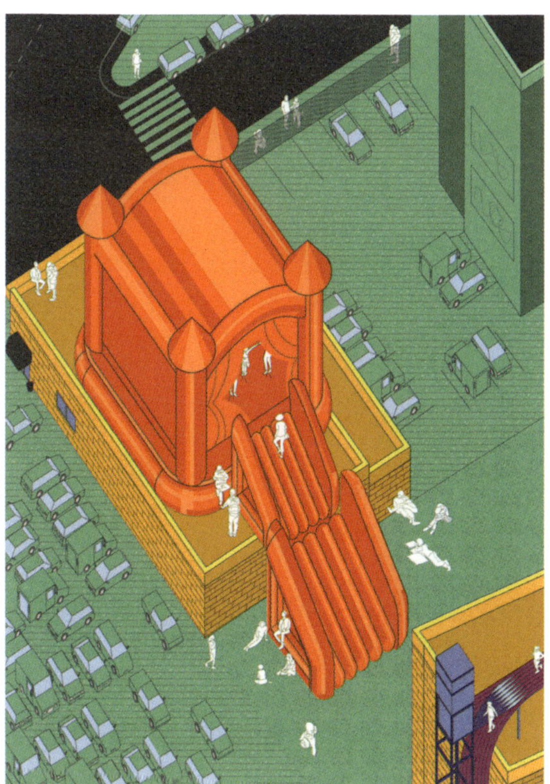

Future Imaginings bounce house mechanic shop

Future Imaginings nighttime bumper cars

"Raise the ..."
A STORY BY ODETTE AND MIRANDA
UPER MARKET
OPEN STREET
Project comic

SPACES NOW!
OPEN STREET
CHAT TRAVIESO

Nonprofit diagram

Future Imaginings Saturday-night theater

Physical model proposal

Physical model proposal

Image Credits

Page 10, 11

Courtesy all(zone)

Page 15

Photograph by Ariel Bintang

Page 16, 17

Photographs by Ariel Bintang, Samantha Ong, Surry Schlabs

Pages 23, 25, 26–27, 29, 30

Courtesy all(zone)

Pages 102, 103

Courtesy Norman Kelley

Pages 110, 111

Photographs by Cal Liang

Page 114, Page 119 (top)

Courtesy Norman Kelley

Page 119 (bottom), 120

Photographs by Kendall McCaugherty

Page 186–187

Courtesy Chat Treviso

Page 193–194, 197–198, 201

Photographs by Chat Treviso

Pages 203, 209, 211, 213

Courtesy of Chat Treviso